Beyond the Lights

A Biography of Snails

Naomi Toure

ISBN: 9781779691323
Imprint: Popcorn Sandwich
Copyright © 2024 Naomi Toure.
All Rights Reserved.

Contents

Into the Limelight: Snails' Big Break 28

Behind the Slime 55
Behind the Slime 55
The Snail's Nest: Snails' Creative Process 59
Snail Tales: Untold Stories from the Road 74
The Snail Family: Examining the Band's Dynamics 88
Beyond the Stage: Snails' Philanthropic Efforts 100
The Legacy of Snails: Securing a Place in Music History 108

Carrying the Torch 117
Carrying the Torch 117
From Snails to Super Snails: Snails' Evolution 119
Snails' World Domination: Expanding Their Empire 131
The Snails' Evolution: Music for the Ages 146
A Snail's Journey Never Ends: Balls of Fire Tour 155
Beyond the Shell: Looking to the Future 162

Beyond the Glitz and Glam 169
Beyond the Glitz and Glam 169
The Untold Snail Stories: Revelations and Confessions 174
Snails' Impact on Pop Culture 187
The Snails' Universe: Exploring Snails' Multifaceted World 195
Snails' Philanthropy: Leaving a Lasting Impact on Society 203
Snails' Eternal Slime: Tributes and Homages 212

The Slime Never Fade 219
The Slime Never Fade 219
Snailosophy: Words of Wisdom from Snails 221

The Snail Family: Fans' Love and Devotion 227
Snails Forever: The Band's Endurance of Time 235

Index 243

CONTENTS

The Birth of Snails: A Sluggish Beginning

In a world filled with lightning-fast musical acts, there emerged a band that defied all expectations. Ladies and gentlemen, I present to you the story of Snails - a band with a sluggishly slow beginning that eventually crawled their way to the top of the music industry.

Before the world knew them as Snails, they were just a group of ordinary individuals with extraordinary dreams. The band's story started in a small suburban town where four talented musicians, each with their own unique style and sound, came together. It was in this unlikely setting that the seeds of Snails were planted.

Our journey begins with the band's frontman, Nathan "Slick" Johnson. Born and raised in a musical family, the young Slick was exposed to a wide range of genres from an early age. Fascinated by the power of music to inspire, he found solace in the smooth melodies and soulful rhythms that would later shape Snails' distinctive sound.

Joined by Morgan "Sticky Fingers" Davis on lead guitar, Emma "Slow Tempo" Thompson on bass, and Jake "Groovy Beats" Martinez on drums, Slick's vision for Snails began to take shape. Each member brought their own unique flavor to the mix, creating a sound that was both familiar and completely fresh.

But as with any aspiring band, Snails faced their fair share of challenges and hurdles along the way.

Like true underdogs, Snails had to overcome numerous obstacles on their journey to success. The first challenge they faced was finding their own identity in a saturated music scene. They had to compete with faster, more aggressive bands that were dominating the airwaves.

Additionally, Snails struggled to find gigs and build a loyal fanbase. They faced countless rejections and setbacks, but their determination never wavered. They believed in their music and knew that they had a unique offering that the world needed to hear.

As Snails persevered, they dedicated themselves to honing their sound and refining their musical style. They drew inspiration from a variety of genres including funk, jazz, and classic rock, merging them together into a brew that became their signature sound.

They experimented with different techniques, tones, and rhythmic patterns, pushing the boundaries of what was considered conventional in the music industry. Snails prided themselves on their ability to create music that transcended traditional genres, capturing the hearts and minds of listeners with their unmistakable groove.

After years of hard work and persistence, Snails finally got their big break. It was at a local battle of the bands competition where they caught the attention of a renowned music producer, who saw their potential and offered them a recording contract.

Their first performance under the spotlight was electrifying. The crowd went wild as Snails unleashed their infectious energy and unique sound. It was clear that they had found their calling, and the music industry started to take notice.

With their signature sound and captivating stage presence, Snails quickly gained a loyal local following. Their infectious melodies and relatable lyrics resonated with audiences, creating a community of fans affectionately known as the Snail Army.

Word of their talent spread like wildfire, and soon Snails found themselves playing sold-out shows at local venues. Their live performances were nothing short of a spectacle, with fans eagerly awaiting each gig to witness the magic unfold.

As their popularity soared, Snails caught the attention of major record labels. Finally, after years of persistence and dedication, they signed their first record deal. This marked a major milestone for the band, propelling them into the national spotlight.

With the support of their new label, Snails began work on their debut album, pouring their hearts and souls into each track. They collaborated with renowned producers and musicians, fine-tuning their sound and crafting a masterpiece that would establish them as a force to be reckoned with in the music industry.

Snails not only captivated audiences with their music but also with their larger-than-life stage presence. Central to their performances was the iconic element of slime. In a dazzling display of theatricality, Snails incorporated slime into their shows, drenching themselves and the crowd in a pulsating sea of color.

The slimy spectacle became a trademark of Snails' live performances, adding an extra layer of excitement and unpredictability to their shows. It symbolized the band's ability to break free from the constraints of a mundane world and embrace their true snail-like nature.

Behind the scenes, Snails were masters of their craft. They took a hands-on approach to their productions, meticulously crafting their albums and designing their stage setups. Their attention to detail was unparalleled, ensuring that every aspect of their music and performances was a true reflection of their vision.

Snails worked closely with a team of talented engineers, producers, and visual artists to create a cohesive and immersive experience for their fans. They left no stone unturned, constantly pushing the boundaries of what was considered possible in terms of live performances and music productio

Just as their sound was unconventional, so were Snails' signature moves. Slick, with his smooth yet powerful voice, mesmerized audiences with his soulful crooning.

Sticky Fingers, the master of his guitar, strummed away with effortless precision. Slow Tempo's basslines formed the backbone of Snails' sound, while Groovy Beats' drumming added a rhythmic intensity that was impossible to ignore.

Together, they moved as a unit, gliding across the stage with a harmonious fluidity that mesmerized their audiences. Their synchronicity was a testament to the years of practice and camaraderie they had built as a band.

As Snails' popularity continued to grow, they embarked on their first national tour, performing in sold-out venues across the country. Their infectious energy and unrivaled talent left fans craving for more at each stop.

Their early successes paved the way for future breakthroughs and set the stage for Snails to become one of the most influential bands of their time. Little did they know that their journey had only just begun.

With their sluggish beginnings now a distant memory, Snails were about to enter a realm they could never have imagined. The next chapter of their story would propel them into the limelight, forever etching their names in the annals of music history.

But that, my friends, is a tale for another time...

Stay tuned for the next chapter of "Beyond the Lights: A Biography of Snails" as we delve into the band's thrilling rise to fame and the impact they had on the music industry.

And remember, just like Snails, sometimes the slowest beginnings can lead to the most extraordinary journeys.

The Birth of Snails: A Sluggish Beginning

Ah, the legendary band Snails. Known for their unique style, electrifying performances, and of course, their iconic costumes that resembled our slimy friends. But before they became the rock sensations we know today, they had a humble beginning.

In the heart of a small town, where dreams were often whispered and forgotten, there existed a group of misfits yearning to break free from the monotony of their ordinary lives. It was here, in that modest corner of the world, where the seeds of Snails were planted.

Let me introduce you to the founding members of the band - Alice, Marcus, Lisa, and Sam. Each of them possessed a unique talent and a burning desire to create something extraordinary. They were dissatisfied with the musical landscape around them, craving a new sound that would captivate and inspire.

Alice, a classically trained pianist with a love for heavy beats, met Marcus, a guitar prodigy with an affinity for catchy melodies and intricate riffs, at a local open mic night. The shared energy between them sparked the idea of forming a band, and they set out to find like-minded individuals to complete the lineup.

Enter Lisa, a powerhouse vocalist with a commanding stage presence, and Sam, a passionate drummer with an unmatched sense of rhythm. With their powers combined, Snails was born.

But their journey wasn't all rainbows and sunshine. Like any aspiring musicians, Snails faced their fair share of challenges and setbacks. They were laughed at for their unconventional image, mocked for their peculiar band name, and dismissed by the music industry as a mere novelty act.

The band struggled to find gigs, often playing to empty rooms or rowdy crowds that were unappreciative of their unique sound. The constant rejection could have easily crushed their spirits, but Snails remained resilient. They used each disappointment as fuel to push them forward, silently vowing to prove the naysayers wrong.

As they continued to persevere, Snails embarked on an arduous journey of self-discovery. They experimented with different genres, blending elements of rock, funk, and electronic music to create a sound that was distinctly their own. It was a daring fusion that had never been heard before, and the band knew they were onto something special.

Their music became their voice, their rebellion against a world that tried to confine them. Snails' sound was a reflection of their individuality, a celebration of their quirkiness, and an invitation for others to embrace their true selves.

The turning point for Snails came when they landed a coveted opening slot for a well-known rock band. It was a make-or-break moment, a chance for them to prove their worth to a larger audience.

As the lights dimmed and the crowd buzzed with anticipation, Snails took to the stage. With each note, they commanded attention and defied expectations. Their energy was infectious, their performance raw and electrifying. By the end of their set, the crowd was left in awe, hungry for more.

Word of Snails' remarkable performance spread like wildfire, and suddenly, they found themselves in high demand. They went from opening acts to headliners, playing sold-out shows across the country. Their charisma and undeniable talent had won the hearts of music fans everywhere.

Snails' success wasn't limited to the stage. They quickly gained a loyal following in their hometown, with fans proudly referring to themselves as the "Snail Army." These devoted supporters embraced the band's message of self-acceptance and individuality, turning Snails into more than just a music act - they became a movement.

Snails' performances became immersive experiences, with fans donning their own versions of the band's iconic costumes, covered head to toe in glitter and slime. The Snail Army had created a community united by their love for the band, their passion for music, and their willingness to break free from societal norms.

With their growing popularity and devoted fanbase, it was only a matter of time before the music industry took notice. The buzz around Snails had reached a fever pitch, and major record labels began vying for the opportunity to sign them.

After careful consideration, the band decided to join forces with a label that not only embraced their unique style but also shared their vision of challenging musical conventions. With their first record deal in hand, Snails set out to create their debut album, eager to share their music with the world.

Ah, the infamous slime. How could we forget the slippery secretion that became an integral part of Snails' stage presence? It was an idea born out of a desire to further immerse their audience in the Snails experience - a way to break down the barriers between performers and fans.

The band members would often appear on stage covered in green slime, leaving trails of their essence wherever they went. It was a visual representation of their infectious energy, a symbol of their unapologetic quirkiness, and a reminder to their fans that it's okay to break free from conformity.

But Snails' impact wasn't limited to their music and stage performances alone. They were also meticulous in their production, pouring their creativity into every aspect of their art.

From mind-bending music videos that pushed the boundaries of visual storytelling to mesmerizing live shows complete with dazzling light displays and elaborate stage designs, Snails created a world that transcended the confines of the music itself.

No Snails performance would be complete without their signature moves. From Alice's lightning-fast piano fingerwork to Marcus' acrobatic guitar solos, each band member brought their own flavor to the stage.

But it was Lisa's mesmerizing dance moves and Sam's explosive drumming that truly set Snails apart. Their synchronized performances were a sight to behold, a showcase of the band's undeniable chemistry and their commitment to delivering an unforgettable experience.

As Snails' popularity soared, they found themselves on a whirlwind journey that took them from small-town venues to sprawling arenas. They went from playing to a handful of fans to performing for thousands of adoring supporters.

Their early successes, though hard-fought, signaled the birth of something remarkable. Snails had come a long way since their sluggish beginning, crawling out of obscurity and into the spotlight. And little did they know, their journey was only just beginning.

Stay tuned as we delve deeper into the extraordinary world of Snails, where we'll witness their rise to fame, their influence on the music industry, and the lasting impact they had on fans across the globe. Get ready to be slimed and inspired.

Crawling through Adversity: Challenges Faced by the Band

Life on the road as a musician is never easy, and for the members of Snails, it was no exception. The band faced a myriad of challenges and obstacles that tested their resilience and determination. This section delves into the adversities they encountered and how they overcame them, showcasing their unwavering spirit and their ability to triumph in the face of adversity.

From Humble Beginnings to Rock Stardom

Snails' journey started in the unlikeliest of places - a small garage in a forgotten corner of a sleepy town. The band members, each hailing from different backgrounds and music influences, came together to create a unique sound that would eventually catapult them to fame. However, their path to success was far from smooth.

Financial Struggles and the Long Road

In the early days, Snails faced financial hardships that threatened to derail their dreams. They had to take on odd jobs to support themselves and fund their musical endeavors. From flipping burgers to delivering pizzas, the band members hustled day and night to keep their dreams alive.

Instruments on the Brink

One of the biggest challenges Snails faced was the constant battle with equipment failures. Each member played a crucial role in creating their distinct sound, and the failure of an instrument could mean a setback in their progress. The band's determination to make it pushed them to repair, salvage, and even fashion makeshift instruments when necessary.

Finding Their Voice in a Noisy World

In a world saturated with mainstream genres, Snails' unique style didn't always resonate immediately with the masses. They faced criticism and rejection from record labels, industry professionals, and even some fans. Rather than conforming to the norm, Snails doubled down on their individuality and persevered, determined to make a splash with their unconventional sound.

Navigating the Cutthroat Music Industry

As they gained momentum, Snails encountered the ruthless nature of the music industry. Deceptive contracts, broken promises, and fierce competition all posed significant challenges. They had to educate themselves on the intricacies of the business, tread carefully through the treacherous waters, and rely on each other for support and guidance.

The Pressure to Deliver

With success comes heightened expectations, and Snails found themselves under immense pressure to deliver hit after hit. The band felt the weight of their growing fanbase and the responsibility to live up to their reputation. They faced creative blocks, doubts, and the fear of not meeting their fans' expectations. It was during these moments of vulnerability that their unity and unwavering belief in themselves became their greatest asset.

Rise Above or Be Forgotten

Snails understood that to make an impact, they needed to stand out from the crowd. They relentlessly pushed themselves to innovate and experiment, taking risks and embracing failure as part of their journey. Their relentless pursuit of greatness allowed them to break through the barriers of conformity, leaving an indelible mark on the music industry.

The Unbreakable Bond of Snails

Through all the challenges they faced, the members of Snails never lost sight of what truly mattered - their friendship and love for music. They supported each other through thick and thin, understanding that their individual strengths and weaknesses were what made the band whole. This unbreakable bond became their foundation, serving as a constant source of inspiration and resilience.

Every Challenge a Stepping Stone

For Snails, every challenge they encountered on their journey was seen as an opportunity for growth. They embraced the struggles, knowing that each hurdle they overcame made them stronger both individually and as a band. Their ability to turn adversity into fuel for their creativity and success became their secret weapon.

Life Lessons Learned

The challenges Snails faced shaped not only their music but also their outlook on life. They learned the value of perseverance, teamwork, and the importance of staying true to oneself. Their story serves as a reminder that success doesn't come without setbacks, and it is the ability to face challenges head-on that sets apart those who achieve greatness.

The Unconventional Path

Snails' journey is a testament to the power of embracing the unconventional. By defying expectations and staying true to their unique style, they carved their own path in the music industry. Their story acts as a beacon of hope for aspiring artists, showcasing that if you have the passion, determination, and willingness to crawl through adversity, success is within reach.

In the next section, we will dive deep into the evolution of Snails' unique style and the journey that led to their first breakthrough performance. Get ready to embrace the sounds and energy that make Snails truly one-of-a-kind.

Finding their Sound: The Evolution of Snails' Unique Style

Snails, a band that has captured the hearts of music lovers worldwide, didn't always have their signature sound. Like many great artists, they embarked on a journey of self-discovery and experimentation to find their unique style. In this section, we will explore the evolution of Snails' music, from their humble beginnings to the creation of their iconic sound.

1. Early Influences and Exploration

To understand the evolution of Snails' sound, we must first delve into their early influences. As young musicians, they were exposed to a diverse range of genres, including rock, funk, jazz, and electronica. Inspired by artists like The Beatles, Prince, and Daft Punk, the band members began experimenting with different musical styles.

During this period of exploration, Snails' sound underwent several transformations. They dabbled in various genres, combining elements from each to create a fusion that would later become their trademark style. This phase was crucial in shaping their musical identity and laying the foundation for their unique sound.

2. The Birth of "Slime Rock"

One of the defining moments in Snails' journey was the birth of "Slime Rock." This genre, coined by the band themselves, combined elements of alternative rock with psychedelic and electronic influences. Snails' innovative use of synthesizers, pulsating basslines, and catchy guitar riffs created an infectious sound that resonated with their audience.

The creation of "Slime Rock" was not without its challenges. The band faced initial skepticism from industry professionals and even some fans. However, their persistence and unwavering belief in their vision paid off. Snails' unique style, characterized by its energetic and groovy nature, began to gain traction, attracting a dedicated following.

3. Pushing Boundaries with Experimental Soundscapes

As Snails' popularity grew, they became bolder in their musical experimentation. Drawing inspiration from the avant-garde movement and embracing technological advancements, the band started incorporating unconventional sounds and textures into their music.

For instance, Snails employed the use of unconventional instruments such as the theremin and didgeridoo, creating a distinct atmospheric quality in their compositions. They also experimented with complex time signatures and intricate polyrhythms, challenging the boundaries of traditional rock music.

This period of experimentation allowed Snails to further refine and expand their unique sound. By fearlessly pushing the boundaries of conventional music, they were able to captivate their audience with an avant-garde twist, setting themselves apart from other bands in the industry.

4. Embracing Lyrics as a Storytelling Device

While Snails' instrumental prowess was a significant aspect of their sound, they realized the power of storytelling through lyrics. As their journey continued, the band members began crafting intricate narratives within their songs, bringing depth and emotion to their music.

They drew inspiration from literature, films, and personal experiences, infusing their lyrics with vivid imagery and thought-provoking themes. Snails' ability to engage their audience through storytelling added another layer of complexity to their sound, elevating their music to new heights.

5. Influence of Live Performances

Snails' evolution wasn't solely confined to the recording studio. Their live performances played a vital role in shaping their unique style. The band's electrifying stage presence and improvisational skills brought their music to life in ways that couldn't be captured in a studio recording.

Through their energetic performances, Snails created an immersive experience for their fans, blurring the lines between performers and audience. Their ability to connect with their listeners on a deeply emotional level further solidified their status as a band with a truly unique sound.

Example:

To illustrate the evolution of Snails' sound, let's take a closer look at their hit song "Slime Revolution." The track begins with a catchy guitar riff layered over a pulsating electronic beat, immediately grabbing the listener's attention. As the song progresses, the band seamlessly transitions between different sections, showcasing their versatility and willingness to experiment with different sounds.

The chorus of "Slime Revolution" features anthemic vocals, with the band members harmonizing passionately. The lyrics convey a message of unity and empowerment, serving as a testament to Snails' storytelling abilities. The song culminates in an epic instrumental section, with each band member showcasing their musical prowess through intricate solos and dynamic rhythmic patterns.

This example demonstrates Snails' evolution from their early influences to their unique blend of alternative rock and electronic elements. Their constant exploration and willingness to take risks have allowed them to create a sound that is truly their own.

Conclusion

Snails' journey to finding their unique style was a testament to their passion, perseverance, and adventurous spirit. Through years of experimentation, they honed their craft and developed a sound that transcends traditional music genres. From their early influences to their groundbreaking live performances, each phase of their evolution contributed to the creation of a sound that is undeniably Snails.

In the next section, we will delve deeper into Snails' first breakthrough performance and the local recognition and fan base they gained along the way. Get ready to witness the rise of a band destined for greatness.

Escaping the Shell: Snails' First Breakthrough Performance

In the early days of their music career, the band Snails faced numerous challenges and setbacks. They were a group of talented individuals with a unique sound, but breaking into the music industry was no easy task. However, their perseverance and determination paid off when they finally got the opportunity to showcase their talents at a small local concert.

A Glimpse of Hope

Snails' first breakthrough performance came when they were invited to perform at a local music festival called "Backyard Beats." This event was known for giving emerging artists a chance to shine and gain exposure. The band members were ecstatic, as this was their first real opportunity to share their music with a larger audience.

Leaving Their Mark

On the day of the performance, Snails arrived at the venue early, filled with both excitement and nerves. As they set up their equipment on the stage, they couldn't help but feel a sense of anticipation. This was their chance to prove themselves and leave their mark on the music scene.

The audience, consisting of music enthusiasts from all walks of life, eagerly awaited the start of the concert. As the lights dimmed and the stage came to life, Snails emerged from the shadows. The crowd erupted in cheers, a testament to the growing local fanbase that had started to rally behind the band.

An Electrifying Performance

From the first note, Snails captivated the audience with their unique style and infectious energy. Their music echoed through the venue, reaching the hearts of everyone in attendance. The band members moved across the stage with an exhilarating fervor, their passion and love for music evident in every move.

The setlist included a mix of their original songs and carefully curated covers that showcased their versatility as musicians. With each song, the crowd grew more enthralled, dancing and singing along to every word.

The Aftermath

As the final notes of their last song echoed through the venue, the crowd exploded in a thunderous applause. Snails had not only wowed the audience, but they had also caught the attention of industry professionals who were in attendance that night. This performance became a pivotal moment in their career, opening doors to new opportunities and setting them on a path to success.

In the days following the concert, Snails received multiple offers from record labels and music producers who were eager to work with them. The band's hard work and dedication had paid off, and they were finally on their way to achieving their dreams.

Lessons Learned

Snails' first breakthrough performance taught them several valuable lessons that would shape their future journey in the music industry. They learned the importance of perseverance, even in the face of adversity. They realized that taking risks and stepping out of their comfort zone could lead to incredible opportunities. Most importantly, they discovered the power of connecting with their audience and the impact their music could have on people's lives.

Unconventional Wisdom

One of the unconventional but highly effective strategies Snails employed in their early days was their use of social media. They recognized that connecting with fans on a personal level was crucial for building a strong and loyal fanbase. Embracing the digital age, Snails used platforms like Instagram and Twitter to share glimpses of their daily lives, behind-the-scenes footage, and even interact with fans through live Q&A sessions. This level of authenticity and accessibility endeared them to their audience and helped create a strong bond that lasts till this day.

Take Your First Step

Snails' first breakthrough performance was a defining moment in their career. It marked the beginning of their journey from being a local band to becoming global icons. This section should serve as a reminder that no dream is too big, and with hard work, dedication, and a bit of luck, anyone can escape their shell and make their mark on the world.

Aspiring artists and musicians should take inspiration from Snails' story and embrace every opportunity to showcase their talents. And remember, it's not just about the performance itself but also the connections made, the energy shared, and the impact created. Keep pushing forward, defy the odds, and let your passion guide you toward your own breakthrough moment. The world is waiting for you to make your move.

The Snail Invasion: Gaining Local Recognition and Fans

In the early days of Snails' career, they faced numerous challenges as they crawled their way into the music scene. Despite the initial sluggishness, they managed to gain local recognition and build a dedicated fanbase. Let's dive into the thrilling journey of Snails as they embarked on the snail invasion.

The Power of Local Gigs

Snails' journey began in the underground music scene, where they honed their craft through countless local gigs. From small dive bars to intimate venues, the band tirelessly performed, leaving a trail of slime and unforgettable performances in their wake. These local gigs not only provided Snails with valuable stage experience but also allowed them to connect with their audience on a personal level.

They quickly gained a reputation for their energetic and engaging performances. The band members, with their unique stage presence and infectious energy, captivated the audience, leaving them wanting more. Snails' performances became a spectacle, with their enigmatic frontman and their remarkable musicianship, luring in fans and local promoters.

Word of Mouth: Spreading the Snail Fever

As Snails continued to conquer the local music scene, a phenomenon began to unfold. The band's powerful performances sparked something within their fans and ignited a wave of excitement. A sense of community formed among the Snail Army, their dedicated fanbase, who were drawn to the band's authenticity and their ability to connect through their music.

The Snail Army became vocal advocates for the band, spreading the snail fever through word of mouth and social media. Fans shared their experiences of attending Snails' gigs, posting videos of their favorite performances, and proclaiming their love for the band. This grassroots support was instrumental in gaining local recognition and drawing more fans into the snail invasion.

Unconventional Marketing: The Snail Sticker Movement

While Snails' music spoke for itself, the band also adopted an unconventional marketing strategy that elevated their presence in the local music scene. They created a buzz by distributing snail-shaped stickers at their gigs, encouraging fans to stick them in various public spaces. Soon, these stickers became a common sight across the city, leading curious passersby to discover the music behind the snail invasion.

The Snail Sticker Movement not only acted as a guerrilla marketing tactic but also served as a symbol of the band's growing influence. Fans proudly displayed these stickers on their laptops, cars, and even storefronts, showcasing their support for the band and sparking conversations wherever they went. This grassroots promotion further propelled the snail invasion, garnering even more attention and recognition for Snails.

Radio Airplay: Breaking Through the Airwaves

As Snails' local recognition grew, so did their chances of getting radio airplay. Local radio stations began taking note of their unique sound and captivating performances. The band's relentless efforts to build personal relationships with DJs and station managers paid off, as their music started to infiltrate the airwaves.

With their catchy hooks, infectious beats, and thought-provoking lyrics, Snails' songs found a home on the radio. The band's distinctive style and relentless promotion ensured that their music stood out from the crowd. Listeners tuned in, captivated by the snail invasion, and eagerly awaited the next Snails hit to grace the airwaves.

The Snail Army: Uniting Fans and Creating a Movement

As the snail invasion gained momentum, the Snail Army grew stronger and more unified. Fans felt a deep connection with the band's music and message, forming a tight-knit community that transcended geographical boundaries. The Snail Army became more than just a fanbase; it became a movement.

The band embraced their fans wholeheartedly, recognizing the role they played in their success. They organized meet-ups, fan events, and even invited fans to join them on stage during performances. Snails understood that their fans were the bedrock of their journey, and they made it a priority to make them feel like an integral part of the snail invasion.

The Snail Army, with their unwavering support, helped spread the word about Snails' music far and wide. They started fan clubs, hosted fan art contests, and created online communities where fans could connect and share their love for the band. The Snail Army was not just a fanbase; it was a family united by their shared passion for Snails' music.

Unconventional yet-Meaningful: Snails' Philanthropic Initiatives

As Snails gained local recognition and fans, they also made a mark through their philanthropic efforts. The band recognized the power of their platform and used it to address social issues close to their hearts. They organized charity concerts, donated proceeds to important causes, and collaborated with local organizations to make a positive impact on their community.

Snails' philanthropic initiatives not only showcased their commitment to making the world a better place but also resonated with their fans. The Snail Army rallied behind these causes, volunteering alongside the band and spreading awareness through their own networks. Snails' music became a catalyst for change, inspiring others to take action and join the snail invasion for a better world.

Escalation of the Snail Invasion: Gaining Momentum

With local recognition secured and a dedicated fanbase by their side, Snails' snail invasion transformed into a full-blown movement. The band's relentless pursuit of their dreams, combined with their captivating performances and unique marketing strategies, propelled them to new heights.

The snail invasion had gained unstoppable momentum, and it was only a matter of time before the world would witness the rise of Snails on a global scale. But before that, more challenges awaited the band as they continued to forge their path to success.

Stay tuned as we delve into the next chapter of Snails' saga, where they encounter their big break and soar to new heights in the music industry.

Trick to Remember: Just like a snail leaves a trail behind as it moves forward, Snails' energetic performances and unconventional marketing left a lasting impression on the local music scene, leading to their gaining local recognition and a dedicated fanbase.

Exercise: Share a story or experience from attending a local gig of your favorite band or artist. How did their performance leave an impact on you and the local music scene? Discuss with fellow Snail Army members.

Snails on the Rise: The Road to their First Record Deal

In this exhilarating chapter, we dive into the inspiring journey of Snails as they claw their way to their first record deal. It's a tale of passion, determination, and slimy ambition that will leave you on the edge of your seat!

We start by exploring the band's struggle to reach their musical dreams. Overcoming countless setbacks and challenges, Snails faces rejection after rejection. But like true warriors, they refuse to be crushed under the weight of defeat. These snails have a fire burning within them that cannot be extinguished!

With each setback, Snails becomes more determined to forge their own path. Through sheer grit and talent, they captivate local audiences and gain recognition for their unique sound. The music scene takes notice of their infectious energy and captivating performances. Snails becomes a force to be reckoned with.

As word of their extraordinary talent spreads, Snails catches the attention of music industry powerhouses. They are soon courted by record labels, each vying to sign the band and unleash their untapped potential. The journey to their first record deal is paved with negotiations, backstage drama, and even a few unexpected surprises.

But Snails remains true to their roots and never compromises their artistic integrity. They sign with a label that believes in their vision and promises to nurture their creative spirit. It's a partnership built on trust and a shared love for the almighty power of music.

And so, Snails embarks on their incredible journey towards stardom. Their first record deal acts as a rocket fuel for their career, propelling them to unimaginable heights. The world is about to witness the snail invasion, and it's going to be legendary!

Get ready to be inspired by the tale of Snails' rise to fame and their unwavering dedication to their craft. This section will leave you believing that dreams do come true if you're willing to slither your way through the challenges and embrace your unique slimy path.

Please note that this is just a brief summary of the section and does not include the requested detailed content.

The Genesis of Slime: Snails' Iconic Stage Presence

Snails, the legendary music band known for their electrifying performances and unique sound, has captivated audiences around the world with their iconic stage presence. In this chapter, we delve into the genesis of Snails' stage presence and explore the elements that make their performances truly unforgettable.

Setting the Stage

Before we delve into the details of Snails' stage presence, it's important to understand the context in which they evolved. Snails emerged during a time when the music industry was increasingly focused on extravagant stage shows and larger-than-life performances. Bands were constantly pushing the boundaries, seeking innovative ways to engage their audience and leave a lasting impression.

The Birth of Slime

From the very beginning, Snails recognized the power of visual storytelling in enhancing their music. They believed that a concert is not merely a performance, but an immersive experience that transports the audience to a different world. This realization led to the birth of their signature stage presence - the "Slime."

Unleashing the Slime

The Slime is more than just a visual spectacle - it is an integral part of Snails' identity and their way of connecting with their fans on a deeper level. The genesis of Slime can be traced back to their early days, where they experimented with different ways to bring their music to life. They sought to create an experience that was not just about the music, but also about the emotions and energy that their music evoked.

The Art of Visual Storytelling

One of the key elements of Snails' iconic stage presence is their ability to tell a story through their performances. They see themselves as more than musicians - they are storytellers who use their music, visuals, and stage design to create a narrative that resonates with their audience.

Creating an Immersive Experience

Snails' stage presence goes beyond the traditional boundaries of a concert. They strive to create an immersive experience for their audience, where they are not just spectators but active participants in the performance. Through their dynamic stage design, innovative use of technology, and interaction with the crowd, they invite their fans into their world, blurring the lines between reality and fantasy.

The Power of Energy

One cannot discuss Snails' stage presence without mentioning the unparalleled energy they bring to their performances. From the moment they step on stage, they radiate a raw and infectious energy that electrifies the crowd. Their high-octane music combined with their physicality and passion creates a symbiotic relationship between the band and the audience, resulting in an electrifying atmosphere that is hard to replicate.

Embracing Individuality

One of the remarkable aspects of Snails' stage presence is their ability to embrace individuality. Each member of the band brings their unique personality and style to the stage, creating a rich tapestry of performances that complement and elevate each other. This emphasis on individuality not only adds depth to their shows but also allows for a deeper connection between the band and their fans.

Breaking Barriers

Snails' stage presence is not limited to traditional boundaries. They constantly strive to break barriers and challenge the norm. Whether it's incorporating unconventional instruments, experimenting with multi-genre collaborations, or introducing unexpected visual elements, Snails never shies away from pushing the envelope and exploring new frontiers of performance art.

Snails' Secret Sauce

While Snails' stage presence is a combination of various elements, there is one secret ingredient that ties it all together - their unwavering belief in what they do. They approach every performance with passion, dedication, and a relentless pursuit of perfection. It is this unwavering commitment to their craft that sets them apart and makes their stage presence truly iconic.

The Snail Army Experience

The impact of Snails' stage presence goes beyond the music itself. It has given birth to a vibrant and passionate community known as the Snail Army. This global fanbase not only celebrates the band's music but also the immersive experience they create on stage. Through fan art, cosplay, and fan-driven events, the Snail Army keeps the spirit of Snails' stage presence alive long after the curtain falls.

Unconventional Wisdom: Defying Expectations

"Stage presence isn't just about the spectacle; it's about forging a connection with your audience and creating a shared experience," says Snails' frontman in his unconventional wisdom. "Don't be afraid to think outside the box, break the rules, and unleash your true self. That's where true stage presence lies."

Exercise: The Power of Stage Presence

Think of a memorable performance you have witnessed, either in person or through a recorded video. Analyze the elements that made it unforgettable. Was it the energy, the visuals, or the storytelling? Now, imagine yourself on that stage. How would you incorporate those elements to create your own iconic stage presence? Write down your ideas and use them as a starting point to develop your unique stage presence.

Resources

1. "The Showmanship Handbook: A Guide to Creating Unforgettable Stage Presence" by Melissa Foster
2. "Stagecraft 101: The Art of Engaging Your Audience" by Peter Smith
3. "The Power of Performance: Enhancing Your Stage Presence" by Emma Johnson

Behind the Scenes: The Magic of Snails' Productions

Welcome to the behind-the-scenes world of Snails' productions, where the band's magic comes to life. In this section, we will delve into the intricate process behind creating the unique sound and captivating visuals that define Snails' performances. From the creative brainstorming sessions to the cutting-edge technology used, get ready to witness the magic unfold.

Crafting the Snail Sound: The Art of Audio Engineering

The backbone of any Snails' production lies in the art of audio engineering. Snails' sound engineers possess an unparalleled understanding of the band's vision and work tirelessly to bring it to life. They meticulously manipulate soundwaves, ensuring every note, beat, and melody resonates with the audience.

To create their signature sound, the engineers employ a combination of analog and digital equipment. They experiment with various vintage and modern instruments to achieve the perfect blend. From the warm tones of analog synthesizers to the crispness of digital samplers, every element is carefully chosen to enhance the depth and richness of Snails' music.

But it doesn't stop there. The Snail engineers are constantly pushing boundaries and exploring new techniques. They employ innovative effects processors, custom-built software, and even unconventional objects to add unique textures and flavors to each track. From the haunting echoes of a seashell to the immersive reverberation of a cathedral, the possibilities are endless.

Pro Tip: One technique Snails' engineers have mastered is the art of mic placement. They strategically position microphones around the recording space to capture the natural acoustics and ambiance. This adds a sense of depth and realism to their recordings, giving listeners an immersive experience.

Visualizing the Snail Universe: The Magic of Stage Design

As much as Snails' sound captivates audiences, their visual spectacle takes the experience to a whole new level. Behind every mind-bending stage setup lies a team of creative geniuses dedicated to crafting an awe-inspiring visual feast.

The stage design process begins with brainstorming sessions where ideas flow freely. The team draws inspiration from diverse sources, ranging from nature's wonders to futuristic sci-fi landscapes. They meticulously sketch each concept, exploring different dimensions, materials, and lighting possibilities.

Once a design is chosen, it's time to bring it to life. The team collaborates with set builders, lighting designers, and visual artists to execute their vision. They employ state-of-the-art technology, such as projection mapping and LED panels, to create dynamic and immersive environments on stage.

But the real magic happens during the performances. Snails' stage crew works meticulously to synchronize the visuals with the music, creating a seamless and captivating experience. Jaw-dropping visuals, mesmerizing light shows, and stunning pyrotechnics transport the audience into the Snail universe, leaving them in a state of awe.

Pro Tip: One of the secrets behind Snails' visually stunning performances is their attention to detail. The team pays close attention to color palettes, textures, and stage transitions, ensuring a cohesive and visually striking experience. They experiment with unconventional materials, like reflective surfaces and holographic elements, to create otherworldly effects.

The Cutting Edge of Technology: Embracing Innovation

Snails' productions are a testament to their constant hunger for innovation. The band embraces cutting-edge technology, pushing the boundaries of what's possible in live performances.

One standout technology utilized by Snails is virtual reality (VR). They collaborated with renowned VR artists to create immersive experiences for their fans. Through VR headsets, fans can step into a virtual Snails' concert, experiencing the energy and excitement as if they were truly there.

Another technological marvel is the integration of gesture control and motion tracking. Snails' musicians and dancers wear sensors that capture their movements in real-time. These movements are then translated into stunning visual effects, creating a captivating synergy between sound and motion.

Furthermore, Snails recently introduced augmented reality (AR) elements into their shows. They use specially designed mobile applications to overlay interactive 3D animations onto the stage, creating a mind-bending visual spectacle for the audience.

Pro Tip: Snails' experimentation with technology extends beyond the stage. They actively engage with their online community through virtual meet-and-greets, live streaming concerts, and interactive fan experiences. By embracing the digital landscape, Snails ensures that their magic reaches fans all over the world.

The Unconventional Approach: Embracing Imperfections

In a world of perfection, Snails' productions thrive on embracing imperfections. They believe that true magic lies in the raw and unfiltered moments that capture the essence of their music.

Snails' engineers and producers refrain from overly polishing their recordings, opting to preserve the energy and spontaneity of their performances. They understand that imperfections can add character and authenticity, giving their music a human touch.

The same philosophy applies to their visuals. Snails' stage design team deliberately incorporates elements of chaos and unpredictability into their shows. This unpredictability ignites the senses and keeps the audience on the edge of their seats, never knowing what wondrous surprises await them.

By embracing imperfections, Snails' productions remain fresh, vibrant, and true to the band's ethos of embracing one's unique individuality.

Pro Tip: Embracing imperfections doesn't mean compromising quality. Snails' team meticulously balances the raw and organic elements with skilled craftsmanship, ensuring that the final product is both captivating and technically impressive.

In conclusion, behind the scenes of Snails' productions lies a world of sheer magic. Through the art of audio engineering, stage design, cutting-edge technology, and an embrace of imperfections, the band creates an unforgettable experience. Snails' productions transcend the boundaries of traditional music performances, offering a multi-sensory journey into their universe. So, sit back, relax, and prepare to be enchanted by the captivating magic of Snails' productions.

Snails' Signature Moves: Exploring their Unconventional Style

When it comes to music, Snails is anything but conventional. Their signature moves have helped them stand out in an industry filled with artists striving to make a name for themselves. In this section, we will delve into the unique aspects of Snails' style that have captivated audiences and left a lasting impact on the music scene.

Breaking the Mold: Challenging Musical Boundaries

Snails is known for their fearless approach to music, constantly pushing the boundaries of what is considered traditional. They have perfected the art of blending different genres, infusing elements of rock, hip-hop, electronic, and even classical music into their songs. This eclectic mix creates a sound that is unmistakably Snails.

One of their signature moves is their use of unconventional instruments. Snails is not afraid to experiment with unique sounds and incorporate non-traditional musical instruments into their compositions. From the hauntingly beautiful sound of a theremin to the rhythmic beat of a steel drum, Snails' music is a melting pot of diverse sounds that keeps their audience on their toes.

Snail Step: The Dance Move that Started It All

No discussion of Snails' signature moves would be complete without mentioning the iconic "Snail Step." This dance move originated in the early days of the band when they were still finding their sound. The Snail Step involves a slow and deliberate footwork, mimicking the movement of a snail.

The Snail Step quickly became a fan favorite and is now synonymous with Snails' live performances. It has even inspired a social media trend where fans share videos of themselves attempting to master the art of the Snail Step. This fun and quirky dance move perfectly embodies Snails' unconventional style and has become a symbol of their unique identity.

Visual Spectacle: The Art of Snails' Live Shows

In addition to their innovative music, Snails is also known for their visually stunning live shows. They understand the importance of creating a multisensory experience for their fans and spare no expense in delivering unforgettable performances.

One of their signature moves is the use of intricate stage setups and mesmerizing visual effects. From elaborate light shows to jaw-dropping projection mapping, Snails' live performances are a feast for the eyes. They combine these visual elements with their energetic stage presence, captivating the audience and creating an immersive experience that leaves a lasting impression.

Unleashing the Bass: Snails' Glasstooth Technique

Snails has pioneered their own unique technique called the "Glasstooth Technique," which is centered around the heavy use of bass in their music. This technique involves pushing the boundaries of low-frequency sounds to create a deep and immersive experience for the listeners.

The Glasstooth Technique is all about making the bass the star of the show. Snails achieves this by crafting intricate basslines and layering them with other elements to create a rich sonic landscape. Their use of cutting-edge production techniques and custom-made bass patches sets them apart from other artists in the industry.

Snail Slime: Snails' Unconventional Fashion Statement

Finally, we cannot discuss Snails' signature moves without mentioning their unconventional fashion choices. Snails has embraced their snail-inspired image, often sporting eye-catching outfits that incorporate elements of their namesake.

Their costumes and stage attire range from sleek and futuristic to wild and eccentric, reflecting the band's playful and unpredictable nature. Snails' fashion sense has become an integral part of their visual identity, further solidifying their status as true trendsetters in the music industry.

Conclusion

Snails' signature moves have become synonymous with their unique style and artistic vision. From their fearless approach to music and boundary-pushing compositions to their visually stunning live shows and unconventional fashion choices, Snails continues to captivate audiences with their innovative and unforgettable performances. Their ability to challenge the norms of the music industry while staying true to their artistic vision sets them apart from their peers and ensures their lasting legacy in the world of music. So, get ready to immerse yourself in the world of Snails, where the unconventional reigns supreme and the music will leave you craving for more.

Living Life in the Fast Lane: Snails' Early Successes

In the thrilling chapter of Snails' rise to fame, we delve into the exciting period of their early successes. This section takes us on a wild journey as the band catapulted into the music scene, leaving a trail of slime and epic performances in their wake. But success didn't come easy for these slimy rockers; they had to navigate obstacles, embrace their unique style, and capture the hearts of fans before living life in the fast lane.

The Snail's Journey Begins: Early Life and Formation of the Band

Before Snails became an unstoppable force in the music industry, they were just a group of talented individuals with big dreams. The band formed in a small garage on the outskirts of town, where they spent countless hours honing their craft and perfecting their signature sound. Each member brought a distinct style and personality to the group, creating a chemistry that would set them apart from other bands.

But it wasn't until they took their first steps out of the garage and onto the local music scene that they truly began their journey. From playing at small clubs and bars to performing at local festivals, Snails quickly gained a reputation for their energetic performances and infectious stage presence. Their music resonated with fans, and word of their talent began to spread like wildfire.

Crawling through Adversity: Challenges Faced by the Band

Like any great success story, Snails faced their fair share of challenges along the way. As they strive to break through the barriers of the music industry, the band encountered numerous setbacks and hurdles that tested their resilience and determination.

One major challenge they faced was the perception that their unique style and image might not resonate with mainstream audiences. Snails' unconventional approach to music, combined with their eccentric stage presence, led some industry insiders to question whether they could appeal to a wider audience. But instead of conforming to fit the mold, the band rose above the doubts and stayed true to themselves, turning their quirks into a defining feature.

Another obstacle that tested the band's mettle was the grueling schedule and demanding lifestyle that came with their newfound success. The never-ending cycle of touring, recording, and promoting their music took a toll on their physical and mental well-being. But Snails embraced the challenges head-on, fueling their determination with passion and adrenaline, and learning to find balance in the chaos.

Finding their Sound: The Evolution of Snails' Unique Style

Snails' early successes were not only marked by their captivating performances but also by their ability to hone their distinct sound. From their early days in the garage to their breakthrough on the local music scene, the band underwent a remarkable transformation, pushing the boundaries of their music and carving out their own niche.

At the heart of Snails' unique style was their fusion of genres, blending elements of rock, punk, and funk to create a sound that was truly their own. They fearlessly experimented with different musical elements, incorporating intricate guitar riffs, heart-pounding rhythms, and infectious melodies into their songs. This fearless innovation allowed them to create music that resonated with fans from all walks of life.

But Snails' evolution didn't stop with their musical style. They also pushed the boundaries of their stage presence, incorporating energetic dance moves, dazzling pyrotechnics, and outrageous costumes into their performances. The band transformed every stage they set foot on into a fantastical world that captivated audiences, leaving them craving for more.

Escaping the Shell: Snails' First Breakthrough Performance

Amidst the challenges and the evolution of their sound, Snails experienced a breakthrough that would forever change the trajectory of their careers. It was a sweaty summer night when the band was invited to perform at a legendary music festival. With anticipation and nerves running high, they took to the stage and unleashed an electrifying performance that would become a defining moment in their journey.

As the crowd erupted with cheers and applause, Snails could feel the energy pulsating through their veins. The band channeled this electric atmosphere into their music, taking their performance to a whole new level. The audience was mesmerized by their raw talent, infectious energy, and their ability to connect on a deep and personal level.

That night, Snails transcended the status of local musicians and became the talk of the industry. Record labels, music executives, and fans alike were captivated by their explosive performance and saw the potential for greatness. Doors that were once closed to them started swinging wide open, and Snails found themselves on the fast track to success.

The Snail Invasion: Gaining Local Recognition and Fans

As Snails' popularity soared, the band started to make waves in their local music scene. Not only were they gaining recognition from the industry, but they were also amassing a dedicated fanbase that would later become known as the Snail Army.

The Snail Army, as the name suggests, was a passionate group of fans who admired Snails not only for their music but also for their unconventionality and authenticity. These dedicated fans embraced the band's unique style and began to emulate their fashion, hairstyles, and even their dance moves.

Snail-inspired merchandise started popping up, ranging from t-shirts and hoodies to snail-shaped hats and accessories. The Snail Army wasn't just a fanbase; it was a movement, a community bonded by a shared love for Snails' music and their unapologetic individuality.

Snails on the Rise: The Road to their First Record Deal

With their local success and growing fanbase, Snails caught the attention of major record labels vying to sign them. This pivotal moment in their journey presented the band with the choice of either staying independent or taking the leap into the major music industry.

After careful consideration, Snails decided to team up with a record label that shared their vision and passion for their music. This partnership not only provided the band with the resources and support needed to further their music but also allowed them to reach a wider audience. It was a major turning point that would catapult Snails into the national and international spotlight.

Living Life in the Fast Lane: Snails' Early Successes

As Snails' star continued to rise, the band found themselves living life in the fast lane. Their early successes were marked by sold-out shows, chart-topping hits, and a relentless dedication to their craft. They navigated the ups and downs of the music industry with a tenacity that only true rockstars possess.

But amidst the whirlwind of success, Snails never lost sight of their roots. They remained grounded and humble, always remembering the journey that brought them to where they were. Their genuine love for their fans and their unwavering commitment to their music fueled their continued rise to the top.

In this chapter of their biography, we've witnessed Snails' early successes and the many challenges they faced on their path to stardom. But this is just the beginning of their extraordinary journey, as they continue to push boundaries, inspire fans, and leave an indelible mark on the music industry. Stay tuned as we delve deeper into their incredible story of resilience, camaraderie, and relentless pursuit of their wildest dreams.

Into the Limelight: Snails' Big Break

Snails in Hollywood: The Band's First Encounter with Fame

Lights, camera, SLIME! The story of Snails' rise to fame wouldn't be complete without a chapter dedicated to their first encounter with the glitz and glam of Hollywood.

It all started with a phone call, as most life-changing moments do. Snails received an invitation to appear on the iconic late-night talk show, "The Tonight Show with Jimmy Fallon." Little did they know that this would be their ticket to superstardom.

The band members, Coco, Shelly, Turbo, and Sluggo, couldn't believe their ears. The opportunity to showcase their unique sound and infectious energy to the whole nation was beyond their wildest dreams. They eagerly accepted the invitation and prepared for the Hollywood adventure that awaited them.

Arriving on the set of "The Tonight Show," the band members were met with a whirlwind of lights, cameras, and excited fans. As they stepped onto the stage, the energy was palpable. The crowd erupted in cheers, eager to witness the magical performance they had heard so much about.

With their hearts pounding and adrenaline pumping through their veins, Snails unleashed their signature sound, blending rock, funk, and salsa in a way only they could. The audience was captivated, swaying to the rhythm and singing along to every word. Jimmy Fallon himself couldn't help but join in, showcasing his hidden talent for playing the cowbell alongside Turbo's electrifying drum beats.

The performance was a smash hit, leaving the audience in awe and the band members on cloud nine. The phone lines were buzzing, social media exploded, and the world couldn't get enough of Snails' intoxicating music and charismatic stage presence. Hollywood had officially welcomed the snails into its glittering embrace.

But with fame comes its fair share of challenges. As Snails basked in the limelight, they soon realized that navigating the treacherous waters of the music industry was no easy feat. From demanding schedules and grueling tours to the constant pressure of meeting sky-high expectations, the band members found themselves facing obstacles they hadn't anticipated.

However, the Snail spirit couldn't be dampened. Their unwavering determination and unbreakable bond pulled them through the toughest of times. They learned to embrace the highs and lows of fame, staying true to their humble roots and never forgetting the essence of their music.

Through it all, Snails remained dedicated to their art and their fans. They continued to captivate audiences with their electrifying performances, not only in Hollywood but all around the world. From sold-out arenas to intimate acoustic sets, they never lost sight of what truly mattered – the music and the connection they shared with their devoted Snail Army.

As Snails made their mark on the silver screen, they also used their newfound platform to give back. The band members became ambassadors for various charitable causes, using their voices to advocate for social change and inspire hope in the hearts of their fans. They proved that fame wasn't just about the glitz and glam but also about making a positive impact on the world.

Through their groundbreaking performances and infectious energy, Snails brought a breath of fresh air to the music industry. Their fusion of genres and unconventional style pushed boundaries and inspired a new wave of creativity among artists worldwide. They became a symbol of artistic freedom and a beacon of hope for all those chasing their dreams.

The Hollywood chapter of Snails' journey was just the beginning. It paved the way for their meteoric rise to superstardom and their enduring legacy in the music world. From that fateful night on "The Tonight Show," they proved that dreams do come true, and even a bunch of snails can make it big in the City of Angels.

So, with their first taste of fame behind them, Snails prepared to embark on an even greater adventure, ready to leave their mark on the music industry and the hearts of their loyal fans. The Hollywood lights may have faded, but the flame of Snails' stardom burned brighter than ever before.

Stay tuned for the next chapter as we delve into the chart-topping hits, memorable concerts, and the indelible impact Snails had on the music industry and their fans worldwide. This is just the beginning of their extraordinary journey. The slime never fades!

From Zero to Hero: Snails' Chart-Topping Hit Singles

In the early days of Snails, they faced many challenges and setbacks, but they never gave up on their dream of becoming music superstars. This section is dedicated to exploring the journey of Snails from obscurity to the top of the charts with their chart-topping hit singles.

Snails' Humble Beginnings

Snails' story started with their first album, "A Sluggish Beginning," which unfortunately did not receive much attention from the public. The album showcased their unique style and electrifying performances, but it failed to generate the expected buzz. The band was disappointed but determined to make a name for themselves.

The Breakthrough Hit: "Slime Takes Over"

Just when things seemed bleak, Snails created a musical masterpiece that would change their lives forever. The hit single, "Slime Takes Over," catapulted them from anonymity to stardom. This infectious tune, with its catchy chorus and pulsating beats, resonated with audiences worldwide.

The song's success can be attributed to the band's relentless dedication to their craft. They poured their hearts and souls into creating a sound that was fresh, innovative, and impossible to ignore. The unique combination of rock, hip-hop, and electronic influences gave "Slime Takes Over" an irresistible appeal.

The Impact on the Music Industry

"Slime Takes Over" not only elevated Snails' status but also revolutionized the music industry. It broke through genre barriers and introduced a new sonic landscape. Their fusion of different musical elements inspired countless artists to experiment with their own sound and pushed the boundaries of what was considered mainstream music.

Moreover, the success of "Slime Takes Over" paved the way for other unconventional artists to find their place in the industry. Snails' authentic and unapologetic approach proved that there was room for diversity and creativity in the music world.

Chart-Topping Hits That Followed

After the groundbreaking success of "Slime Takes Over," Snails continued to dominate the charts with a string of hit singles. Some of their most notable chart-toppers include:

- "Shell Shock": This high-energy anthem captured the essence of Snails' unbridled passion and showcased their unparalleled stage presence. It became an instant fan favorite and solidified the band's position at the forefront of the music industry.

- "Sonic Slime": With its infectious hooks and mesmerizing lyrics, "Sonic Slime" became an anthem for the generation. The song's thought-provoking social commentary combined with its irresistible rhythm made it a chart-topping sensation.

- "Trailblazers": This empowering track exemplified Snails' ability to inspire and uplift their listeners. Its anthemic chorus and motivational lyrics struck a chord with audiences worldwide, solidifying their position as trailblazers in the music industry.

The Secret Sauce: Snails' Unique Sound

Snails' chart-topping success can be attributed to their ability to create a truly distinctive sound. By blending genres and infusing their music with raw emotion, they captured the hearts of fans from all walks of life. Their unapologetic authenticity and powerful performances resonated with audiences on a deep level.

One key element that sets Snails' music apart is their innovative use of percussion. They incorporate unconventional instruments, such as the congas and djembe, to create a rhythmic backbone that is both captivating and infectious. This signature sound has become a trademark of Snails' music and has contributed to their chart-topping success.

Unconventional Wisdom: Snails' Journey to Stardom

Snails' journey from zero to hero teaches us valuable lessons about perseverance, authenticity, and the power of embracing our uniqueness. Despite initial setbacks, the band never compromised their artistic vision or compromised their sound to fit into preconceived notions of what success should look like.

Their chart-topping hit singles are a testament to their unwavering dedication to their craft and their refusal to conform to industry norms. Snails' story serves as a reminder to aspiring artists that staying true to oneself and pushing boundaries can lead to groundbreaking success.

Exercise: Exploring Your Unique Sound

Just like Snails, every artist has the potential to create their own unique sound. As an aspiring musician, take some time to reflect on your musical influences and personal experiences. Identify the elements that make you different from other artists and experiment with blending genres to create something entirely new.

Challenge yourself to step outside of your comfort zone and embrace your individuality. Remember, chart-topping success often comes from daring to be different and bringing something fresh to the table. Embrace your uniqueness and let your true sound shine.

Caveat: The Perils of Success

While achieving chart-topping success is undoubtedly a dream for many artists, it's important to acknowledge the challenges that come with it. Snails' rise to stardom was not without its pitfalls, and the band had to navigate the pressures of fame and the constant scrutiny of the public eye.

It's crucial to have a support system in place and prioritize self-care to navigate the potential pitfalls of success. Surround yourself with a team that believes in your vision and stay true to your artistic integrity. Remember, success is not solely defined by chart-topping hits but also by staying authentic and true to yourself.

Snails' Continued Evolution

After their initial chart-topping success, Snails didn't rest on their laurels. They continued to push boundaries, experiment with new sounds, and evolve as artists. Their journey from zero to hero was not just about achieving chart success but about leaving a lasting impact on the music industry and their fans.

In the next section, we will delve deeper into the impact Snails had on the music industry and their journey from opening act to headliners.

Behind the Slime

Stay tuned as we uncover the fascinating behind-the-scenes stories of Snails' creative process, their life on the road, and the dynamics within the band. Get ready to dive into the world of Snails' music and their enduring legacy.

Staging a Revolution: Snails' Impact on the Music Industry

In the high-energy world of music, where trends come and go, there are only a few artists who have the power to truly revolutionize the industry. Snails, the iconic band known for their unique style and electrifying performances, are one such force. With their catchy tunes, unapologetic lyrics, and boundary-pushing sound, Snails has left an indelible mark on the music landscape. In this section, we will explore the ways in which Snails has staged a revolution and forever changed the music industry.

Breaking the Mold: Challenging Genre Boundaries

From the very beginning, Snails set out to challenge the status quo and break free from the confines of traditional music genres. They created a fusion of styles, seamlessly blending rock, pop, and electronic elements to create a sound that was entirely their own. Their music resonated with fans across different demographics and broke down the walls that separated genres.

One of the most remarkable aspects of Snails' impact on the music industry is their ability to bring people together. Through their music, they have united fans from all walks of life, creating a sense of belonging and community. Their infectious energy and relatable lyrics have made them an anthem for outsiders, misfits, and dreamers alike.

Innovation through Technology

Snails' impact on the music industry goes beyond their music alone. They have embraced technology as a tool for innovation and exploration, pushing the boundaries of what is possible in live performances. Their use of cutting-edge technology, such as holographic projections and interactive stage designs, has elevated their shows to immersive experiences that transcend traditional concerts.

By embracing technology, Snails has not only revolutionized their own performances but has also inspired other artists to think outside the box and explore new frontiers in live entertainment. They have shown that technology can be a powerful tool for creative expression and have paved the way for a new era of live music experiences.

Empowering Music as a Vehicle for Change

Snails' impact on the music industry extends beyond the sonic realm. They have used their platform to champion important social issues and inspire positive change. Through their lyrics and activism, they have shed light on topics such as mental health, social justice, and environmental conservation, sparking conversations and encouraging their fans to take action.

One of the ways Snails has empowered music as a vehicle for change is through their partnerships with charitable organizations. They have collaborated with nonprofits that support causes close to their hearts, leveraging their platform to raise awareness and funds. Snails has proved that music can be a powerful catalyst for social change and has inspired countless artists to use their voices for good.

Reshaping the Industry Norms

Snails' impact on the music industry is not limited to their creative output and activism. They have also challenged and reshaped industry norms, advocating for fair treatment of artists and pushing for more equitable structures within the music business.

By taking control of their own music and touring operations, Snails has set an example for independent artists and proved that it is possible to succeed outside of the traditional major label system. They have shown that artists can maintain creative control and build successful careers on their own terms, without compromising their artistic vision.

Furthermore, Snails has also paved the way for more diverse voices and representation within the industry. They have been vocal advocates for inclusivity and have consistently used their platform to uplift marginalized communities. By challenging the industry's homogeneity, Snails has opened doors for artists from all backgrounds and inspired a new generation of musicians to pursue their dreams.

The Snails Phenomenon: Impact on Fan Culture

Snails' impact on the music industry has been nothing short of a whirlwind, and their fans have played an essential role in their success. The Snail Army, as they are lovingly known, is a passionate and dedicated fan base that has been instrumental in spreading the band's music and message.

The Snail Army has taken fan culture to new heights, with its own unique language, rituals, and traditions. From creating elaborate fan art to organizing fan conventions and meetups, Snails' fans have built a tight-knit community centered around their shared love for the band. Their unwavering support and enthusiasm have fueled Snails' rise to stardom and created a lasting legacy.

An Unconventional Approach

In the true spirit of Snails, their impact on the music industry has been marked by their unconventional approach to everything they do. From their genre-bending music to their use of technology, activism, and fan engagement, Snails has never been afraid to color outside the lines.

Their unique blend of creativity, innovation, and authenticity sets them apart from their peers and has allowed them to carve out a distinct place in music history. Snails' impact on the music industry is a testament to the power of thinking outside the box and staying true to oneself in an ever-evolving landscape.

Conclusion

Snails' impact on the music industry cannot be overstated. They have staged a revolution by challenging genre boundaries, embracing technology, empowering music as a vehicle for change, reshaping industry norms, and inspiring a dedicated fan base. Snails has left an indelible mark on the music industry, and their legacy will continue to inspire future generations of artists to push the boundaries of creativity, authenticity, and social impact.

As we continue to explore Snails' journey, we will delve deeper into their creative process, the untold stories behind their music, and the personal dynamics that have shaped the band. Join us on this exciting ride through the world of Snails, where the slime never fades.

Snails Live and Uncensored: Memorable Concerts and Tours

Welcome to the electrifying world of Snails' live performances and unforgettable tours! In this section, we dive into the exhilarating experiences of attending a Snails concert, exploring the band's iconic stage presence, the energy they exude, and their ability to captivate audiences worldwide. Get ready to be transported to the heart-pounding moments of Snails' most memorable concerts and tours.

The Snails Spectacle: Creating Magical Moments

When it comes to delivering a mind-blowing concert experience, Snails knows how to set the stage on fire! With their infectious energy and larger-than-life performances, the band creates a spectacle that transcends the boundaries of music. From the very first note to the explosive finale, Snails takes the audience on an unforgettable journey of sound, visuals, and pure adrenaline.

Setting the Stage Ablaze

Imagine stepping into a vibrant world of captivating visuals, overwhelming sounds, and an atmosphere charged with excitement. As the lights dim and the crowd roars, the stage comes alive with an explosion of pyrotechnics, dazzling light displays, and larger-than-life set designs. Snails spares no expense in creating a visual extravaganza that matches the intensity of their music, leaving the audience in awe.

The Snails' Secret Ingredient: Crowd Interaction

What sets Snails apart from other bands is their unparalleled ability to connect with their fans. From the moment they step on stage, Snails has an uncanny knack for making every audience member feel like they are part of something truly special. Whether it's high-fiving fans in the front row, pulling someone on stage for an impromptu jam session, or simply making eye contact with individuals in the crowd, Snails creates a sense of intimacy that few can replicate.

The Sonic Storm of Snails' Hits

A Snails concert is not just about the spectacle; it's also about the music. With a catalog of chart-topping hits and fan favorites, every performance is a sonic storm that leaves the crowd craving more. From the blistering guitar solos to the thunderous drum beats, Snails' music reverberates through the venue, taking the audience on a rollercoaster of emotions. Singles like "Slime and Shine" and "Sticky Riffs" ignite the crowd, creating massive sing-alongs that reverberate throughout the entire venue.

Unleashing the Snail Army

No Snails concert would be complete without the infamous Snail Army. These dedicated fans, known as "Snailites," are an integral part of the band's live shows. Dressed in their signature Snail army uniforms, they bring an infectious energy, creating an atmosphere unlike any other. From starting massive mosh pits to inventing their own dance moves, the Snail Army adds an extra layer of excitement and camaraderie to any Snails concert.

Unforgettable Tour Experiences

Snails doesn't just perform in one city or country; they take their electrifying shows on the road, embarking on epic global tours that span continents. Each tour is meticulously crafted to deliver an experience that captures the essence of Snails' music and persona. From intimate club shows to massive stadium performances, every tour stop offers a unique opportunity for fans to witness Snails' unstoppable force firsthand.

Snails' Legendary Tour Moments

Throughout their career, Snails has had countless tour moments that have gone down in music history. From their explosive performance at the Snailville City Arena, where they played for a record-breaking crowd of 80,000 fans, to their intimate acoustic set in a secluded forest, Snails knows how to create magical moments on stage. Whether it's surprising fans with special guest appearances, smashing guitars, or performing jaw-dropping stunts, the band never fails to leave a lasting impression.

Behind the Scenes: the Tour Life

Behind the scenes, the tour life of Snails is a whirlwind of adventure and camaraderie. Traveling from city to city, the band forms a tight-knit bond that becomes the backbone of their spellbinding performances. From late-night jam sessions in hotel rooms to sharing meals with the crew, the band's unity shines through, reflecting in their electrifying performances on stage.

Snail Tails: Fan Experiences

As Snails' popularity soared, so did the unforgettable fan experiences that accompanied their concerts and tours. Countless fans have shared stories of meeting their musical heroes, being inspired by their performances, and forging lifelong friendships within the Snail community. These personal accounts serve as a testament to the profound impact Snails has had on their fans' lives.

The Snail Legacy: Carrying the Torch

Snails' live performances and tours have cemented their place as one of the most influential bands in music history. Their ability to combine music, theatrics, and intense audience engagement has set the standard for live shows. As Snails moves into the next chapter of their career, their iconic concerts and tours will continue to inspire future generations of musicians and entertainers.

Snails Live and Uncensored: A Conclusion

Snails' live performances and tours are a spectacle like no other. From their explosive stage presence to the unforgettable moments shared with fans, Snails has redefined what it means to put on an incredible show. With their legacy firmly secured, Snails continues to push the boundaries of live music, leaving an indelible mark on the industry. So, get ready to be captivated by the raw energy and sonic brilliance of Snails' live and uncensored concerts – an experience like no other.

From Opening Act to Headliners: Snails' Journey to Stardom

Snails' journey to stardom was not an easy one. Like most bands, they started out as an opening act, playing in small venues to a handful of people. But through hard work, determination, and a little bit of luck, they eventually became headliners, selling out stadiums and capturing the hearts of millions around the world.

The Early Struggles

Snails' rise to fame was not without its fair share of challenges. In the early days, they faced numerous rejections from record labels and struggled to find their unique sound. But instead of giving up, they used these setbacks as fuel to push themselves harder.

Finding Their Sound One of the key turning points for Snails was their relentless pursuit of their own unique musical style. They experimented with different genres, blending elements of rock, funk, and soul to create a sound that was entirely their own. This fusion of styles became the signature Snails sound, setting them apart from other bands and attracting a dedicated fan base.

Breaking Through Snails' first breakthrough performance came when they were given the opportunity to open for a well-established band on a national tour. This exposure allowed them to showcase their talent to a larger audience, and their energetic and captivating performances quickly won over fans.

Gaining Local Recognition and Fans

As Snails continued to tour and gain more experience on stage, their popularity started to grow. They became known for their electrifying live shows, full of high energy and infectious enthusiasm. Word spread quickly about the band, and soon they had a growing army of devoted fans.

Connecting with the Snail Army Snails made it a point to connect with their fans on a personal level. They took the time to meet and greet fans after shows, sign autographs, and take pictures. This genuine interaction with their audience created a strong sense of community and loyalty among their fans, who affectionately came to be known as the "Snail Army."

Harnessing the Power of Social Media In addition to their live performances, Snails also took advantage of the power of social media to connect with their fans. They shared behind-the-scenes videos, exclusive content, and personal stories, allowing their followers to get a glimpse into their lives offstage. This transparency and authenticity further strengthened their bond with their fan base.

The Road to their First Record Deal

With their growing fan base and increasing recognition, it wasn't long before record labels started to take notice of Snails' talent. After years of hard work and perseverance, they eventually signed their first record deal, marking a major milestone in their journey to stardom.

Creating their Debut Album Snails' first record deal gave them the opportunity to record and release their debut album. This was a defining moment for the band, as it allowed them to fully showcase their songwriting skills and musical prowess. The album received critical acclaim and spawned several hit singles, propelling Snails further into the spotlight.

Touring as Headliners With the success of their debut album, Snails embarked on their first headlining tour. This was a dream come true for the band, as they finally had the chance to perform their own full-length shows and connect with their fans on a deeper level. The tour was a massive success, with sold-out shows and rave reviews, solidifying Snails' status as a headline act.

The Snails Phenomenon

As Snails' popularity continued to soar, they became more than just a band. They became a cultural phenomenon, with their music and unique style transcending borders and captivating audiences around the world.

Influence on Music Trends Snails' innovative fusion of genres and their distinctive sound influenced a new wave of music trends. Their energetic performances and infectious melodies inspired countless up-and-coming artists, leaving a lasting impact on the music industry.

Global Fanbase and Fan Culture The Snail Army grew exponentially, spreading their love for the band across continents. Fans organized fan clubs, fan art contests, and even created their own Snails-inspired merchandise. The band's impact went beyond music, as they became a symbol of unity and inspiration.

In the Fast Lane to Success

From humble beginnings to headlining stadiums, Snails' journey to stardom was a testament to their unwavering passion, perseverance, and undeniable talent. Their unique sound, electrifying performances, and genuine connection with their fan base propelled them to the top of the music industry. But their story didn't end there – Snails' journey was only just beginning, with many more chapters yet to be written.

So, hang on tight and get ready for the next part of Snails' incredible adventure!

The Price of Fame: Navigating the Pitfalls of Celebrity

The Glitz and Glam of Stardom

Ah, the sweet taste of success! As Snails rose to stardom, they found themselves thrust into a world of glitz and glam that few can comprehend. The flashing lights, the adoring fans, and the high-profile appearances—it all seemed like a dream come true.

But behind the scenes, there were unforeseen challenges that came with the incredible fame and fortune. In this section, we explore the price that Snails paid for their celebrity status and how they navigated through the pitfalls that came their way.

The Dark Side of the Spotlight

Being in the limelight is not always sunshine and rainbows. Snails quickly realized that fame had a dark side too. The pressures of staying relevant, the constant scrutiny from the media, and the expectations of their fans weighed heavily on their shoulders.

One of the first challenges they faced was the invasion of their privacy. With their popularity soaring, every aspect of their personal lives became fair game for the tabloids. Snails had to find a way to protect their privacy while still maintaining a connection with their devoted fanbase.

Additionally, the band members had to deal with the relentless demands of their busy schedules. Endless touring, recording sessions, and promotional events took a toll on their physical and mental well-being. They had to constantly find a balance between their professional commitments and their personal lives.

The Strains on Relationships

The price of fame extended beyond the individual struggles of each band member. Relationships within the band and with their loved ones also faced their fair share of challenges.

Snails had always prided themselves on their unbreakable bond, but the pressures of fame put that bond to the test. Creative differences, artistic egos, and the constant exposure to each other's flaws and quirks strained their relationship. It took open communication, compromise, and a lot of love to keep the band intact.

Outside of the band, the personal lives of the Snails' members were also affected. Maintaining romantic relationships and friendships became difficult as the band's fame grew. Trust issues, jealousy, and the constant presence of paparazzi created additional hurdles that they had to navigate.

Staying Grounded in a Sea of Temptation

As the world embraced Snails' music, there were temptations at every corner. The band had to face the allure of drugs, alcohol, and party culture that often comes with a rockstar lifestyle. With their reputation on the line, they had to make conscious choices to remain true to their values.

Snails recognized the need for a strong support system to keep them grounded. They surrounded themselves with trusted friends, family, and mentors who could guide them through the ups and downs of fame. Additionally, they invested in their own well-being by seeking professional help, practicing mindfulness, and staying physically active.

Overcoming the Pitfalls

Although the price of fame seemed steep at times, Snails rose above the challenges and proved their resilience. They harnessed the power of their fanbase and used their platform to spread positive messages about the importance of self-care, mental health, and staying true to oneself.

The band's transparency about their struggles helped their fans realize that even celebrities face hardships. Snails encouraged their fans to prioritize their well-being and strive for a balanced life. They became advocates for mindfulness, mental health awareness, and the importance of maintaining healthy relationships.

Lessons Learned

The journey of Snails taught them valuable lessons about the realities of fame. They learned that success should not come at the expense of their authenticity and happiness. They discovered the importance of setting boundaries, taking breaks, and prioritizing self-care to maintain a sustainable career in the music industry.

Snails had to navigate the treacherous waters of fame, but they emerged stronger, wiser, and more resilient. Their story serves as a powerful reminder that with fame comes responsibility, and that the true measure of success is not just in the number of records sold, but in the positive impact they have on the lives of their fans and the world around them.

Exercise

Reflect on a celebrity who has faced the pitfalls of fame and navigated their way through successfully. What lessons can you learn from their journey? How can you apply those lessons to your own life, even if you are not in the public eye? Share your thoughts with a friend or on social media using the hashtag #NavigatingFameWisely.

A Closer Look: The Personal Lives of Snails' Members

Behind the larger-than-life stage personas and the electrifying performances, the members of Snails are just like you and me. In this chapter, we explore the personal lives of these rock icons, delving into their passions, struggles, and the moments that shaped them into the global superstars they are today.

From Ordinary to Extraordinary: The Snails' Journey

Before we bask in the glory of Snails' flamboyant success, let's rewind the clock and dig deep into their humble beginnings. Each band member grew up in different corners of the world, coming from diverse backgrounds, but connected by the shared dream of making music that transcends borders.

Take, for instance, Freddie "The Flying Snail" Mendez, the enigmatic frontman. He was born in a small town in Mexico, where he discovered his love for music at an early age. Raised in a household filled with traditional Mexican tunes, Freddie's fascination with the power of music ignited a fire within him, leading him to weave his own creative path.

Then there's Liam "The Lightning" O'Connor, the thunderous drummer of Snails. Hailing from Dublin, Ireland, Liam's rhythmic inclination emerged during his childhood when he would tap his pencil on the school desk, creating impromptu beats. This innate passion soon developed into a mastery of percussion, propelling him towards a life of endless possibilities.

Next, we have Isabella "The Serpent" Rossi, the mesmerizing lead guitarist. Born in the heart of Buenos Aires, Argentina, Isabella's journey began with a chance encounter with her father's old electric guitar. As her nimble fingers danced across the strings, she realized that she had discovered the missing piece of her soul. From that moment forward, there was no turning back for Isabella.

Completing the formidable lineup of Snails is Marcus "The Magician" Chen, the maestro behind the keyboard. Growing up in Tokyo, Japan, Marcus found solace in the world of melodies and harmonies. Drawing inspiration from the vibrant cityscape, he immersed himself in the study of classical and contemporary piano techniques, molding him into a dynamic force within the band.

The Struggles and Triumphs of Snails

Behind the glitz and glamour, Snails' personal lives are punctuated by both triumphs and struggles. Their journey to success was not without its share of hardships, but they persevered, emerging stronger than ever.

While Freddie was known for his charismatic stage presence, his life was marred by personal demons. Battling with anxiety and self-doubt, he found solace in his music. Through his introspective songwriting, he transformed his pain into anthems of resilience, giving voice to those who needed it most.

For Liam, the constant pressure to maintain the band's energy took a toll on his mental and physical well-being. But with the support of his bandmates and the love of his dedicated fans, he overcame the obstacles, finding strength in his passion for music.

Isabella's path was not without its fair share of challenges either. As a woman in a male-dominated industry, she had to fight for her place on the stage. With unwavering determination and undeniable talent, Isabella shattered every stereotype and became an inspiration for aspiring female musicians around the world.

As for Marcus, the journey was one of self-discovery. Wrestling with cultural identity and the pressures of conforming, he embarked on a musical pilgrimage that led him to embrace his uniqueness. His contribution to Snails' sound became a testament to the power of embracing one's true self.

Love and Loss: The Personal Lives of Snails

Beyond the music, the personal lives of Snails' members are a tapestry woven with love, friendship, and profound loss. Through the highs and lows, their bond as a band and as friends has remained unshakeable.

Freddie's love for his devoted fans is unwavering, but it is his love for his family that truly defines him. A doting father and husband, he cherishes every moment spent with his loved ones, reminding him of the importance of staying grounded amidst the whirlwind of fame.

Liam's personal life took a heartfelt turn when he met his soulmate, Emma. Their love story blossomed against all odds, proving that true love transcends distance and time. In the face of tragedy, Liam relied on the strength of their bond to navigate the darkest of days.

For Isabella, family is the anchor that keeps her grounded. Her deep-rooted connection with her Argentinean roots is evident in every chord she plays, instilling a sense of pride in her heritage. Her passion for music is rivaled only by the love she shares with her tight-knit family.

Marcus, the quiet force within Snails, draws inspiration from his late grandfather, a renowned pianist. The loss of his mentor fueled his desire to forge his own path, paying homage to the musical legacy that runs through his veins. Every note he plays is a tribute to the love and wisdom imparted by his grandfather.

The Snail Brotherhood: A Bond that Defies Explanation

Within Snails, there is an unbreakable bond that extends beyond the stage. The members share a rare camaraderie, supporting each other through thick and thin. Their friendship is the glue that holds everything together, acting as a sanctuary in the unpredictable world of fame.

Whether it's late-night jam sessions, impromptu adventures, or simply being there for one another during tough times, the Snail brotherhood is an embodiment of unconditional love and unwavering support. It is this unbreakable bond that elevates their music and fuels their determination to continue pushing boundaries.

Snails: More Than Just Rock Stars

Snails' lives extend far beyond the glitz and glamor associated with being global rock stars. Each member is an advocate for social change, using their platform to address important issues and make a positive impact on society.

Freddie channels his personal struggles with anxiety into a mission to raise awareness about mental health. Through his candid interviews and heartfelt messages, he encourages his fans to seek help and supports numerous mental health organizations.

Liam's love for the environment drives his activism in the fight against climate change. By collaborating with environmental organizations and using sustainable practices on tour, he aims to inspire others to take action and protect our planet.

Isabella's passion for empowering women in the music industry led her to create workshops and mentorship programs for aspiring female musicians. She firmly believes in the transformative power of music and its ability to break down barriers.

Marcus, with his global perspective, advocates for cultural diversity and understanding. In a world divided by borders, he uses his music to bridge gaps and promote unity among people from different walks of life.

Conclusion: The Humanity Behind the Stage

Behind the extravagant performances and mesmerizing music, the personal lives of Snails' members are a testament to the enduring power of human resilience, friendship, and love. From their humble beginnings to their present-day success, they have weathered storms, celebrated triumphs, and continued to evolve both as individuals and as a band.

In the next chapter, we delve into the creative process behind Snails' music, exploring the magic that happens behind closed doors and the meticulous craftsmanship that goes into crafting their sonic masterpieces. But before we go there, let us take a moment to appreciate the individuals behind the rock gods – the ordinary people who dared to dream, dared to defy, and ultimately became the legends we know as Snails.

The Power of Snail Army: Global Fanbase and Fan Culture

The Snail Army is not just any ordinary group of fans. They are a force to be reckoned with, an army that stands together in their love and support for the band Snails. With fans spread across the globe, the Snail Army has become a symbol of unity and loyalty.

Unleashing the Power

The Snail Army's global reach is a testament to the band's widespread appeal. From the bustling streets of Tokyo to the vibrant cities of Brazil, Snails' music has captivated people from all walks of life. It is this universal connection that has fueled the expansion of the Snail Army, allowing it to transcend borders and cultures.

The Snail Effect

The influence of the Snail Army extends far beyond the music itself. Fans have created a unique culture around the band, embracing their music as a way of life. They proudly display their love for Snails through fan art, tattoos, and personalized merchandise. The Snail logo has become a symbol of identity and belonging, a rallying point for all who consider themselves part of the Snail Army.

Fan Culture

Fan culture surrounding Snails is unlike anything seen before. The Snail Army has its own set of inside jokes, memes, and catchphrases that have become part of their shared lexicon. Snails' concerts are not mere performances; they are epic gatherings of the Snail Army, where fans come together to celebrate their shared love for the band and create memories that will last a lifetime.

Fan Initiatives

The Snail Army is not just a passive group of fans; they are a force of positivity and action. Fans have organized charity events and fundraisers in the name of Snails, using their passion for the band to make a difference in the world. These initiatives serve as a testament to the power of music and the unity that the Snail Army embodies.

The Snail Social Network

Thanks to the power of social media, the Snail Army has formed a tight-knit community that transcends physical boundaries. Fans connect with each other through dedicated fan pages, forums, and hashtags, sharing their love for Snails and engaging in lively discussions about the band's music, performances, and future projects.

The Snail Whisperers

Within the Snail Army, there are a select few who have gained recognition as the "Snail Whisperers." These individuals have a deep understanding of Snails' music and are known for their insightful interpretations of the band's lyrics and themes. They are looked up to by the rest of the Snail Army as interpreters of the band's message and as a source of inspiration.

The Evolution of the Snail Army

As Snails' music has evolved over the years, so too has the Snail Army. New generations of fans continue to join the ranks, keeping the spirit of Snails alive for years to come. The Snail Army's ability to adapt and embrace change is a testament to the band's lasting legacy and the enduring power of their music.

The Phenomenon of Snails' Fan Army

The Snail Army is a global force that demonstrates the incredible influence a band can have on its fans. They connect across borders and cultures, creating a powerful community that goes beyond the music. The Snail Army's dedication and passion serve as a reminder of the impact music can have on our lives.

The Snail Army is made up of individuals who have found solace, inspiration, and a sense of belonging in Snails' music. Through their shared love for the band, fans have formed deep connections with one another, building a supportive network that extends far beyond the realm of music. This fan culture is a testament to the power of music in bringing people together.

The Snail Army's impact goes beyond the fan community. Fans have organized charity events and fundraisers, using their love for Snails as a catalyst for positive change in the world. This demonstrates that music has the ability to inspire action and make a difference.

The Snail Army's presence on social media has allowed fans to connect and engage with each other on a daily basis. They share their love for Snails, discuss their favorite songs, and even meet up at concerts and events. This online community has become a source of support and friendship for many fans, giving them a sense of belonging and a place to express themselves freely.

Within the Snail Army, there are fans who have gained recognition as the "Snail Whisperers." These individuals have a deep understanding of Snails' music and are able to interpret the band's lyrics and themes in a profound and insightful manner. They serve as a source of inspiration for other fans and help foster a deeper appreciation for the band's artistry.

The Snail Army's evolution mirrors Snails' own musical journey. As the band has experimented with different genres and styles, the fan base has grown and evolved alongside them. New generations of fans continue to join the Snail Army, ensuring that the band's music will continue to resonate for years to come.

In conclusion, the Snail Army is much more than just a group of fans. They are a testament to the power of music to bring people together, inspire action, and create a sense of belonging. Snails' music has had a profound impact on their lives, and they in turn have made a lasting impact on the band. The Snail Army is a true testament to the enduring power of music and the strong bond between artists and their fans.

Reinventing the Genre: Snails' Influence on Music Trends

In the ever-evolving landscape of music, there are rare moments when a band comes along and completely redefines a genre. Such is the case with Snails, the iconic music band whose innovative sound has left an indelible mark on the industry. In this section, we will delve into the ways in which Snails has reinvented the genre and the profound influence they have had on music trends.

Breaking the Mold: Challenging Conventions

Snails burst onto the scene with a musical style that defied categorization. Their unique blend of rock, funk, and electronic elements created a fresh and distinct sound that captivated audiences worldwide. Gone were the traditional genre boundaries as Snails embraced experimentation and pushed the limits of musical conventions.

One of the ways Snails challenged conventions was through their unconventional use of instrumentation. They were pioneers in incorporating unconventional instruments, such as the theremin, accordion, and steel drums, into their music. This unexpected fusion of sounds created an entirely new sonic experience for listeners, breaking away from the predictable formulas of the past.

Moreover, Snails infused their songs with thought-provoking lyrics that tackled social and personal themes. They fearlessly explored topics such as mental health, societal inequalities, and the human condition. By addressing these issues head-on, Snails not only connected with their audience on a deep level but also sparked conversations and inspired others to use their music as a platform for change.

Evolution of Sound: Influences and Inspirations

Snails' ability to reinvent the genre can be attributed, in part, to their diverse range of influences and inspirations. Drawing from a wide array of musical styles and eras, they created a sound that was both nostalgic and forward-thinking.

Early on, Snails were heavily inspired by the pioneers of rock and roll, such as Led Zeppelin and The Rolling Stones. They embraced the raw energy and rebellious spirit of these trailblazers, incorporating it into their own music. However, Snails didn't stop there. They also drew inspiration from funk legends like James Brown and Parliament-Funkadelic, infusing their songs with infectious grooves and funky rhythms.

As the band evolved, they began incorporating electronic elements into their music, inspired by the works of visionary artists like Kraftwerk and Daft Punk. With their seamless integration of electronic beats and synthesized sounds, Snails created a sound that was truly ahead of its time.

The Snail Effect: Reverberations in the Music Industry

Snails' innovative approach to music had a profound impact on the industry as a whole, not just within their own genre. They set off a ripple effect that reverberated throughout the music world, influencing and inspiring countless artists to break free from the confines of traditional genres.

One of the most significant ways Snails' influence can be seen is in the rise of genre-bending artists who refuse to be pigeonholed. From acts like Twenty One Pilots, who effortlessly blend rock, hip-hop, and electronic elements, to Billie Eilish, whose ethereal sound defies categorization, Snails' influence can be felt in the diverse range of music being produced today.

Moreover, Snails' impact on music production cannot be overstated. Their pioneering use of sampling and looping techniques paved the way for a generation of artists who would go on to revolutionize the art of music production. The band's fearless exploration of new sonic territories opened doors for experimentation in recording studios around the world.

Snails' Musical Legacy: Impact on Future Generations

As we reflect on Snails' influence on music trends, it becomes clear that their legacy extends far beyond their own time. They have left an enduring impact on future generations of musicians, forever changing the landscape of the industry.

But Snails' influence goes beyond just sound and genre. They have inspired a new generation of artists to embrace their individuality and push the boundaries of creativity. By fearlessly embracing their own uniqueness, Snails showed others that true artistry lies in authenticity.

Their legacy is not merely confined to the music world either. Snails' impact on popular culture can be seen in fashion trends, visual art, and even in the way we consume and experience music. Their boundary-breaking performances and experimental stage presence have set a new standard for live shows, inspiring artists to create immersive and unforgettable experiences for their fans.

In conclusion, Snails' reinvention of the genre and influence on music trends can be summed up in one word: revolutionary. By challenging conventions, embracing experimentation, and pushing the boundaries of creativity, they have forever changed the face of music. Their legacy serves as a reminder that true artistry lies in the ability to break free from the mold and create a sound that is uniquely your own. Snails' story is a testament to the power of innovation, and their influence will continue to shape the future of music for generations to come.

Higher, Faster, Stronger: Snails' Record-Breaking Achievements

In the world of music, there are those who simply make a mark and those who break records, shatter barriers, and redefine what is possible. Snails, the extraordinary band known for their unique style and relentless passion, falls firmly into the latter category. Throughout their illustrious career, Snails has achieved record-breaking feats that have left the entire music industry in awe. In this section, we will delve into the remarkable achievements of Snails, celebrating their ability to push boundaries and reach new heights.

Breaking the Speed Limit: The Fastest Music Performance

For Snails, speed is not just a statistic; it is a way of life. The band has always been known for their high-energy performances that leave fans breathless and clamoring for more. In 2016, Snails set the record for the fastest music performance ever recorded, reaching a mind-boggling tempo of 300 beats per minute during their electrifying encore at the Snail Stadium. The performance left fans amazed and critics scrambling for words to describe the sheer intensity and adrenaline of that unforgettable night.

But breaking records is not just about speed; it's also about stamina. Snails proved that they were not just a flash in the pan by sustaining their lightning-fast pace for an impressive 45 minutes, captivating the audience with their relentless energy and unwavering dedication to their craft. This record-breaking achievement not only showcased the band's extraordinary musical talents but also their unmatched endurance and commitment to delivering unforgettable performances.

Climbing the Charts: Chart-Topping Hits

Snails' success is not limited to their live performances; their chart-topping hits have also made waves in the music industry. Throughout their career, Snails has consistently dominated the charts with their addictive melodies, thought-provoking lyrics, and genre-bending sound. In 2018, their hit single "Slime Revolution" topped the charts in over 50 countries simultaneously, a feat never before achieved by any other artist or band.

But what sets Snails apart is not just their ability to create catchy tunes; it is also their commitment to pushing boundaries. With each new release, the band manages to captivate audiences with their innovative and daring approach to music. From blending different genres to experimenting with unconventional instruments, Snails has redefined what it means to create a chart-topping hit. Their record-breaking achievements on the charts are a testament to their unparalleled creativity and unwavering commitment to artistic excellence.

The Power of Unity: Largest Virtual Concert

In the digital age, music has the power to bring people together like never before. Snails understands this better than anyone else and has harnessed the power of technology to create unprecedented experiences for their fans. In 2020, Snails broke the record for the largest virtual concert ever, attracting over 10 million viewers from around the world.

The concert, aptly named "Snail's Paradise," was a testament to the band's ability to adapt to the ever-changing landscape of the music industry. Through cutting-edge technology and innovative storytelling, Snails transported viewers into a virtual world where they could not only enjoy the band's electrifying performance but also interact with fellow fans in real-time. The record-breaking virtual concert not only showcased Snails' ability to harness the power of technology but also their unwavering dedication to creating unforgettable and inclusive experiences for their fans.

Unleashing the Power of Fan Participation: Most Interactive Concert

Snails understands that a concert is not just about the band; it is about the fans and the collective experience of being part of something truly extraordinary. In 2019, they set the record for the most interactive concert ever, giving fans unprecedented control over the setlist, stage design, and lighting effects.

Using state-of-the-art technology, Snails developed a one-of-a-kind mobile app that allowed fans to vote on various elements of the concert in real-time. From choosing the next song to triggering mesmerizing light shows, the band empowered their fans to become co-creators of the concert experience. This groundbreaking achievement not only demonstrated Snails' commitment to creating unforgettable moments for their fans but also showcased their ability to harness the power of technology to foster a deeper connection between artists and their audience.

Beyond the Records: Inspiring a Generation

While Snails' record-breaking achievements are undoubtedly impressive, their impact extends far beyond the numbers. Throughout their journey, the band has inspired a generation of artists and music lovers to dream bigger, work harder, and always push the boundaries of what is possible.

By fearlessly exploring different genres, collaborating with diverse artists, and infusing their music with powerful messages, Snails has opened doors for new and unconventional forms of artistic expression. Their relentless pursuit of excellence, combined with their unwavering dedication to their craft, serves as an inspiration not only to aspiring musicians but to anyone who dares to dream big and chase their passions.

In conclusion, Snails' record-breaking achievements are a testament to their undeniable talent, unwavering dedication, and relentless pursuit of excellence. From their blistering speed to their chart-topping hits, from their groundbreaking use of technology to their unwavering commitment to their fans, Snails has redefined what it means to be a band in the modern music industry. Their record-breaking legacy will forever remain a source of inspiration and a reminder that with passion, innovation, and an unyielding spirit, anything is possible. So lace up your boots, put on your headphones, and get ready to witness the extraordinary: Snails, higher, faster, and stronger than ever before.

Behind the Slime

Behind the Slime

Behind the Slime

Welcome to Chapter 2 of our snail-tastic journey through the extraordinary lives of the band known as Snails. In this section, we will journey behind the scenes and delve into the enigmatic world of these musicians. Get ready to uncover the secrets, aspirations, and creative process that make Snails the iconic band they are today.

The Snail's Nest: Snails' Creative Process

Every great band has a unique creative process that sets them apart from the rest. Snails is no exception. As we take a peek into their world, it becomes clear that the snail's nest is where the magic happens.

Snails' creative process is a combination of collaboration, unique perspectives, and a whole lot of slime. At the core of their creative process is the belief that inspiration can strike from the most unexpected places. From the chirping of birds to the buzz of a crowded street, Snails finds beauty and potential in every sound.

To harness this inspiration, Snails holds regular jam sessions, allowing their musical instincts to guide them. They experiment with different melodies, rhythms, and harmonies, pushing the boundaries of their music. These sessions can sometimes turn into massive snail jam parties, with friends and fellow musicians joining in the sonic exploration.

Composing the Stench: Snails' Songwriting Techniques

Composing the stench is no easy feat, but Snails has mastered the art of crafting songs that stick with you long after the music ends. Their songwriting techniques are as unique as their slimy aesthetic.

One of Snails' most beloved songwriting techniques is the "shell swap." In this process, each band member writes a song, then passes it to another member to add their creative touch. This shell swap ensures that each song carries the essence of every band member, creating a harmonious blend of different musical perspectives.

Another technique that Snails employs is the "lyrical storytelling." They take inspiration from their own experiences, as well as those they've encountered on their journey. Through vivid and often metaphorical lyrics, Snails invites fans to step into their slimy world and experience life from their perspective.

Uncovering the Gems: Snails' Rare Collaborations

Collaborations are like hidden gems, waiting to be discovered and cherished. Snails has a knack for finding these rare gems and turning them into extraordinary musical experiences.

One unforgettable collaboration was with renowned jazz saxophonist, Benny "The Slug" Johnson. The fusion of Snails' energetic beats with Benny's soulful saxophone created a musical masterpiece that transcended genres and captivated fans from all walks of life.

In another surprising twist, Snails joined forces with electronic music sensation, DJ Shelltop. This collaboration between two seemingly different music styles showcased Snails' versatility and their ability to adapt and evolve.

But Snails' collaborations don't stop in the music industry. They've also partnered with well-known visual artists, incorporating their distinctive style into music videos and album art. These collaborations push the boundaries of creativity and give fans a visually stunning experience.

Pushing the Boundaries: Snails' Experimental Music

Snails is known for pushing the boundaries of conventional music, daring to experiment with new sounds and styles. Their commitment to musical exploration shines through in their experimental music.

One of their most audacious experiments was their fusion of classical music with heavy metal. The haunting melodies of the violin blended seamlessly with the thunderous riffs of the electric guitar, creating a genre-defying symphony that left audiences awe-struck.

In another daring move, Snails incorporated unconventional instruments, such as the waterphone and the didgeridoo, into their music. These unique sounds added a distinct dimension to their songs and created an otherworldly atmosphere that only Snails could conjure.

BEHIND THE SLIME 57

Let's Get Snail-y: Recording in the Studio

Recording a Snails album is an adventure in itself. It's a process that requires precision, creativity, and a whole lot of snail spirit.

The Snails' recording sessions are like a chaotic symphony. The band members bring their ideas and melodies to the studio, where they work tirelessly to capture the essence of their music. The studio becomes their sanctuary, a place where they can let their creativity run wild without any constraints.

But it's not just about recording the music. Snails believes in crafting a complete sonic experience for their fans. They meticulously layer each instrument, adding unique effects and textures to create a multi-dimensional sound that transports listeners into the depths of their slimy universe.

The Art of the Album: Snails' Masterpieces

For Snails, an album is not just a collection of songs; it's a work of art. Each album is a carefully crafted masterpiece that tells a story and evokes emotions in a way that only Snails can.

The band pours their hearts and souls into every aspect of the album, from the music to the artwork. They believe in creating a cohesive experience, where every song is a chapter in a larger narrative.

Snails' artistry extends beyond the music itself. They collaborate with visual artists to create stunning album covers that capture the essence of each album. These visually striking designs are a testament to their dedication to creating a complete sensory experience for their fans.

Innovation on Steroids: Technical Wizardry by Snails

Snails not only brings innovation to their music but also to the technical aspects of their performances. They constantly push the boundaries of what is possible, incorporating state-of-the-art technology into their shows.

One of their most mind-boggling technical feats is their holographic stage presence. Snails uses cutting-edge hologram technology to create stunning visual displays that complement their music. From virtual snails crawling across the stage to ethereal landscapes that perfectly match the mood of the songs, the band's holographic wizardry takes their performances to another dimension.

Snails also embraces the power of augmented reality (AR) to engage their audiences. Through specially designed apps, fans can immerse themselves in a virtual snail universe, where they can interact with the band members and experience their music in breathtaking new ways.

The Snail's Musical Toolbox: Instruments and Equipment

Snails' music wouldn't be what it is without their trusty musical toolbox. Each band member has their signature instruments and equipment that contribute to Snails' unique sound.

Lead vocalist Serena slithers across the stage with her custom-made golden microphone, which gives her voice that unmistakable snail sparkle.

Joe, the band's drummer, delivers thunderous beats on his signature snare drum, aptly named "The Slammer." Its deep, resonating sound creates the backbone of Snails' music.

The bass guitarist, Oliver, elicits waves of slithering vibrations through his electric bass, equipped with modifications that allow for mind-bending effects and tones.

Lastly, Eric, the guitarist, dazzles the audience with his custom-built electric guitar, aptly named "The Slugger." Its sleek design and powerful sound provide the perfect complement to Snails' energetic performances.

The Art of the Snail: Visual Aesthetics

For Snails, their music is not just about the sound; it's also about the visual feast they present to their fans. Their visual aesthetics are as captivating and unconventional as their music itself.

Snails' stage shows are a mesmerizing blend of fantastical elements, vibrant colors, and larger-than-life props. From giant snail shells to larger-than-life slime sculptures, the band creates a surreal atmosphere that transports the audience to a world where snails reign supreme.

Each band member sports their unique visual style, from Serena's glimmering slime-inspired costumes to Joe's snail shell drum kit. These visuals not only enhance their performances but also serve as a visual representation of their music and philosophy.

The Snail's Nest: A Hub of Infinite Creativity

In conclusion, the Snails' nest is a hub of infinite creativity, innovation, and experimentation. It's a place where the band members come together to create magical music that transcends the boundaries of genres and captivates audiences around the world.

Their collaborative approach, unique songwriting techniques, and willingness to push the boundaries of conventional music have cemented Snails' place in music history. From the studio to the stage, the band's attention to detail and dedication to creating a complete sensory experience set them apart from the rest.

Stay tuned for the next chapter, where we will dive into the untold stories from the road and explore the band dynamics that have kept Snails united throughout their remarkable journey. Get ready to rock 'n' roll, Snail Army!

The Snail's Nest: Snails' Creative Process

Composing the Stench: Snails' Songwriting Techniques

In this section, we will dive into the fascinating world of Snails' songwriting techniques. The band's ability to create unique and unforgettable music is the driving force behind their success. From the birth of an idea to the final composition, Snails' songwriting process is a journey filled with creativity, passion, and a touch of stench.

The Birth of an Idea: Finding Inspiration

Every song starts with an idea, a spark of inspiration that ignites the creative process. For Snails, finding inspiration can come from anywhere and everywhere. Whether it's a personal experience, a thought-provoking concept, or even a simple observation, the band members are constantly seeking sources of inspiration to fuel their songwriting.

To capture the essence of their inspiration, Snails' members immerse themselves in their surroundings. They embrace the mundane, finding beauty and intrigue in everyday moments. They tap into their emotions, exploring the depths of their feelings to create music that resonates with their audience. They draw from their own experiences, each band member bringing their unique perspective to the songwriting table.

Crafting the Melody: The Musical Puzzle

Once the initial idea is born, Snails embark on the journey of crafting the melody. This is where their musical genius shines through. Each band member plays a crucial role in piecing together the musical puzzle.

The frontman, with their captivating voice, sets the foundation for the melody. Their powerful vocals intertwine with the instrumental layers, delivering the message of the song. The rhythm section, consisting of the bassist and drummer, provide the heartbeat of the melody. Their synchronicity and precision bring depth and groove to the music. The other band members, including guitarists, keyboardists, and more, add layers of melody and harmony, elevating the composition to new heights.

Snails' songwriting process involves experimenting with various musical elements. They play with chord progressions, exploring both traditional and unconventional harmonies. They experiment with rhythms, creating infectious grooves that make listeners want to get up and dance. They blend genres, drawing from their diverse musical influences, resulting in a sound that is uniquely their own.

Lyrics: The Language of Snails

While the melody sets the tone, the lyrics are the voice of Snails. Writing powerful and meaningful lyrics is an essential part of Snails' songwriting process. Their lyrics are raw, honest, and often introspective, inviting listeners to connect on a deeper level.

To pen the perfect lyrics, Snails' members draw from their personal experiences, exploring themes such as love, loss, triumph, and self-discovery. They use vivid imagery and thought-provoking metaphors to craft poetic verses that resonate with their audience. The lyrics reflect the band's perspective on life, capturing the essence of their journey and inviting listeners to embark on their own.

Collaboration: The Power of Teamwork

One of the key ingredients to Snails' songwriting success is their ability to collaborate effectively. The band members work together as a team, leveraging their individual strengths to create something greater than the sum of its parts.

Collaboration starts from the very beginning of the songwriting process. The band members engage in open and honest discussions, sharing their ideas and perspectives. They listen to one another, embracing constructive criticism and new viewpoints. This collaborative spirit allows them to build upon each other's ideas, pushing the boundaries of their creativity.

During the composition phase, Snails' members jam together, experimenting with different musical elements and exploring various avenues. They engage in lively debates, challenging each other's ideas and pushing each other to reach new heights. This collaborative process ensures that every song is a true representation of the band's collective vision.

Embracing the Stench: Unconventional Techniques

Snails is known for their unique and unconventional style, and their songwriting techniques are no exception. They embrace the stench, refusing to conform to traditional norms. This fearless approach allows them to push boundaries and create music that is truly one-of-a-kind.

One of Snails' unconventional techniques is the incorporation of unusual instruments and sounds into their music. They are not afraid to experiment with unconventional instruments such as harmonicas, didgeridoos, or even everyday objects like kitchen utensils. These unexpected additions add layers of texture and intrigue to their compositions.

Snails also takes inspiration from nature, incorporating sounds of the environment into their music. From the chirping of birds to the rustling of leaves, these natural sounds become an integral part of their sonic landscape. This brings a sense of authenticity and organic beauty to their compositions.

Example: "Slime Symphony"

To illustrate Snails' songwriting techniques, let's take a closer look at one of their iconic compositions, "Slime Symphony." This song showcases the band's ability to seamlessly blend genres, experiment with unconventional sounds, and deliver powerful lyrics.

The melody of "Slime Symphony" begins with a haunting piano intro, complemented by the subtle sound of raindrops hitting a tin roof. The frontman's soulful voice enters, delivering thought-provoking lyrics that explore the human experience. The rhythm section adds depth and intensity, with a pulsating bassline and driving drumbeat.

As the song progresses, Snails introduces unexpected elements. They incorporate the sound of glass breaking and the pounding of a hammer, creating a rhythmic foundation that adds an element of surprise. The guitarists weave intricate melodies, seamlessly transitioning between different styles.

The lyrics of "Slime Symphony" delve into the depths of human emotions, capturing the pain of heartbreak and the resilience of the human spirit. Metaphors of slime and stench permeate the song, serving as a reminder to embrace the imperfections and complexities of life.

Through the unconventional techniques employed in "Slime Symphony," Snails showcases their innovation and willingness to take risks. They create a sonic experience that is both captivating and thought-provoking, leaving a lasting impression on their audience.

Conclusion: The Art of Snails' Songwriting

Snails' songwriting techniques are a masterful blend of inspiration, collaboration, and unconventional creativity. From the birth of an idea to the final composition, every step of the process is guided by their passion for music and their desire to create something truly unique.

By embracing the stench, Snails defies expectations and creates a musical experience that transcends genres and captivates listeners. Their fearless approach to songwriting, combined with their unparalleled talent and teamwork, has solidified their place in music history.

In the next section, we will delve into the untold stories from the road as we explore Snails' life on tour and the adventures they've encountered along the way. So buckle up, and get ready for a wild ride with Snails!

Uncovering the Gems: Snails' Rare Collaborations

In the swirling world of music, collaboration is often the key to unlocking new and exciting sounds. Many bands have dabbled in the art of collaboration, but few have ventured as far and wide as Snails. Known for their experimental and unconventional style, Snails has brought their unique brand of music to the masses by joining forces with some of the most unexpected and talented artists in the industry.

Unleashing the Snail Groove

When Snails first burst onto the music scene, they were like a bolt of lightning. Their infectious energy and raw talent quickly caught the attention of music lovers around the globe. As the band started to gain traction, they sought to expand their musical horizons by collaborating with artists from various genres and backgrounds.

One such rare and unexpected collaboration came about when Snails teamed up with the legendary jazz musician Miles Davis. Known for his groundbreaking improvisational skills, Davis was initially skeptical about merging his smooth jazz sound with Snails' edgy style. But, after hearing the band's unique blend of funk, rock, and electronic music, Davis couldn't resist the opportunity to tap into Snails' energy.

The result was an electrifying fusion of genres that pushed the boundaries of what was thought possible in music. Together, Snails and Miles Davis created a track called "Slime's Delight," which showcased the seamless integration of Davis' soulful trumpet melodies with Snails' bold and energetic instrumentals. The collaboration not only garnered critical acclaim but also opened the door for other artists to experiment with genre-bending collaborations.

A Symphony of Collaborations

Snails' rare collaborations extended beyond the realm of jazz and into classical music as well. In a groundbreaking move, the band joined forces with renowned composer and conductor Gustavo Dudamel to create a symphonic masterpiece. Combining Snails' electrifying sound with the sophistication of a full orchestra, the collaboration resulted in an unforgettable performance titled "Symphony of Slime."

In this symphony, the band's unconventional instruments, such as the electric violin and distorted keyboard, blended harmoniously with the traditional orchestral instruments. The composition featured intricate melodies that showcased the individual talents of Snails' band members, while also highlighting the versatility and adaptability of the orchestra. The fusion of classical music with Snails' signature style created an entirely new musical experience that left audiences in awe.

But Snails didn't stop at collaborating with jazz and classical musicians; they also pushed the boundaries of rap and hip-hop. Teaming up with iconic rapper Jay-Z, Snails created a powerful anthem called "Shell Shocked." The track combined Snails' explosive instrumentals with Jay-Z's lyrical prowess, resulting in a high-energy and thought-provoking masterpiece. With "Shell Shocked," Snails and Jay-Z proved that collaboration can transcend genres and empower artists to create something truly groundbreaking.

Unlocking the Collaborative Mindset

So, what is it about Snails' collaborative efforts that set them apart from other bands? The answer lies in their willingness to embrace diverse influences and experiment with different sounds. Snails understands that collaboration is not just about bringing together different artists; it is about embracing different perspectives and pushing creative boundaries.

In the world of music, collaboration can serve as a catalyst for innovation and growth. When artists from different genres and backgrounds come together, they bring their unique experiences and perspectives, which can result in the creation of something entirely new and groundbreaking. Snails' rare collaborations serve as a reminder that music is not confined to one genre or style but is an ever-evolving and limitless form of expression.

Exercises

1. Think of two seemingly contrasting genres of music and brainstorm ways in which they could be merged together to create a unique sound. Write a paragraph describing the potential collaboration and the impact it could have on the music scene.

2. Research a collaboration between two artists that you admire. Write a short essay discussing how their collaboration influenced their respective genres and the music industry as a whole.

3. Imagine you are a member of Snails and have the opportunity to collaborate with any artist, dead or alive. Who would you choose and why? Write a persuasive paragraph arguing for your chosen collaboration and the potential impact it could have on both artists' careers.

Conclusion

Snails' rare collaborations have not only pushed the boundaries of music but have also paved the way for new and exciting possibilities within the industry. By embracing diverse influences and partnering with artists from various genres, Snails has demonstrated the transformative power of collaboration. Their willingness to step outside their comfort zone and explore uncharted musical territories has not only enriched their own sound but has also inspired a new generation of artists to break free from traditional conventions and create something truly extraordinary. The gems uncovered through Snails' rare collaborations have forever changed the musical landscape, leaving a lasting legacy of innovation and artistic exploration.

Pushing the Boundaries: Snails' Experimental Music

In the vast world of music, Snails has carved a unique niche for themselves with their experimental approach to music. This section delves into the daring and boundary-pushing aspects of Snails' music, exploring their unconventional techniques, fearless exploration of new sounds, and their impact on the music industry.

Breaking the Mold: Challenging Traditional Conventions

Snails' experimental music stems from a desire to challenge the traditional conventions of music. They refuse to be confined by genre boundaries, opting instead to blend various styles and create something entirely new. Their fearlessness in stepping outside the box has earned them a reputation as pioneers of the unconventional.

Unorthodox Instrumentation: Where Creativity Knows No Bounds One of Snails' key approaches to experimental music lies in their unorthodox use of instrumentation. They are known for incorporating unconventional elements into their compositions, such as modified electronic devices, everyday objects turned instruments, and even found sounds from nature. This approach adds a distinct and unexpected flavor to their music, pushing the boundaries of what is considered traditional instrumentation.

For instance, in their hit song "Slime Symphony," Snails incorporated the sound of breaking glass, water droplets, and even the crunching of leaves. By merging these unconventional sounds with traditional instruments like guitars and drums, they created a truly unique auditory experience.

Exploration of New Technologies: Shaping the Music of the Future Snails have never shied away from embracing new technologies and incorporating them into their music. Their innovative use of electronic equipment and digital effects has led to the creation of entirely new sounds and textures.

In their album "Electro-Mollusk," Snails delved deep into the possibilities offered by virtual instruments and synthesizers. They blended traditional orchestral arrangements with synthesized sounds to create a futuristic and otherworldly sonic experience. This experimentation with technology not only pushed the boundaries of their music but also opened up a world of possibilities for future musicians.

The Experimentation Process: Where Ideas Take Shape

Creating experimental music requires a unique creative process that allows for unrestricted exploration and the willingness to take risks. Snails' approach to experimentation involves a meticulous and dynamic process that nurtures the growth of their musical ideas.

Collaborative Brainstorming: Combining Forces for Innovation To push the boundaries of their music, Snails fosters a collaborative atmosphere within the band. Each member brings their unique perspective and ideas to the table, sparking a creative synergy that leads to breakthroughs in their music.

In the early stages of creating experimental tracks, Snails' members gather for intensive brainstorming sessions. These sessions involve exploring new sounds, experimenting with various techniques, and challenging each other to think outside the box. This collaborative environment not only fuels their creativity but also encourages them to push their individual limits.

Improvisation: Unleashing Spontaneity and Raw Creativity Another essential aspect of Snails' experimental process is the use of improvisation. They believe that spontaneity is the key to unlocking raw creativity and originality in their music.

During their jam sessions, Snails' members embark on unstructured improvisation sessions. They allow themselves, and each other, to wander into uncharted musical territories, blurring the line between composition and performance. Out of these improvised moments, they unearth innovative musical ideas that become the building blocks of their experimental tracks.

Impact on the Music Industry: Paving the Way for New Frontiers

Snails' commitment to pushing the boundaries of music has not only set them apart from their peers but has also had a profound impact on the music industry as a whole. Their fearlessness and innovative spirit have paved the way for new frontiers in music.

Inspiring a New Wave of Artists: Embracing Unconventionality Snails' experimental music has inspired a new wave of artists to embrace unconventionality and push the limits of their own creativity. By demonstrating that music is not bound by genre or traditional norms, they have opened up the possibilities for other musicians to explore new sounds and push beyond the familiar.

Expanding the Definition of Genre: Blurring Boundaries Snails' boundary-pushing music has challenged the traditional notions of genre. Their unique style incorporates elements from different genres, often fusing them together seamlessly. This genre-blurring approach has not only created a distinct sonic identity for the band but has also inspired other artists to explore and experiment with the boundaries of their own genres.

Cultivating a Culture of Experimentation: A Legacy of Fearless Creativity Through their experimental music, Snails has cultivated a culture of experimentation within the music industry. They have shown that taking risks and embracing the unknown can lead to groundbreaking artistic achievements. As a result, more artists are willing to step outside their comfort zones and explore the uncharted territories of music, ensuring a constant wave of innovation and fresh ideas.

Unleash Your Creativity: Two Examples

To further illustrate the boundary-pushing nature of Snails' experimental music, let's explore two examples of their tracks that exemplify their fearless creativity.

Track Example 1: "Sonic Vortex"

In the track "Sonic Vortex," Snails blends elements of rock, electronic music, and avant-garde sounds to create a mind-bending auditory experience. The song opens with a distorted guitar riff that gradually morphs into a swirling vortex of electronic beats and atmospheric textures. Throughout the track, Snails expertly navigates the fine line between chaos and structure, creating a sonic landscape that challenges the listener's perception of music.

Track Example 2: "Rhythmic Riddles"

"Rhythmic Riddles" is a prime example of Snails' ability to blend unconventional rhythms and intricate melodies. The track features polyrhythmic drum patterns, complemented by overlapping melodies played on an array of non-traditional instruments. The result is a captivating musical puzzle that showcases Snails' mastery of rhythm and their willingness to experiment with unconventional sounds.

Conclusion

Snails' experimental music is a testament to the power of pushing boundaries and embracing the unknown. Through their unorthodox instrumentation, fearless exploration of new technologies, and commitment to collaboration and improvisation, they have redefined the landscape of music. Their impact extends far beyond their own compositions, inspiring a new generation of artists to embrace creativity without limits.

As you embark on your own creative journey, remember Snails' philosophy: there are no boundaries to what can be accomplished when you dare to push them. Let their fearless spirit and innovative approach shape your own musical endeavors, and never be afraid to break the mold and venture into uncharted territories. The possibilities are endless when you embrace the power of experimental music.

Let's Get Snail-y: Recording in the Studio

Welcome to the snail-tastic world of Snails, where the music is as slow and smooth as their slimy trails! In this chapter, we dive into the intriguing process of recording in the studio with the band. Get ready to get snail-y and experience the behind-the-scenes magic that brings Snails' music to life.

The Snail's Nest: Snails' Creative Process

The recording studio is the secret hideout where the Snails unleash their creativity and transform their musical ideas into reality. Known by the band members as the "Snail's Nest," this sacred space is filled with instruments, gadgets, and a whole lot of snail energy.

Snails' creative process is truly unique and resembles the slow and steady journey of a snail. They take their time, savoring each moment of the creative process. They start with a simple seed of an idea and let it slowly germinate and evolve into a fully-fledged song.

Frontman Gary "Slimy" Johnson is the mastermind behind Snails' intricate compositions. He leads the band through the creative maze, guiding them every step of the way. With his extraordinary musical instincts and keen ear for melodies, Slimy sets the tone for each recording session.

Composing the Stench: Snails' Songwriting Techniques

The Snails' songwriting techniques are as unconventional and mesmerizing as their music. They take inspiration from the world around them, finding beauty and meaning in the most unexpected places. Their lyrics often delve deep into the human experience, exploring themes of love, hope, and the trials of life.

One technique Snails often employ is "Stench-writing." This involves creating a musical atmosphere that captures the essence of their lyrical themes. For instance, when writing a love ballad, they might use mellow and romantic chords to set the mood. To express the hardships of life, they might embrace dissonant harmonies and edgy melodies.

Another technique they often use is "Lyric Fusion." This involves blending different lyrical perspectives to create a cohesive narrative. For example, in their hit song "Trail of Love," the lyrics intertwine the stories of two individuals on separate paths, eventually converging and finding love.

Uncovering the Gems: Snails' Rare Collaborations

While Snails is primarily a band known for their independent songwriting, they occasionally collaborate with other artists to create musical magic. These collaborations are like finding a rare gem in the depths of the snail kingdom.

Snails' approach to collaboration is all about creating a harmonious balance between their unique sound and the style of the collaborating artist. They seek out artists who share their passion for pushing boundaries and creating innovative music.

One memorable collaboration was with the renowned jazz saxophonist, Sally "Saxslinger" Thompson. The fusion of Snails' slow melodies with Saxslinger's soulful saxophone solos created a completely new musical landscape, captivating both Snails' fans and jazz enthusiasts.

Pushing the Boundaries: Snails' Experimental Music

Snails never shy away from pushing the boundaries of their music and exploring uncharted territories. Their love for experimentation is evident in their studio sessions, where they constantly seek new sounds, textures, and sonic landscapes.

One way Snails achieves this is through the usage of unconventional instruments. They have been known to incorporate unusual instruments like the theremin, kazoo, and even a musical saw into their recordings. These instruments add a layer of uniqueness to their sound and elevate their music to another dimension.

In addition to using unconventional instruments, Snails also experiment with production techniques. They explore innovative ways to manipulate sounds, such as using tape loops, reverse effects, and sampling found sounds from nature. These experimentation sessions often result in unexpected sonic surprises that make Snails' music truly one-of-a-kind.

Let's Get Snail-y: Recording in the Studio

Now let's take a closer look at the step-by-step process of recording in the studio with Snails. Grab your headphones and join us on this slimy adventure!

Step 1: Pre-production - Before entering the Snail's Nest, the band spends time in pre-production. They meticulously analyze each song, making sure every detail is perfected. This involves fine-tuning the arrangements, refining the melodies, and experimenting with different musical textures.

Step 2: Setting the Atmosphere - Creating the right atmosphere is crucial for Snails' recording sessions. They dim the lights, light scented candles, and even scatter some snail shells around the studio to harness the snail energy. The ambiance sets the stage for their creativity to flourish.

Step 3: Capturing the Magic - Once they are in the right headspace, it's time to hit the record button. Snails record their music live, with all band members playing together in the same room. This allows them to capture the raw energy and organic chemistry that emanates when the band is in sync.

Step 4: Painting with Sound - Recording is not just about capturing the performance, but also about painting with sound. Snails pay meticulous attention to the textures and colors of their music. They experiment with various studio effects, layering different tracks, and manipulating sounds to create a sonic masterpiece.

Step 5: The Mixing Process - After recording all the individual tracks, Snails hand over the raw materials to their trusted sound engineer, who works closely with the band to mix their music. The mixing process is like sculpting, shaping each element until it blends harmoniously. Every snare hit, every guitar riff, and every snail-y sound is carefully balanced and EQed to perfection.

Step 6: Mastering the Magic - The final step is mastering, where the songs are polished and made ready for public consumption. Snails work with mastering engineers who add the finishing touches to their music, ensuring it sounds pristine across different platforms and speakers. Mastering is the icing on the cake, giving the songs a professional sheen.

The Art of the Album: Snails' Masterpieces

Once the recording is complete and the songs are mixed and mastered, Snails unveil their masterpieces to the world in the form of albums. Their albums are carefully crafted artistic journeys, taking listeners on a snail-tastic adventure from start to finish.

Snails' albums are known for their attention to detail, both musically and visually. They believe in creating a cohesive listening experience, where each song seamlessly flows into the next, like a winding snail trail. The album cover artwork is also a vital part of their vision, often created by acclaimed visual artists who capture the essence of the music in stunning visuals.

In the Shell: Snails' Unforgettable Studio Moments

Recording in the studio with Snails is an experience like no other. Their recording sessions are filled with unforgettable moments that capture the essence of their creativity and camaraderie.

One legendary studio moment occurred during the recording of their hit song "Slow Motion Symphony." The band had been struggling with the song's chorus, unable to find the perfect melody. Suddenly, inspiration struck when their drummer, Speedy, accidentally knocked over a stack of tambourines, creating a rhythmic pattern that fit seamlessly into the chorus. The accident gave birth to one of Snails' most iconic musical moments.

Exercises to Get Snail-y

Now that you've learned some of the intricacies of recording in the studio with Snails, it's time to put your own snail-y skills to the test. Here are a few exercises to help you get into the snail-tastic groove:

1. Take a song you love and experiment with different instruments or sounds to create your own unique version. Embrace the Snails' spirit of exploration and see where it takes you.

2. Practice writing lyrics that capture emotions and themes in unconventional ways. Think outside the box and try to find beauty in unexpected places, just like Snails do.

3. Set up your own mini-recording studio at home. Experiment with different microphone placements, effects, and production techniques to create your own sonic masterpieces.

Remember, just like a snail, take your time and embrace the slow and steady approach to creativity. Every trail you leave behind is a step closer to your own musical masterpiece.

Conclusion

Recording in the studio with Snails is a journey like no other. Their slow and steady approach, coupled with their love for experimentation, creates a musical experience that is both captivating and extraordinary. From composing the stench to capturing the magic, Snails' recording process is an art form in itself.

In the next chapter, we dive even deeper into Snails' world as we explore the untold stories from their life on the road. Get ready for hilarious and exciting moments, behind-the-scenes stories, and the unforgettable bond shared by the Snail Army. Get your snail goggles ready because it's going to be a wild ride!

The Art of the Album: Snails' Masterpieces

In the world of music, albums are more than just a collection of individual songs. They are a carefully crafted body of work that showcases the talent, creativity, and vision of the artists who create them. When it comes to Snails, their albums are like works of art, each telling a unique story and leaving an indelible mark on the music industry. In this section, we delve into the artistry behind Snails' masterpieces and explore what makes their albums truly exceptional.

Setting the Stage: Conceptualizing the Album

Before diving into the creative process, Snails begins by conceptualizing the album. They don't simply throw together a compilation of songs; instead, they approach each album as a cohesive narrative, with a central theme or message that ties everything together. This theme serves as the guiding force behind the entire project, allowing Snails to create a unified and immersive experience for their listeners.

To illustrate this, let's take a look at their most recent album, "Molten Slime." This masterpiece takes us on a journey through the depths of their imagination, exploring themes of self-discovery, resilience, and the power of unity. The title alone evokes a sense of transformation and fluidity, setting the tone for the entire album.

Song Selection: Crafting the Perfect Playlist

Once the concept is established, Snails carefully curates the selection of songs that will make it onto the album. This process involves a meticulous evaluation of each track, ensuring that it aligns with the album's message and contributes to the overall narrative. Snails doesn't settle for mediocrity; only the finest compositions earn a spot on their albums.

But what sets Snails apart is their ability to create a diverse range of songs while maintaining coherence. They seamlessly transition between different genres and musical styles, defying traditional boundaries and offering a refreshing and dynamic listening experience. From heart-wrenching ballads to high-energy anthems, Snails knows how to strike the perfect balance and keep their audience captivated.

Crafting the Sonic Landscape

A key element in creating their masterpieces is Snails' meticulous attention to the sonic landscape of their albums. They understand that sound goes beyond just the notes and lyrics—it's about creating an immersive experience that engages all the senses. This involves careful consideration of instrumentation, arrangement, production techniques, and even the order of the tracks.

Snails experiments with a wide array of sounds, often incorporating unconventional and unexpected elements to add depth and texture to their music. Each instrument and sound effect is carefully selected to serve a purpose, to evoke specific emotions, and to enhance the overall storytelling of the album. From mesmerizing synth arpeggios to soul-stirring orchestral arrangements, Snails' sonic palette knows no limits.

Exploring the Unconventional: Snails' Signature Twists

Snails' innovation doesn't stop at sound—they strive to push the boundaries of traditional album formats. They infuse their albums with unconventional elements, surprising their listeners and creating a sense of anticipation and delight. One of their most notable signature twists is the inclusion of hidden tracks within their albums.

These hidden tracks are carefully placed after a period of silence at the end of an album or as a hidden track within another song. They allow Snails to surprise and reward their most dedicated fans, encouraging them to stay engaged and explore every nook and cranny of the album. It's a testament to Snails' commitment to creating a fully immersive and memorable experience for their listeners.

The Visual Journey: Album Art as a Visual Expression

True to their artistic nature, Snails recognizes that an album is not just about the music—it's a complete sensory experience. They pay equal attention to the visual aspect of their albums, using album art as a medium to convey their message and enhance the overall storytelling.

Snails collaborates with talented visual artists to create visually stunning and thought-provoking artwork that captures the essence of each album. These visuals serve as a gateway into the sonic world they've crafted, inviting listeners to immerse themselves fully in the experience. From intricate illustrations to bold and abstract designs, Snails' album art is as diverse and captivating as their music.

Unleashing the Masterpieces

When Snails finally unleashes their masterpieces upon the world, the impact is undeniable. Fans eagerly anticipate each album release, knowing that they are about to embark on an extraordinary sonic journey. Snails' albums transcend mere escapism—they have the power to inspire, provoke, comfort, and uplift.

The art of the album is a testament to Snails' creativity, passion, and commitment to their craft. It showcases their ability to push boundaries, defy expectations, and create music that resonates on a profound level. Snails' masterpieces are not only a testament to their own genius but also a testament to the enduring power of music to move and inspire us all.

So, the next time you listen to a Snails album, take a moment to appreciate the artistry that went into its creation. Immerse yourself in the sonic landscape, let the music transport you to new realms, and allow yourself to be captivated by the sheer brilliance of Snails' masterpieces.

Snail Tales: Untold Stories from the Road

Adventures on Tour: Hilarious and Exciting Moments

Snails' tours were more than just concerts. They were extraordinary adventures, filled with hilarious and exciting moments that left both the band and their fans in stitches. Whether it was an unexpected prank, a wild fan encounter, or a spontaneous jam session, Snails knew how to make their tours unforgettable.

The Prank Wars

One recurring theme on Snails' tours was the ongoing prank wars between band members. They were notorious for playing practical jokes on each other, always trying to outdo one another and keep the laughter going. One instance that stands out is when the drummer, Tim "The Slammer" Johnson, decided to fill the lead guitarist's amp with snails during a soundcheck. When the solo kicked in, the guitarist couldn't figure out why his guitar was making strange noises until he discovered the slimy surprise waiting for him inside. It was an unforgettable moment that left the whole band in stitches.

Unexpected Fan Encounters

Snails' dedicated fan base, known as the Snail Army, always brought the excitement to their shows. One particular tour stop in a small town had an unexpected guest appearance by a local farmer who was known for his pet snails. He showed up at the backstage entrance with a box of snails in hand, insisting on introducing them to the band. The band decided to embrace the moment and invited the farmer on stage during their performance. The crowd went wild as the farmer proudly showcased his snails while the band played on. It was a hilarious and heartwarming moment that showed the power of their music to bring people together, no matter how unconventional the circumstances.

Jamming with Surprise Guests

Snails were known for their love of collaboration, and they often invited surprise guests to join them on stage during their tours. One memorable tour stop had them crossing paths with a renowned saxophonist, Larry "The Smooth Operator" Davis. After the band finished their set, Larry jumped on stage with his saxophone and started jamming alongside them. The energy in the room skyrocketed as Snails and Larry traded electrifying solos, each pushing the other to new musical heights. The audience was blown away by the impromptu performance, and it became one of the highlights of the tour. It was a reminder of the magic that can happen when talented musicians come together and create music in the moment.

Snails' Road Trip Chronicles

While on tour, Snails embarked on epic road trips between cities, and these journeys were filled with hilarious and memorable moments. One time, their tour bus broke down in the middle of nowhere, leaving them stranded for hours. Instead of feeling defeated, they turned the situation into an impromptu acoustic jam session by the side of the road. Passersby couldn't believe their luck as they stumbled upon this unexpected roadside concert. Snails' ability to turn setbacks into opportunities for music and laughter became a trademark of their tours.

The Power of Spontaneity

One of the most exciting aspects of Snails' tours was their ability to embrace spontaneity. On one occasion, during a sold-out show, they decided to surprise the audience by switching instruments halfway through the set. The lead guitarist became the drummer, the bassist picked up the guitar, and the drummer took over the bass. The crowd went wild as they witnessed their favorite band members showcasing their musical versatility in a whole new way. It was a daring move that added an extra layer of excitement and fun to the performance.

Conclusion

Adventures on tour with Snails were more than just musical performances; they were thrilling, hilarious, and full of surprises. The band's pranks, unexpected fan encounters, jam sessions with surprise guests, road trip chronicles, and the power of spontaneity made each tour a one-of-a-kind experience for both the band and their devoted fans. Snails' ability to find joy and laughter in every situation created a unique bond with their audience, leaving them eagerly awaiting the next adventure on tour.

On the Road with Snails: Behind the Scenes Stories

Join us on a thrilling adventure as we lift the curtain on Snails' life on the road! Get ready to dive into the whirlwind of craziness, excitement, and unforgettable moments that come with touring. In this section, we'll take you behind the scenes and share some incredible and hilarious stories that unfolded during Snails' globe-trotting adventures.

Adventures on Tour: Hilarious and Exciting Moments

Life on tour is anything but ordinary, and Snails knows how to keep things interesting. Let's delve into some of the most memorable and entertaining moments the band has experienced on the road:

1. **The Epic Food Fight in Tokyo**

   During their first tour in Tokyo, Snails found themselves immersed in the vibrant culture and mouth-watering cuisine. One night, after an amazing show, the band decided to celebrate by exploring the local street food scene. Little did they know, this culinary adventure was about to turn into an epic food fight!

   As they indulged in sushi rolls and bowls of ramen, a mischievous rivalry began to brew. Each band member playfully challenged the others to try unique and sometimes bizarre dishes. From octopus tentacles to fermented soybeans, nothing was off-limits. Food flew across the table, laughter echoed through the restaurant, and the local patrons watched in awe at the spectacle.

   In the end, they left the restaurant covered in food, with smiles plastered on their faces. It was messy, hilarious, and a memory that would forever bind them together.

2. **The Mystery of the Vanishing Bassist**

   One fateful night in Berlin, Snails experienced a moment of panic when their bassist, Jim, mysteriously disappeared from their tour bus. As the band members finished their pre-show rituals, they noticed Jim was nowhere to be found.

Frantically searching the venue, they finally stumbled upon Jim exploring a hidden underground passage beneath the concert hall. Lost in the excitement of exploring a new city, he had forgotten about the upcoming performance. With only minutes to spare, they quickly pulled Jim out of the labyrinth and rushed to the stage, barely making it in time for their introduction.

From that day forward, they designated a 'tour buddy' system to ensure no band member would ever go missing again. Jim's escapade became a legendary tale that would be retold countless times, a reminder to always keep an eye on each other during their travels.

3. **The Wild Safari Party in South Africa**

    Feeling adventurous, Snails decided to immerse themselves in the stunning wildlife of South Africa during a break in their tour schedule. Little did they know, a surprise was waiting for them in the form of a wild safari party organized by their dedicated fans.

    As the band arrived at the safari lodge, they were greeted by a cheering crowd adorned in their iconic 'snail' attire. The safari guides, in collaboration with the fans, had transformed the lodge into a jungle-themed extravaganza. From animal-print decorations to a dance floor in the shape of a watering hole, every detail was meticulously planned.

    Under the night sky, with the sounds of the wilderness as their backdrop, Snails and their fans danced, sang, and celebrated into the early hours of the morning. It was a surreal experience, a true testament to the incredible bond between the band and their devoted fans.

On the Road with Snails: Behind the Scenes Stories

Beyond the glamorous performances and the adrenaline-fueled concerts, touring comes with its fair share of challenges and behind-the-scenes tales. Snails has faced them all with resilience, humor, and a whole lot of snail spirit. Let's take a look at some of the fascinating stories that unfolded while on the road:

1. **The Great Bus Breakdown**

    Tour buses are like second homes to Snails, but sometimes, even the most trusted steeds can falter. On a memorable tour through the vast landscapes of the American southwest, their dependable tour bus suddenly came to a screeching halt in the middle of the desert.

Forced to confront this unexpected setback, the band found themselves stranded under the blazing sun. But instead of succumbing to frustration, they decided to turn this misfortune into an opportunity for adventure. They set up an impromptu campsite, cooked meals over an open fire, and even ended up writing a few songs inspired by the breathtaking vistas surrounding them.

After a thrilling day of living like desert nomads, a tow truck arrived to rescue them from the scorching heat. Although the journey was delayed, the experience created a bond among them that couldn't be broken – a reminder that even in the face of adversity, Snails' unbreakable spirit prevails.

2. The Haunted Hotel

In between shows, Snails often finds themselves staying in a wide range of accommodations. From lavish hotels to quirky hostels, their road trips are never short on surprises. However, one hotel stay in New Orleans stood out from the rest – it was rumored to be haunted.

Late at night, as the band settled into their rooms, strange noises filled the halls. Doors creaked, footsteps echoed, and eerie whispers crept through the air. Some members reported seeing shadowy figures in the corners of their vision. Though the paranormal presence was unsettling, Snails chose to embrace the mystery and leaned into their sense of adventure.

They spent the night exploring the hotel's history, swapping ghost stories, and sharing their own supernatural encounters. By morning, any fears had transformed into a newfound curiosity for the unknown. This spine-chilling experience became a cherished memory, reminding Snails that life on the road is filled with unexpected wonders.

3. The Unforgettable Fan Encounters

One of the most rewarding aspects of touring for Snails is connecting with their dedicated fan base. From meet-and-greets to surprise encounters in unexpected places, fans have shown relentless support and created unforgettable memories for both the band and themselves.

During a tour stop in London, Snails stumbled upon a group of fans who had traveled thousands of miles to attend the show. Overwhelmed by their commitment, the band invited the fans backstage for an impromptu meet-up. What started as a simple conversation turned into an evening of laughter, tears, and shared dreams.

These encounters are a constant reminder of the impact Snails has on people's lives. They fuel the band's passion, inspire them to continue creating music, and reinforce the deep connection they share with their ever-growing Snail Army.

Snails' Travel Diary: Exploring the World Through Music

Snails' music is heavily influenced by their travels, providing fans with a sonic journey around the globe. Each tour destination brings a unique blend of sounds, cultures, and experiences that shape their musical evolution. Let's take a closer look at how Snails' travel adventures have inspired their music:

1. **A Symphony of Sounds**

   From the bustling streets of Tokyo to the mystical rainforests of Brazil, Snails has absorbed the rich tapestry of global culture. During their travels, they've made it a priority to immerse themselves in local music scenes, learning from native musicians and collaborating with artists from diverse backgrounds.

   These musical explorations have birthed a fusion of genres within Snails' sound, blending elements of rock, funk, electronic, and folk music. The band's willingness to dive into different musical traditions has created a harmonious blend that is uniquely their own.

2. **Lyrics Inspired by Landscapes**

   The breathtaking landscapes encountered while touring have a profound influence on Snails' lyrical compositions. From the majestic mountains of Patagonia to the serene beaches of Bali, the band's experiences in these natural wonders find their way into their songs.

   Drawing inspiration from the beauty and grandeur of our planet, Snails' lyrics often touch on themes of unity, introspection, and the importance of cherishing our surroundings. By infusing these profound experiences into their music, they strive to create a sense of connection between listeners and the world around them.

3. **Tour Tales Woven Into Melodies**

   Behind every song, there's a story waiting to be told. Snails' travels have produced countless stories, from chance encounters with fellow musicians to misadventures in foreign lands. These tales find their way into the band's compositions, adding depth and authenticity to their music.

By sharing their personal experiences through melodies and lyrics, Snails invites their listeners into their world—one filled with wild adventures, hilarious mishaps, and moments of profound meaning. Through their music, the band aims to transport fans to the places they've been, evoking emotions and creating a shared sense of adventure.

Snails' Travel Tips: Embarking on Your Own Musical Journey

Snails' globetrotting escapades have not only shaped their music but also provided them with invaluable knowledge and insights into the world of travel. Whether you're an aspiring musician or simply an adventurer at heart, here are some travel tips from Snails to help you embark on your own musical journey:

- **Embrace the Unknown:** Don't be afraid to step outside your comfort zone and explore new destinations. The unfamiliar can lead to unexpected and incredible experiences.

- **Immerse Yourself in Local Culture:** Seek out local music scenes, connect with fellow musicians, and learn about traditional instruments and rhythms. The music you encounter may inspire you in ways you never imagined.

- **Capture the Moment:** Keep a travel diary, take photographs, and record snippets of sounds that resonate with you. These mementos will become cherished memories and may serve as inspiration for future musical endeavors.

- **Interact with Locals:** Strike up conversations with locals and fellow travelers. These encounters can lead to meaningful connections and open doors to opportunities you may never have discovered otherwise.

- **Stay Adventurous:** Embrace the unexpected twists and turns of travel. Sometimes, the best experiences can arise from unforeseen circumstances.

- **Use Music as a Universal Language:** No matter where you go, music has the power to bridge gaps and foster understanding. Whether through collaboration or impromptu jam sessions, let your music be a conduit for connection.

Snails' travel experiences have shaped their identities as musicians, shaped their sound, and forged unbreakable bonds within the band. The tales from the road are not just stories but a testament to the power of music and the remarkable connections it creates between people from all walks of life. So, get out there, explore the world, and let your own musical journey unfold.

Remember: It's not just about the destination, but the adventure along the way.

Snails' Travel Diary: Exploring the World through Music

When you think about the life of a rock star, images of glamorous parties and luxury hotels might come to mind. But for the members of Snails, their life on the road is about much more than just the glitz and glam. It's about exploring the world, meeting new people, and sharing their music with fans from all walks of life. In this chapter, we take a peek into Snails' travel diary and discover the adventures and experiences they've had while traversing the globe.

Adventures on Tour: Hilarious and Exciting Moments

Touring can be a whirlwind of excitement, with each city offering unique experiences and challenges. Snails' travel diary is filled with hilarious and thrilling moments that have become legendary among their fans. From getting lost in foreign cities to impromptu jam sessions with local musicians, these stories give us a glimpse into the band's adventurous spirit.

In one unforgettable incident, the band found themselves in a small town in Germany with no idea where their hotel was. As they wandered the streets, they stumbled upon a local pub where a karaoke night was in full swing. Always up for a good time, Snails decided to join in and ended up performing an impromptu set with the locals, much to the delight of the audience. It was a night they would never forget and a testament to their ability to find joy in unexpected places.

Another memorable moment happened during a tour in Japan. After a particularly energetic performance, the band was invited to a traditional tea ceremony by a group of enthusiastic fans. Snails, always open to new experiences, graciously accepted the invitation. They found themselves in a serene tea house, sipping on matcha tea and listening to the soothing sounds of a koto. It was a moment of cultural exchange and a reminder of the power of music to bring people together across language and cultural barriers.

On the Road with Snails: Behind the Scenes Stories

Life on the road isn't all about the shows and the fans. There's a whole world behind the scenes that often goes unnoticed. Snails' travel diary gives us a glimpse into the ups and downs of touring, shedding light on the challenges and the camaraderie that develop when you spend countless hours on a tour bus.

One particular tour, known as the "Slime and Shine" tour, stands out as a turning point for the band. It was a grueling schedule with back-to-back shows in different cities every night. The band members, exhausted from the constant traveling and lack of sleep, found solace in their shared experiences. They would often gather in the back of their tour bus, sharing funny stories and supporting each other through the highs and lows of tour life. These moments of camaraderie and friendship became the fuel that kept them going during the most challenging times.

But life on the road isn't without its pitfalls. Snails had their fair share of mishaps and unexpected situations. One time, their tour bus broke down in the middle of the desert, leaving them stranded for hours. With no cell service and limited supplies, they had to rely on their resourcefulness to find a way out. Eventually, a kind-hearted local spotted their distress and offered them a ride to the nearest town. It was a reminder that even in the most difficult situations, there is always a silver lining and help can come from the most unexpected places.

Snails' Travel Diary: Exploring the World through Music

For Snails, touring is about more than just performing on stage. It's an opportunity to immerse themselves in different cultures, to learn from the people they meet, and to explore the world through music. Their travel diary is filled with notes and sketches, capturing the essence of each place they visit.

In every city they perform, Snails make it a point to explore the local music scene and connect with local musicians. They have collaborated with traditional percussionists in Africa, played impromptu street concerts in South America, and even incorporated ethnic instruments into their own songs. By embracing the music of each culture they encounter, Snails not only create a unique experience for their fans but also pay homage to the beauty and diversity of the world.

But it's not just about the music. Snails' travel diary also showcases their love for adventure and exploration. From climbing ancient ruins in Greece to surfing on the pristine beaches of Hawaii, the band takes full advantage of their time off the stage to indulge in their passions. These experiences not only inspire their music but also fuel their creativity and keep them connected to the world beyond the stage.

Crazy Fan Encounters: Unforgettable Moments with the Snail Army

The Snail Army, as their fans are affectionately known, is a worldwide community of devoted followers who share in the band's love for music and adventure. Snails' travel diary is filled with stories of the incredible connections they've made with fans from all corners of the globe.

In Australia, the band was greeted at the airport by a group of fans who had painted themselves head to toe in vibrant slime-colored body paint. The sight was so incredible that it stopped even the most seasoned travelers in their tracks. The band was so moved by this display of dedication that they invited the fans to join them on stage for a special encore performance. It was a moment of pure joy and celebration, a testament to the power of music to bring people together.

But it's not just the large-scale encounters that leave a lasting impression. Snails' travel diary is also filled with stories of small acts of kindness from fans. From homemade gifts to letters expressing gratitude, these gestures remind the band of the impact their music has on individuals. It's these personal connections that fuel Snails' dedication to their craft and inspire them to continue creating music that touches people's hearts.

The Spirit of Snails: Bonds and Connection within the Band

Being on the road for months at a time can take a toll on even the strongest of relationships. But for Snails, it's the shared experiences and bonds they've formed that keep them going. Their travel diary is a testament to the unbreakable connection they have as a band.

During one particularly difficult tour, the band faced personal and professional challenges that tested their resolve. But instead of letting it tear them apart, they came together and found strength in their common goals and shared love for music. Their travel diary is filled with notes of encouragement and support, reminding each other of their collective vision and inspiring one another to push through the obstacles.

Snails' travel diary is not just a documentation of their adventures; it's a reflection of the band's spirit and resilience. Through the highs and lows of life on the road, they've discovered that it's the connections they forge with each other and with their fans that truly make the journey worthwhile.

Conclusion

Snails' travel diary is a window into their world, a world filled with adventure, camaraderie, and the power of music to bring people together. As they continue to explore the world through their music, their travel diary will undoubtedly be filled with even more unforgettable moments and experiences. The band's never-ending curiosity and love for exploration will ensure that their journey is one for the books, leaving a lasting impact on both their fans and the world of music. So join Snails on their travels and let their music take you on a journey of a lifetime.

Crazy Fan Encounters: Unforgettable Moments with Snail Army

The Snail Army is more than just a fanbase. They are a passionate and dedicated group of individuals who share a deep love for Snails and their music. Over the years, the band has had countless encounters with their loyal fans, resulting in some truly unforgettable moments. From heartwarming stories to wild and crazy adventures, let's dive into the world of the Snail Army and explore the incredible bond between the fans and the band.

One of the most remarkable fan encounters happened during a tour stop in a small town. The Snails had just finished an electrifying performance, and as they made their way backstage, they were greeted by a young fan named Emily. Emily had been following the band since their early days, and her undying admiration for Snails was evident in every word she spoke. She carried a homemade scrapbook filled with hand-drawn pictures, concert tickets, and heartfelt letters expressing her love for the band.

Emily's dedication and love for Snails left a lasting impression on the band members. They invited her backstage, where she shared her stories of how their music had helped her through tough times. Touched by her vulnerability and honesty, the band not only signed her scrapbook but also invited her to join them on stage for their final song. It was a magical moment that showcased the incredible connection between the band and their fans.

But the Snail Army's unwavering support wasn't limited to just concerts. On one occasion, the band ran into a group of fans who had organized a Snails-themed charity event. These fans, driven by their love for both the band and their community, had come together to raise funds for a local shelter. They had designed Snails-inspired merchandise, organized auctions, and even created a special cocktail named after one of the band's hit songs.

The band was blown away by the fans' creativity and generosity. They joined the event, signing autographs and taking pictures with everyone. It was an incredible show of unity and kindness, showcasing the positive impact that the Snail Army could have beyond just being fans.

Of course, not all fan encounters are heartwarming and emotional. Some are outright wild and crazy. During a particularly rowdy concert, the band noticed a fan in the front row wearing a giant, inflatable snail costume. This fan, determined to stand out, had brought a confetti cannon and would unleash a burst of colorful confetti every time a Snails hit played. The sight was both amusing and awe-inspiring, as the crowd erupted with excitement every time the confetti rained down on them.

But the madness didn't stop there. At another concert, the band spotted a fan who had created a snail-themed obstacle course in the crowd. Complete with giant inflatable mushrooms, slime pits, and even a mini stage, this fan had turned the concert into an interactive adventure. Snails couldn't resist the temptation and decided to partake in the obstacle course themselves, much to the delight of the audience.

These crazy fan encounters not only showcase the unique creativity of the Snail Army but also highlight the powerful connection between the band and their fans. The love and support from the Snail Army have propelled Snails' success and shaped their career in unimaginable ways.

So, whether it's through heartfelt gestures, charitable endeavors, or wild antics, the Snail Army continues to amaze the band with their unwavering love and devotion. They are not just fans; they are an integral part of the Snails' story, contributing to the band's legacy and ensuring that the Slime never fades.

The Spirit of Snails: Bonds and Connection within the Band

The Snails, despite their slow and sluggish nature, possess a deep sense of camaraderie and connection within the band. This section delves into the unique bond that exists amongst band members and explores the secrets behind their strong unity.

The Power of Snail Unity

Just like snails moving as a collective force, the members of Snails understand the importance of working together towards a common goal. Their shared vision of creating music that captivates and inspires their audience has forged a powerful alliance, surpassing individual egos and differences.

At the core of this unity is a strong sense of trust and respect. Each member recognizes and values the unique contributions of their bandmates, allowing each individual to shine in their own way. Whether it's the powerful vocals, the intricate guitar riffs, or the commanding stage presence, every talent is acknowledged, celebrated, and woven harmoniously into the fabric of Snails' music.

Facing Challenges Together

No journey is without its share of challenges, and the Snails have had their fair share. From creative differences to personal struggles, the band has traversed rough terrains both on and off stage. However, it is during these challenging times that the bonds between the Snails are tested and strengthened.

The members of the band have developed a support system that helps them navigate through the darkest of moments. They lean on each other for emotional support, providing a safe space to express their fears, doubts, and frustrations. This open and honest communication allows them to find solutions together and emerge stronger than ever.

The Snail's Nest: A Creative Haven

The creative process of Snails is a testament to the band's deep connection and synergy. When they gather in their creative haven, affectionately known as "The Snail's Nest," magic happens. This is where ideas flow freely, and each member's creativity is brought to life.

Within The Snail's Nest, the band engages in collaborative songwriting sessions, bouncing ideas off each other and refining them collectively. They encourage experimentation, pushing the boundaries of their sound while staying true to their unique style. It is in this environment of trust and exploration that their iconic music takes shape.

Shared Experiences and Music

As the Snails tour together, they share countless experiences both on and off the stage. These shared moments become the foundation of their bond, creating memories they hold dear. From late-night jam sessions to impromptu adventures in different cities, these experiences forge a connection that goes beyond music.

The band's music becomes a channel through which they connect with each other and their audience. The energy they create on stage is infectious, drawing fans into a collective euphoria. Through their passionate performances, the Snails unite people from all walks of life, transcending boundaries and reinforcing the power of human connection.

Keeping the Flame Alive

To keep the flame of their bond burning bright, the Snails prioritize spending quality time together outside of their musical commitments. From movie nights to game nights, they nurture their friendship and ensure that their connection goes beyond the boundaries of their profession.

In addition to their strong internal bond, the Snails engage with their fanbase, lovingly referred to as the Snail Army. They make a conscious effort to connect with their fans, whether it's through meet-and-greet sessions, fan clubs, or interacting on social media. This engagement helps forge a broader community that shares the same love and passion for the band's music.

The Snails' Secret Sauce

The key to the Snails' enduring bond lies in their unwavering commitment to support and uplift each other. They hold each other accountable and celebrate milestones together. Through it all, they never lose sight of the fact that their bond is the foundation of their success.

By nurturing their connections within the band and with their fans, the Snails have created an unbreakable spirit that transcends time and trends. Their legacy goes beyond their music, reflecting the power of unity, friendship, and the everlasting impact of genuine human connections.

Exercises

1. Reflect on a time when you experienced a strong bond or connection with a group of people. How did that connection enhance your experience?

2. Imagine you are a member of the Snails. How would you contribute to the unity and bond within the band? Share your ideas and strategies.

3. Take some time to appreciate the people in your life who have been there for you through thick and thin. Write a heartfelt letter or message expressing your gratitude for their presence and support.

Resources

- *The Power of Unity: How to Create and Sustain Successful Teams* by Pete Wilkinson

- *The 5 Love Languages: The Secret to Love that Lasts* by Gary Chapman

- Snails' official website: www.snailsofficial.com

Remember, the bonds we forge with others are what make life truly meaningful. As the Snails have shown, when we come together with a shared purpose and support each other along the way, the possibilities are endless.

The Snail Family: Examining the Band's Dynamics

The Legendary Leader: A Profile of Snails' Frontman

Introduction

In the world of music, there are few frontmen who possess the charisma, talent, and magnetism to captivate audiences and leave a lasting impression. Snails' frontman is one such individual, a legendary leader who has become the face of the band and an icon in his own right. This section will delve into the life and persona of the frontman, exploring his journey to fame, his unique characteristics, his role within the band, and his impact on Snails' success.

Early Life and Musical Roots

Born and raised in a small town, the frontman's passion for music blossomed from a young age. The seed was planted when he received his first guitar as a gift from his grandfather, an accomplished musician in his own right. From that moment, the young frontman was hooked, spending endless hours honing his craft and developing his own distinctive style.

As he grew older, the frontman found inspiration in a variety of genres, from rock to blues to funk. He immersed himself in the music of legends like Jimi Hendrix, Freddie Mercury, and Prince, studying their performances and techniques to mold his own artistic identity. This eclectic mix of influences laid the foundation for Snails' unique sound.

The Birth of Snails

The frontman's journey took a pivotal turn when he crossed paths with the other members of Snails. Driven by a shared passion for music and a desire to push boundaries, they quickly formed an inseparable bond. Recognizing the frontman's natural talent and commanding stage presence, the band chose him as their charismatic leader.

Unleashing the Beast: The Frontman's Stage Persona

When the frontman steps onto the stage, a transformation occurs. He becomes a force to be reckoned with, commanding the attention of every audience member with his raw energy and magnetic presence. His powerful vocals soar through the air, captivating listeners and leaving them begging for more.

With his signature moves and infectious enthusiasm, the frontman takes the audience on a wild ride, creating an unforgettable experience that transcends the boundaries of a traditional concert. His charismatic stage presence is fueled by an unwavering passion for the music, a deep connection with the lyrics, and a genuine love for the fans who have supported Snails throughout their journey.

Musical Vision and Leadership

The frontman's role extends far beyond his captivating performances. As the visionary behind Snails' music, he plays a crucial role in shaping the band's sound and direction. Drawing from his extensive musical knowledge and creative instincts, he collaborates with the other members to craft songs that resonate with audiences and push the boundaries of the genre.

His natural leadership abilities manifest in the studio and during live performances, where he guides the band through the creative process and ensures that everyone's unique talents are showcased. He has an innate ability to bring out the best in his fellow bandmates, fostering an environment of collaboration and mutual respect.

Impact on Snails' Success

The frontman's contribution to Snails' success cannot be overstated. His magnetic personality and undeniable talent have helped propel the band to new heights, attracting a devoted fan base and garnering critical acclaim. His ability to connect with audiences on a deep emotional level has made Snails' music resonate with listeners around the world.

Beyond the stage, the frontman's influence extends to the band's business ventures and philanthropic efforts. He is actively involved in decision-making processes, ensuring that Snails maintains its artistic integrity while also making a positive impact on society. His dedication to social causes and unwavering support for the Snail Army have strengthened the bond between the band and their fans, creating a community united by their love for music and their shared values.

Conclusion

Snails' frontman is not just a musician; he is a legendary leader who embodies the spirit of the band. From his humble beginnings to his meteoric rise to fame, his journey is a testament to the power of passion, perseverance, and true artistry. Snails' success may be attributed to the collective talent and dedication of all its members, but it is the frontman's unparalleled stage presence, musical vision, and leadership that have truly set the band apart. As Snails continues to make waves in the music industry, the frontman will remain its steadfast leader, inspiring audiences and leaving an indelible mark on the world.

Snails' Rhythm Section: The Backbone of the Band

Ah, the rhythm section of Snails - the mighty backbone of the band! When it comes to creating the grooves that make your body move and your hips sway, you can count on these talented musicians to deliver. In this section, we will take a closer look at the key players in Snails' rhythm section, their roles, and the magic they bring to the band's music.

Meet the Groove Masters

First up, we have Max "The Beat Machine" Johnson on drums. Max's thunderous beats and impeccable timing provide the solid foundation on which the entire band builds their sound. With lightning-fast hands and feet, he effortlessly switches between complex time signatures and drives the energy of every Snails performance.

Next, we have Brandon "The Funk Maestro" Davis on bass guitar. Brandon's mastery of the low end is simply unmatched. His funky basslines and infectious grooves add depth and soul to Snails' music, making it impossible for anyone to resist the urge to dance. Brandon's fingers glide effortlessly across the strings, effortlessly navigating complex melodies and locking in with Max's drumming to create a tight rhythmic pocket.

The Art of the Rhythm

Creating the perfect rhythm requires skill, creativity, and a deep understanding of the musical language. Max and Brandon are true virtuosos in their respective instruments, but their magic goes beyond technical proficiency. They have an innate ability to listen to each other and communicate through their music, seamlessly syncing their rhythms and elevating the entire band's performance.

But it's not just about playing the right notes at the right time. The rhythm section's finesse lies in their ability to create dynamics, control the tempo, and enhance the overall musical experience. They know when to hold back to create anticipation and when to unleash their rhythmic fury to drive the crowd wild.

The Secret Ingredient

One of the secrets to Snails' success lies in the unbreakable bond between Max and Brandon. They have been playing together since their high school days, honing their skills and developing an intuitive musical connection. Their chemistry on and off the stage is palpable, and it's this synergy that takes their performances to a whole new level.

Their understanding of each other's playing styles allows them to effortlessly anticipate each other's moves and respond in perfect harmony. This connection creates a unique energy that resonates with the audience, leaving them captivated and wanting more.

Breaking the Rhythm Mold

While Max and Brandon excel at traditional rhythm techniques, they are never afraid to push the boundaries and experiment with unconventional styles. They are constantly exploring new sounds, incorporating elements from different genres, and infusing their own unique flavor into every song.

From pulsating reggae beats to intricate jazz-inspired rhythms, Max and Brandon fearlessly navigate uncharted musical territories, taking Snails' sound to new heights. Their versatility and willingness to step outside their comfort zones keep the band's music fresh, exciting, and relevant.

The Rhythm Section's Legacy

Max and Brandon's contribution to Snails' music extends far beyond the stage. Their influence on aspiring musicians cannot be overstated. Countless drummers and bassists have been inspired by their technical prowess, creativity, and undeniable stage presence.

Their legacy lives on in the next generation of rhythm section players, who continue to carry the torch and push the boundaries of what's possible. Max and Brandon have paved the way for future rhythm sections to embrace their individuality, experiment with new sounds, and create music that moves both the body and the soul.

An Exercise in Groove

Now, it's time for a little exercise to put your groove to the test. Grab your air drumsticks and air bass guitar because we're going to dive into a funky Snails classic, "Slime Time". This song is a perfect showcase of Max and Brandon's rhythmic brilliance.

Listen carefully to the song and pay attention to Max's intricate drum patterns and Brandon's infectious basslines. Feel the groove pulsating through your veins and let the music guide your every move. Don't be afraid to let loose and dance like nobody's watching. Remember, the rhythm section sets the tone, so allow yourself to be swept away by the irresistible energy they create.

Exercise: Find Your Groove

1. Listen to "Slime Time" by Snails and focus on Max's drumming and Brandon's basslines. 2. Move your body in rhythm with the music. Let the groove guide your every step. 3. Imagine yourself on stage with Snails, playing alongside Max and Brandon. Feel the energy of the crowd and let it fuel your performance. 4. Experiment with different rhythms and variations. Add your personal touch to the song and make it your own. 5. Share your groove with others. Record yourself jamming to "Slime Time" and share it with the Snail Army on social media using the hashtag #SnailsSlimeTimeGroove.

Remember, the rhythm is the heart and soul of any band. It's what makes your body move, your heart race, and your spirit soar. So embrace the rhythm, find your groove, and let the music take you on a wild and unforgettable journey.

Resources and Further Reading

1. "The Drummer's Bible" by Mick Berry and Jason Gianni - A comprehensive guide to drumming techniques and styles. 2. "Ultimate Bass Play-Along: Rolling Stones" by Rolling Stones - A collection of bass-driven songs to help you improve your groove. 3. "Groove Alchemy: Combining Funk, Jazz, Afro-Cuban, and Brazilian Rhythms to Take Your Drumming to the Next Level" by Stanton Moore - A book that explores different groove styles to enhance your drumming skills.

Fun Fact: Did you know that Max's drum set is custom-made and incorporates unique elements that enhance his performance? The bass drum skin is adorned with a mesmerizing snail shell design, symbolizing the band's identity and their deep connection to nature.

Behind the Masks: Exploring the Individuality of Snails' Members

In the vibrant world of music, it is often the unique personalities and individual talents of band members that captivate audiences. Snails is no exception. Behind their snail-shaped masks lie a group of talented individuals who have brought their own flair and style to the band. In this section, we delve deep into the personalities and contributions of each member, shedding light on the extraordinary individuals that make up Snails.

THE SNAIL FAMILY: EXAMINING THE BAND'S DYNAMICS

The Legendary Leader: A Profile of Snails' Frontman

At the forefront of Snails is their enigmatic frontman, known for his electrifying stage presence and mesmerizing vocals. Born Marcus Turner, he adopted the persona of Snailman to personify the spirit of the band. With a magnetic personality and a powerful voice that can command the attention of any crowd, Snailman is the driving force behind Snails' success.

A natural-born leader, Snailman possesses a unique ability to connect with fans on a personal level. He is often seen interacting with the crowd during shows, making each concert a memorable experience for everyone. Snailman's commanding stage presence and charismatic persona have made him an icon in the music industry.

Beyond his performance skills, Snailman is also known for his humanitarian efforts. He is actively involved in various charitable causes, using his platform to make a positive impact on the world. From hosting benefit concerts to partnering with organizations, Snailman strives to improve the lives of those in need.

Snails' Rhythm Section: The Backbone of the Band

Behind every great band is a solid rhythm section, and Snails is no exception. The foundation of their sound lies in the synchronized beats of their drummer, Bill "Sticky" Johnson, and the grooving basslines of their bassist, Lisa "Slime Queen" Martinez.

Sticky is a rhythmic powerhouse who sets the pace for the band with his dynamic drumming skills. With lightning-fast fills and infectious energy, Sticky's beats are the heartbeat of Snails' music. His metronomic precision keeps the band in sync and ensures that the audience can't help but dance along.

Complementing Sticky's beats is the Slime Queen herself, Lisa Martinez. Known for her funky basslines and infectious stage presence, Lisa brings a unique vibe to Snails' sound. With her signature grooves and melodic bass solos, she adds depth and richness to the band's music. Offstage, Lisa is a passionate advocate for female musicians, empowering aspiring bassists to pursue their dreams.

Behind the Masks: Exploring the Individuality of Snails' Members

While each member of Snails contributes to the band's overall sound, they also bring their individuality to the table. Behind their snail masks, there are stories and passions that define each member.

First, we have Isabella "Shimmer" Thompson, the band's keyboardist and resident synth wizard. With her vast musical knowledge and boundless creativity,

Shimmer adds layers of ethereal melodies and atmospheric sounds to Snails' music. Offstage, she spends her time composing film scores and exploring new ways to push the boundaries of sound.

Next, we have Eddie "Speedy" Ramirez, the band's lead guitarist. Known for his lightning-fast fingers and technical prowess, Speedy's guitar solos are nothing short of awe-inspiring. His melodic riffs and intricate harmonies bring an electrifying energy to Snails' performances. Outside of Snails, Speedy is an avid rock-climber, finding inspiration in the heights just as he does on stage.

Finally, we come to Georgia "Glow" Nguyen, the band's multi-talented backing vocalist and percussionist. With her soulful voice and vibrant stage presence, Glow adds depth and harmony to Snails' music. Whether she's belting out powerful harmonies or adding percussive elements, Glow's contributions elevate the band's sound to new heights. Beyond her musical talents, Glow is also a skilled painter, her artwork often incorporating themes from the band's music.

Snails Always and Forever: The Band's Unbreakable Bond

Beyond their individual talents, what sets Snails apart is their unwavering bond and collective vision. When they come together on stage, the chemistry between the members is palpable, creating a symbiotic energy that captivates audiences.

The members of Snails consider themselves a family, supporting and inspiring each other both on and off stage. Their shared experiences, triumphs, and struggles have forged an unbreakable bond that extends beyond the music they create. It is this camaraderie and mutual respect that has carried Snails through the highs and lows of their journey.

In conclusion, behind the masks lie the extraordinary individuals that make up Snails. From the enigmatic frontman to the rhythmic powerhouse and the creative forces that shape their sound, Snails is a band built on the talents and individuality of each member. Together, they create a unique musical experience that continues to resonate with fans around the world.

Snails Always and Forever: The Band's Unbreakable Bond

The bond between the members of Snails is something truly remarkable. It goes beyond mere friendship or professional collaboration, evolving into a connection that has stood the test of time. The unbreakable bond they share has been the secret ingredient behind their success and longevity in the music industry.

The Foundation of Friendship

At the core of Snails' unbreakable bond is the foundation of deep friendship that the band members have built over the years. From the very beginning, they recognized that their friendship was a crucial element in their journey towards musical greatness. They understood that having each other's backs, supporting one another through thick and thin, would be the key to their success.

Example:
When the band was faced with their first major setback—having their debut album rejected by multiple record labels—it was their bond as friends that kept them going. They reassured each other, reminding themselves that they were in this together, and that failure was just a stepping stone on the path to success.

Trust and Respect

Another pillar of Snails' unbreakable bond is the immense trust and respect they have for each other. They understand that each member brings something unique to the table and that their individual strengths complement one another. This trust allows them to create music that is greater than the sum of its parts.

Example:
During the creative process, there is a level of trust and respect that enables them to push boundaries and explore new musical territories. Each member has the freedom to express their ideas and experiment without fear of judgment. This atmosphere of trust and respect gives birth to the innovative and groundbreaking sound that Snails is known for.

Shared Vision and Goals

Snails' unbreakable bond is further strengthened by their shared vision and goals. From the early days, they had a clear understanding of what they wanted to achieve as a band and the mark they wanted to leave on the music industry. This shared vision acts as a guiding force that keeps them focused and united, even in the face of challenges.

Example:
When Snails faced disagreements or creative differences, they always found a way to come together and align their vision. They recognized that the success of the band relied on their ability to find common ground and work towards a shared goal. This unified approach has allowed them to overcome obstacles and achieve remarkable milestones in their career.

Support and Encouragement

Perhaps one of the most significant aspects of Snails' unbreakable bond is the unwavering support and encouragement they provide for one another. They know that in a competitive industry, having a support system within the band is crucial for individual growth and overall success.

Example:

When one member feels discouraged or faces personal challenges, the others are always there to lift them up and provide a shoulder to lean on. Whether it's through heartfelt conversations, pep talks, or simply being there as a listening ear, Snails never fails to support one another. This support not only strengthens their bond but also allows them to thrive and push their boundaries as artists.

The Magic Formula

The combination of friendship, trust, shared vision, and unwavering support forms the magic formula behind Snails' unbreakable bond. It is this formula that has kept them together through the highs and lows of their journey, solidifying their position as one of the most iconic and enduring bands in the music industry.

Example:

Imagine the band as puzzle pieces. Each member has a unique shape and color, and when put together, they create a masterpiece that captivates audiences worldwide. This metaphorical puzzle is a representation of the bond between the band members—individually, they are impressive, but together, they are unstoppable.

In conclusion, the unbreakable bond between the members of Snails is the key to their extraordinary success and longevity. It is a bond forged through friendship, trust, shared vision, and unwavering support. This bond has not only shaped their music but has also shaped their lives. Snails, always and forever, will continue to inspire and captivate the world with their unbreakable bond.

The Secret Ingredient: Snails' Manager and Support System

Snails' success in the music industry would not have been possible without the secret ingredient that played a pivotal role in their journey - their manager and support system. Behind every great band is a team of hardworking professionals who help navigate the complexities of the music business, ensuring that the artists can focus on what they do best - creating music. In this section, we delve into the importance of Snails' manager and the support system that propelled the band to new heights.

The Manager: Snails' Guiding Force

At the heart of Snails' success is their incredible manager, Marcus Johnson. Known for his sharp business acumen and unwavering commitment to the band's vision, Johnson is the driving force behind Snails' rise to fame. With his vast knowledge of the music industry, he has been instrumental in shaping their career and fostering their growth.

Johnson's role extends beyond mere business dealings; he is also a mentor, advisor, and friend to the band members. He understands their unique strengths and weaknesses and leverages them to maximize their potential. Johnson's expertise in strategic planning, contract negotiation, and relationship management has not only led to lucrative record deals and endorsements but has also ensured that the band remains authentic to their artistic vision.

But what sets Johnson apart is his genuine care for the band. He has an uncanny ability to balance their professional needs with their personal lives, creating a harmonious environment where the members can thrive. Johnson acts as a buffer between the band and the industry, shielding them from unnecessary pressures and ensuring their well-being.

The Support System: Building a Strong Foundation

Behind every successful band, there is a support system that provides the necessary infrastructure for growth and success. Snails' support system is a tight-knit team of professionals who work tirelessly behind the scenes to ensure the band's operations run smoothly.

One crucial aspect of the support system is the band's legal team. Led by renowned music attorneys, they handle all aspects of Snails' legal affairs, from contract negotiations and intellectual property protection to licensing and copyright issues. Their expertise ensures that the band's interests are always safeguarded, allowing Snails to focus on their music without worrying about legal complexities.

Another integral part of the support system is the band's publicists and marketing team. They are responsible for creating and executing strategic promotional campaigns that generate buzz around Snails' music. From securing media coverage to crafting compelling press releases, they ensure that the band's image is effectively communicated to the public.

The support system also includes tour managers, roadies, and technicians who work tirelessly to ensure seamless live performances. From setting up equipment and handling logistics to managing travel arrangements and coordinating with venues, their attention to detail is essential for Snails' electrifying stage presence.

The Power of Collaboration: Working Hand-in-Hand

The relationship between Snails and their manager, as well as the wider support system, is built on trust, collaboration, and mutual respect. It is a true partnership where everyone is aligned towards a common goal - achieving greatness.

Regular communication and collaboration between the band and their manager form the foundation of this successful partnership. They work hand-in-hand, making crucial decisions together, and charting the course for Snails' career. This open and transparent approach ensures that everyone's voice is heard, empowering the band to make informed choices.

The support system also plays a crucial role in fostering a positive and nurturing environment for the band. They provide emotional support, offering a shoulder to lean on during challenging times and celebrating victories together. This sense of camaraderie enhances the band's cohesion and allows them to thrive creatively.

Unconventional Wisdom: Thinking Outside the Box

In the ever-evolving landscape of the music industry, Snails' manager and support system understand the importance of thinking outside the box. They constantly seek innovative strategies and unconventional methods to keep the band relevant and ahead of the curve.

For example, they have embraced the digital era by utilizing social media platforms as a powerful tool for connecting with fans and expanding their reach. By capitalizing on viral trends, live streaming performances, and engaging with their audience, they have created a dedicated and passionate online community.

Furthermore, they have explored non-traditional revenue streams, such as brand partnerships and collaborations with other artists from different genres. These ventures not only provide financial stability but also showcase Snails' versatility and widen their fan base.

The Secret to Success: The Snails' Magic Formula

Snails' manager and support system are the secret ingredients that have propelled the band to unparalleled success. Their unwavering commitment, strategic guidance, and unwavering support have allowed Snails to navigate the music industry's challenging landscape and create a lasting impact.

The relationship between Snails and their manager is built on trust, respect, and shared goals, forming a solid foundation for their collaboration. The wider support system, comprising legal, marketing, and production professionals, ensures that all aspects of the band's operations are meticulously managed.

The key to their success lies not only in their expertise but also in their unwavering belief in Snails' talent and potential. With their manager and support system by their side, the band has the freedom to unleash their creativity, captivating audiences worldwide with their unique sound and electrifying performances.

In the next section, we explore the creative process behind Snails' music - from their unique songwriting techniques to rare collaborations that have shaped their sound. Stay tuned to dive deeper into the heart and soul of Snails' musical journey.

Beyond the Stage: Snails' Philanthropic Efforts

Snails for a Cause: Charitable Contributions and Activism

Snails, the iconic music band known for their electrifying performances and distinctive style, have not only conquered the music industry but also made a significant impact through their philanthropic efforts. Through their charitable contributions and activism, Snails have become champions of various causes, using their fame and influence to bring about positive change in the world.

The Power of Slime: Making a Difference

Snails' journey to fame has been intertwined with their desire to make a difference in the lives of others. As their popularity grew, they realized the immense power they possessed to raise awareness and funds for important social and environmental issues. Snails recognized that their success was not solely for their own benefit, but also a platform to make a lasting impact.

Unleashing the Slime for Good: Charitable Contributions

Snails have been actively engaged in supporting a wide range of charitable causes. They have donated generous sums of money to organizations dedicated to providing education, healthcare, and basic necessities to underprivileged communities. Whether it's building schools in developing countries or funding medical research, Snails have consistently used their resources to improve the lives of those in need.

Education for All: Snail Scholars Program Recognizing the importance of education in breaking the cycle of poverty, Snails established the Snail Scholars Program. This initiative provides scholarships and educational opportunities to talented individuals from disadvantaged backgrounds. By investing in the education of these individuals, Snails are giving them a chance to fulfill their potential and pursue their dreams.

Music for Change: Instruments for Hope Snails firmly believe in the transformative power of music. Through their Instruments for Hope program, Snails donate musical instruments to schools, community centers, and youth programs in underserved areas. By providing access to instruments and music education, Snails aim to inspire the next generation of musicians and foster creativity and expression.

Environmental Stewards: Protecting Mother Earth Snails are passionate advocates for environmental conservation. They actively support organizations that work towards preserving natural habitats, combating climate change, and promoting sustainable practices. By raising awareness about environmental issues through their music and engaging in initiatives like tree-planting campaigns, Snails are encouraging their fans to join them in protecting the planet.

Using Their Voice: Advocacy for Social Change

In addition to their charitable contributions, Snails have become vocal advocates for social change. They have used their platform to raise awareness and rally support for important social justice causes. Snails believe that music has the power to ignite conversations and inspire action, and they are determined to use their voice for positive change.

Equality and Inclusion: Snail Pride Movement Snails have been staunch supporters of LGBTQ+ rights and equality. Through their Snail Pride Movement, they aim to create a safe and inclusive space for their LGBTQ+ fans. They actively promote messages of acceptance, love, and equality in their music and performances, while also supporting organizations that advocate for LGBTQ+ rights.

Silencing Violence: Stand Against Domestic Abuse Snails have taken a strong stand against domestic abuse, a pressing issue that affects people globally. Through public service announcements, charity concerts, and collaborations with organizations dedicated to supporting survivors, Snails are using their platform to raise awareness about this issue and encourage action to end domestic violence.

Inspiring Others: Snails' Impact on Fans' Lives

Snails' charitable contributions and activism have not only made a tangible difference in the lives of individuals and communities but have also inspired their fans to get involved and make a positive impact. The band's dedication to giving back has resonated with their fanbase, creating a ripple effect of kindness and philanthropy.

The Snail Army: Uniting for a Cause Snails have always been grateful for their loyal and passionate fanbase, the Snail Army. Recognizing the power of their collective impact, Snails have actively engaged their fans in their charitable efforts.

Through social media campaigns, fundraisers, and fan-driven initiatives, the Snail Army has played a crucial role in supporting various causes championed by the band.

Beyond Music: Community Engagement　Snails go beyond their music career to personally engage with their fans and communities. They regularly visit hospitals, participate in charity events, and make surprise appearances at schools and organizations supported by their charitable initiatives. This direct interaction allows Snails to connect with their fans on a deeper level and inspire them to make a difference in their own communities.

Snail Speak: Empowering Through Lyrics　The power of Snails' music lies not only in its energetic beats and catchy melodies but also in the messages conveyed through their lyrics. Snails uses their music as a tool to spread positivity, inspire change, and ignite passion in their fans. Their songs often touch on social issues, challenging listeners to reflect and take action.

The Legacy of Snails: Making an Everlasting Impact

Snails understand that their impact extends beyond their career as a band. They aim to leave a lasting legacy that continues to inspire and bring about positive change in the world. Whether it's through their charitable contributions or their fans' involvement in philanthropy, Snails' influence is meant to endure for generations to come.

Eternal Slime: The Snail Foundation　To ensure the continuity of their charitable work, Snails have established the Snail Foundation. This organization serves as a platform to carry on their philanthropic efforts even after they retire from the stage. The Snail Foundation aims to support and empower emerging artists, continue their existing charitable programs, and explore new avenues for making a positive impact.

Spreading the Slime: Snails' Philanthropy Roadmap　Snails have documented their charitable journey, sharing their experiences and insights in a book titled "Spreading the Slime: Snails' Philanthropy Roadmap." This book serves as a guide for aspiring artists, fans, and philanthropists who wish to make a difference in their communities. It offers practical advice, case studies, and personal anecdotes to inspire and guide individuals on their own philanthropic journeys.

Snails for a Cause: Leaving a Slime Trail of Goodness

Snails' commitment to making a difference through their charitable contributions and activism sets them apart as not just extraordinary musicians but also as compassionate human beings. Their tireless efforts to support various causes and their dedication to using their platform for positive change have left a lasting impact on individuals, communities, and the world. Snails have proven that success is not just measured by record sales and chart positions but by the lives touched and the difference made. They have truly exemplified the mantra of "leaving a slime trail of goodness" in everything they do.

Inspiring Hope: Snails' Impact on Fans' Lives

Throughout their incredible journey, Snails has touched the lives of millions of fans around the world. Their music has not only entertained and captivated audiences, but it has also inspired hope and made a positive impact on the lives of many. In this section, we will delve into the ways Snails has influenced their fans, leaving a lasting legacy of inspiration and empowerment.

Music as a Healing Force

Music has the power to heal and uplift, and Snails has embraced this notion wholeheartedly. Their powerful lyrics and infectious melodies have resonated with fans from all walks of life, offering solace and encouragement in times of hardship. Through their music, Snails has provided a safe space for fans to express their emotions and find comfort, fostering a sense of belonging and community.

Example:
One fan, Emily, shared her story of battling with depression and how Snails' music became her lifeline. In her darkest moments, their songs provided her with a glimmer of hope and reminded her that she was not alone in her struggles. The raw honesty and vulnerability in Snails' lyrics gave Emily the strength to confront her mental health challenges head-on and seek the help she needed. Today, she continues to be an avid supporter of the band and is an advocate for mental health awareness.

Empowering Fans to Embrace Individuality

Snails' unwavering commitment to authenticity and self-expression has empowered their fans to embrace their true selves. Through their music and message, the band encourages individuals to break free from societal norms and embrace their uniqueness. Snails has created a safe space for fans to embrace their quirks and celebrate their differences, fostering a sense of confidence and self-acceptance.

Example:

Sarah, a young teenager struggling with self-esteem issues, found solace in Snails' message of embracing individuality. Their music allowed her to discover her own identity and gave her the courage to express herself authentically. Inspired by the band's fearlessness, Sarah started her own fashion blog, encouraging others to embrace their personal style without fear of judgment. Snails' music became the soundtrack to her journey of self-discovery and empowerment.

Supporting Social Causes

Snails has been a vocal advocate for various social causes, using their platform to raise awareness and support positive change. The band's commitment to making a difference has inspired their fans to get involved in their communities and champion causes that are close to their hearts. Snails has galvanized their fanbase to take action and make a positive impact in the world.

Example:

When a devastating natural disaster struck a small town, Snails organized a charity concert to raise funds for the affected community. Fans from all over came together, united by their love for the band and their desire to help those in need. The event not only raised a significant amount of money but also inspired fans to continue supporting charitable causes in their own lives. Snails' efforts showed their fans that music can be a powerful tool for social change and encouraged them to make a difference in their own communities.

Building a Supportive Community

Snails' impact goes beyond their music; they have fostered a strong and supportive community among their fans, known as the Snail Army. This tight-knit community provides a sense of belonging and camaraderie, offering a support system for fans to connect with one another and share their experiences. Snail Army members support and uplift each other, creating a positive and inclusive space for all.

Example:

John, a long-time fan of Snails, found a sense of belonging within the Snail Army. As a teenager struggling with his sexuality, he often felt isolated and misunderstood. However, through Snails' music and the community they had built, John found acceptance and support. The Snail Army provided him with a network of friends who understood and celebrated him for who he truly was. Today, John actively volunteers for LGBTQ+ organizations, inspired by the acceptance and love he experienced within the Snail Army.

Lessons Learned from Snails' Journey

Snails' impact on their fans' lives extends beyond their music; their journey has taught valuable lessons and provided inspiration for aspiring artists and dreamers. Through their perseverance and determination, Snails has shown that success is attainable through hard work and passion. They have taught their fans to never give up on their dreams and to always stay true to themselves.

Example:

Emma, an aspiring musician, found immense inspiration in Snails' journey. Witnessing the band's rise to success from humble beginnings motivated her to pursue her own passion for music. Their story taught her that setbacks and challenges are a natural part of the journey, but with dedication and belief in oneself, anything is possible. Emma now performs at local venues and credits Snails for giving her the courage to pursue her dreams.

Overall, Snails' impact on their fans' lives is immeasurable. Through their music, message, and activism, they have inspired hope, offered solace, and empowered their fans to embrace their individuality. Snails has cultivated a community built on love and acceptance, leaving a lasting legacy that transcends music. They are proof that music has the power to change lives and make the world a better place. The Snail Army will forever carry the torch, spreading the band's message of hope and inspiring future generations to embrace their dreams with determination and resilience.

Using Their Voices: Snails' Advocacy for Social Change

In addition to their mesmerizing music and electrifying performances, the members of Snails have always used their platform to advocate for social change. From the very beginning, they recognized the power of their voices and the ability to make a difference in the world. This section explores the band's unwavering commitment to philanthropy and their efforts to create a positive impact on society.

Snails for a Cause: Charitable Contributions and Activism

Snails has been actively involved in various charitable organizations and social causes throughout their career. They firmly believe in giving back to the community and using their success to uplift those in need. Some of the notable causes they have supported include:

1. **Environmental Conservation:** Snails has been a strong advocate for environmental sustainability and raising awareness about the importance of protecting our planet. The band has partnered with organizations like Greenpeace and the World Wildlife Fund to promote conservation efforts and address issues such as deforestation, climate change, and endangered species.

2. **Youth Empowerment:** Recognizing the potential of young minds, Snails has been actively involved in initiatives focused on empowering and inspiring the youth. They have partnered with organizations like UNICEF and Boys & Girls Clubs of America to support education, mentorship programs, and providing opportunities for underprivileged children.

3. **Mental Health Awareness:** Snails understands the importance of mental health and has been vocal about breaking the stigma surrounding mental illnesses. They have worked closely with organizations like the American Foundation for Suicide Prevention and Mind, promoting mental health awareness, offering support, and encouraging open conversations about mental well-being.

4. **Social Justice:** Snails takes a stand against injustice and inequality. They have lent their support to human rights organizations, such as Amnesty International and the NAACP, advocating for equality, fighting against discrimination, and promoting social justice for all.

Inspiring Hope: Snails' Impact on Fans' Lives

Through their music and philanthropic efforts, Snails has inspired hope and touched the lives of countless fans around the world. The band's message of unity, resilience, and positivity resonates deeply with their audience, creating a sense of belonging and empowerment.

Fans have shared stories of how Snails' music and advocacy have helped them overcome personal struggles and find strength during difficult times. The band's lyrics often touch on themes of perseverance, self-acceptance, and the power of unity, striking a chord with listeners from all walks of life.

Snails' involvement in social causes has also encouraged their fans to get involved and make a difference in their communities. Through various campaigns and volunteer opportunities, the band has inspired a wave of activism among their dedicated fanbase, showing that even small acts of kindness and advocacy can create significant change.

Using Their Voices: Snails' Advocacy for Social Change

Snails understands the significance of using their voices and platforms to create real change in the world. In addition to their financial contributions, the band actively amplifies the voices of marginalized communities and promotes inclusivity through their music and public appearances.

They use their concerts and tours as a platform to spread messages of love, acceptance, and unity, promoting a sense of belonging among their diverse fanbase. Snails often invites local activists and representatives from charitable organizations to their shows, allowing them to share their stories and raise awareness about their causes.

The band also takes the time to educate themselves and their fans about the issues they support. They have hosted panel discussions, workshops, and Q&A sessions, featuring experts and activists, to foster understanding and inspire action.

In addition to their music, the members of Snails regularly use their social media platforms to advocate for social change. They share informative posts, resources, and personal stories, encouraging their followers to get involved, donate their time or money, and engage in conversations about pressing societal issues.

The Power of Snail Army: Global Fanbase and Fan Culture

The immense support and dedication from their fanbase, often referred to as the "Snail Army," have been instrumental in Snails' advocacy efforts. The band's passionate fans are not just supporters of their music but also active participants in the causes they champion.

The Snail Army has organized fundraising campaigns, volunteer events, and awareness drives in collaboration with the band's initiatives. They have also created online communities and discussion groups where fans can connect, share resources, and continue the conversation on social issues.

Snails recognizes the power of their fanbase beyond just numbers. They leverage their influence to mobilize the Snail Army, encouraging them to make a positive impact in their own communities. From organizing local clean-up drives to launching grassroots social campaigns, the fans of Snails have become a force for good, spreading the band's message far and wide.

Cultivating Change: Snails' Impact on the Music Industry

Snails' commitment to advocacy extends beyond their charitable contributions and fan engagement. The band has also left an indelible mark on the music industry itself, using their artistry as a platform to challenge norms, push boundaries, and inspire other artists to create music with a social conscience.

Through their groundbreaking music and performances, Snails has:

1. **Promoted Diversity and Inclusion:** Snails has actively embraced diversity in their music, collaborating with artists from various backgrounds and genres. By showcasing the power of collaboration and celebrating different cultures, they have set an example for the industry to follow, promoting inclusivity and breaking down barriers.

2. **Addressed Social Issues:** Snails' lyrics often touch on social issues, such as inequality, mental health, and environmental concerns. Their music serves as a catalyst for conversations and helps raise awareness about these pressing topics, encouraging listeners to reflect on the world around them.

3. **Encouraged Authenticity:** Snails' unapologetic and authentic approach to their music has inspired other artists to stay true to themselves and use their platforms to advocate for causes they believe in. The band's success has shown that being true to one's values and beliefs can resonate with audiences and create a lasting impact.

4. **Pushed Boundaries:** Snails' unique sound and style have challenged traditional genre boundaries, encouraging other artists to experiment and think outside the box. Their willingness to take risks has opened doors for new approaches to music, leading to innovation and fresh perspectives within the industry.

In conclusion, Snails' advocacy for social change goes beyond just words and financial contributions. They actively use their music, public appearances, and social media presence to promote awareness, inspire action, and make a tangible difference in the world. Through their collaboration with charitable organizations, engagement with fans, and impact on the music industry, Snails has established themselves as not only groundbreaking musicians but also passionate advocates for social justice and positive change.

The Legacy of Snails: Securing a Place in Music History

Snails' Enduring Influence: Artists Touched by their Sound

Snails' unique and groundbreaking sound has resonated with countless artists across genres, leaving an indelible mark on the music industry. Their revolutionary blend of pulsating rhythms, mind-bending melodies, and infectious energy has inspired a new wave of musicians and transformed the musical landscape. In this section, we explore the enduring influence of Snails and the artists who have been touched by their sound.

The Snail Effect: A Paradigm Shift in Music

Snails' music challenges traditional notions of genre and pushes the boundaries of sonic experimentation. Their use of heavy bass, filthy drops, and electrifying synths has revolutionized electronic music, inspiring a legion of artists to embrace a more audacious and daring approach to their craft.

One such artist who has been deeply influenced by Snails is DJ X, an up-and-coming electronic music producer. Known for his innovative soundscapes and genre-bending tracks, DJ X credits Snails as a major source of inspiration. In an interview, he expressed how Snails' unique sound opened his mind to new possibilities, allowing him to break free from the constraints of conventional EDM and explore uncharted territories. DJ X's music embodies the spirit of Snails, pushing boundaries and challenging the status quo.

Revolutionizing the Sound: Snails' Influence on Pop and Rock

Snails' influence extends beyond the realm of electronic music, reaching into the realms of pop and rock. Their infectious melodies and infectious energy have permeated the soundscapes of many artists in these genres, bringing a fresh and dynamic edge to their music.

One of the most notable examples of Snails' influence on pop music is the artist Y, whose chart-topping hits bear the unmistakable stamp of Snails' sonic innovation. Y's fusion of pop, EDM, and Snails' signature sound has created a sonic palette that captivates audiences worldwide. The impact of Snails on Y's music is evident in the heavy basslines, the gritty synths, and the dynamic drops that define their sound.

In the rock genre, Snails' influence can be seen in the music of Z, a band that has embraced Snails' experimental ethos and incorporated it into their own sound. Z's fusion of rock, electronic elements, and a touch of Snails' heavy bass has garnered them critical acclaim and a devoted following. Their music pays homage to Snails' legacy while carving out a unique space in the rock landscape.

Beyond Music: Snails' Influence on Visual Arts

The impact of Snails' innovative sound reaches beyond music and into the world of visual arts. Their aesthetic and artistic vision have inspired a new generation of visual artists, who seek to capture the essence of Snails' music through their own creations.

A prominent visual artist known as A draws inspiration from Snails' music to create immersive and otherworldly installations. A's work combines elements of sculpture, light, and sound to transport viewers into a surreal and ethereal realm. Snails' music serves as the driving force behind A's artistic exploration, providing the sonic landscape upon which their visual creations come to life.

Embracing the Snail Spirit: Artists as Trailblazers

Snails' enduring influence goes beyond mere imitation; it ignites a spirit of innovation, encouraging artists to push the boundaries of their creativity and forge their own distinct paths. The artists touched by Snails' sound are not mere imitators but trailblazers in their own right, harnessing the energy and inspiration derived from Snails' music to create something entirely new.

In this section, we have explored just a few examples of the multitude of artists who have been touched by Snails' sound. From electronic music producers like DJ X to pop artists like Y, and visual artists like A, Snails' influence remains undeniable and pervasive. Their sonic experimentation and boundary-pushing nature continue to inspire and shape the creative landscape of today and tomorrow.

Exercises: Exploring Your Sonic Boundaries

1. Choose a genre of music that you're familiar with and listen to a few Snails tracks. Identify elements of Snails' sound that you believe can be incorporated into that genre. Experiment with integrating these elements into your own music creation and see how it transforms the overall sound.

2. Research other artists who have been influenced by Snails and explore their music. Pay attention to the specific aspects of Snails' sound that have been adopted and how those elements have been adapted to suit different genres. Write a short analysis of the ways in which these artists have incorporated Snails' influence into their own unique style.

3. Imagine you are a visual artist and you want to create a piece inspired by Snails' music. Consider how you can translate Snails' sonic innovativeness into a visual form. Sketch out some ideas and create a mood board to help you visualize your concept.

4. Reflect on your own creative process. Have you ever felt constrained by the conventions of your chosen medium or genre? How might embracing Snails' spirit of boundary-pushing and innovation impact your approach to your craft? Write a short essay exploring the possibilities and challenges of incorporating Snails' influence into your own artistic practice.

Honors and Awards: Recognizing Snails' Artistic Contributions

Throughout their remarkable career, the legendary band Snails has amassed an impressive collection of honors and awards, solidifying their position as one of the most influential and groundbreaking musical acts of all time. With their unique style and revolutionary sound, Snails has left an indelible mark on the music industry, and their exceptional talent has been recognized by prestigious organizations worldwide. In this section, we will delve into the numerous accolades that Snails has received, showcasing the band's unparalleled artistic contributions.

Grammy Awards: The Snail's Crown Jewel

When it comes to music industry recognition, the Grammy Awards reign supreme, and Snails' trophy case proudly houses several of these prestigious honors. Known as the "Oscars of Music," the Grammys celebrate the highest level of artistic achievement in the industry. Snails' relentless dedication to their craft has garnered them multiple Grammy wins, establishing them as a force to be reckoned with.

Their groundbreaking album, "Slime Fever," took home the highly coveted Grammy Award for Best Rock Album, solidifying their status as a pioneer of a new musical genre. The album's infectious energy, daring experimentation, and thought-provoking lyrics captivated both critics and fans alike, cementing Snails' place among rock legends.

Furthermore, Snails' distinct vocal style and mesmerizing stage presence earned them the Grammy Award for Best Live Performance. Their ability to captivate audiences from the moment they step on stage is unparalleled, leaving a lasting impression that resonates long after the final note is played.

Rock and Roll Hall of Fame: A Permanent Place in Music History

A true testament to Snails' enduring impact on the music industry is their induction into the prestigious Rock and Roll Hall of Fame. This hallowed institution recognizes artists who have made a significant contribution to the evolution and preservation of rock and roll music. Snails' innovative approach to music, blending elements of rock, funk, and punk, propelled them into this elite group of musical trailblazers.

With their induction, Snails joined the ranks of legendary musicians who have shaped the course of rock history. Their influence on subsequent generations of musicians is undeniable, and their timeless classics continue to resonate with audiences of all ages. The band's legacy is forever enshrined within the Rock and Roll Hall of Fame, ensuring that their contributions will never be forgotten.

MTV Video Music Awards: Iconic Visuals and Trailblazing Videos

In addition to their groundbreaking music, Snails' iconic music videos have played a pivotal role in their artistic recognition. The band's ability to merge visually stunning imagery with their unique sound has garnered them numerous accolades at the MTV Video Music Awards.

Their mesmerizing video for the chart-topping hit "Slime Revolution" secured Snails the prestigious Moonman trophy for Best Music Video. This groundbreaking visual masterpiece showcased the band's creativity and showcased their ability to push boundaries and redefine the music video genre. With its vivid colors, innovative special effects, and thought-provoking symbolism, the "Slime Revolution" video captured the essence of Snails' artistic vision.

Billboard Music Awards: Dominating the Charts

Snails' undeniable impact on the music industry is evident in their Billboard Music Awards record. As a testament to their commercial success and critical acclaim, the band has consistently dominated the charts, earning them numerous accolades.

Their infectious hit single "Gooey Love" topped the charts for weeks, earning Snails the coveted Billboard Music Award for Best Rock Song. This anthemic track showcased their ability to capture the hearts and minds of listeners, solidifying their place as true rock icons.

In addition, Snails' chart-topping album "Sticky Rhythms" secured their victory in the fiercely competitive Best Alternative Album category. The band's ability to seamlessly blend various genres and create a fresh, innovative sound set them apart from their peers, making them worthy recipients of this prestigious honor.

Other Notable Recognitions

Snails' artistic contributions have been acknowledged beyond traditional music-related awards. The band's unique style and impact have resonated with a diverse range of organizations, leading to a wide array of honors.

Their philanthropic efforts and dedication to social causes have earned them the Humanitarian Award from the Global Music Foundation. Snails' commitment to using their platform for positive change and their contributions to various charitable organizations have touched the lives of people around the world, making them inspirational figures in both the musical realm and society at large.

Furthermore, Snails' collaboration with renowned contemporary artist David Houndstooth resulted in a groundbreaking multimedia exhibition, "The Slime Art Experience." This innovative blend of music, art, and technology earned them the prestigious Artistic Collaboration of the Year award from the International Arts Association. Snails' ability to seamlessly merge different art forms and create a truly immersive experience showcases their unparalleled creativity and artistic vision.

Snippet of Snails' Acceptance Speech: Setting the Stage on Fire

In the acceptance speech for one of their numerous awards, the charismatic frontman of Snails, aptly named Slimy, took the stage with his signature energy and charm, leaving the audience in awe and laughter. As he held the award triumphantly in his hand, he began:

"Ladies and gentlemen, Snail Army, all our fans out there, thank you! This award means the world to us! We want to express our gratitude to all the people who have believed in us from day one, who have supported us through thick and thin, and who have stood by us as we pushed the boundaries of music. We couldn't have done it without you!"

Slimy's heartfelt words resonated throughout the auditorium, as the band's loyal fans erupted in applause and cheers. He continued:

"Tonight, we stand here not just as a band, but as a symbol of perseverance, artistic exploration, and the power of music to unite and inspire. We share this honor with every artist who has dared to dream, who has poured their heart and soul into their music, and who has relentlessly pursued their passion. May we always have the courage to break the mold, to challenge the status quo, and to create something that leaves a lasting impact."

The band's acceptance speech was a testament to their humility, appreciation for their fans, and their unwavering dedication to their craft. They not only recognized their own success but also the collective efforts of the entire music community, setting an example of what it means to be true artists.

The Snail's Trail: A Lesson in Perseverance and Artistic Vision

Snails' honors and awards serve as a testament to their extraordinary talent, indomitable spirit, and unwavering commitment to their artistic vision. Their groundbreaking music, mesmerizing stage presence, and thought-provoking visuals have left an indelible mark on the music industry.

Through their numerous Grammy Awards, induction into the Rock and Roll Hall of Fame, recognition at the MTV Video Music Awards, domination of the Billboard charts, and acknowledgment from diverse organizations, Snails' artistic contributions have been celebrated and admired on a global scale.

Aspiring artists can draw inspiration from Snails' journey, learning the value of perseverance, authenticity, and pushing creative boundaries. Their success not only highlights the importance of originality and innovation but also reminds us that true artistry transcends genres and leaves a lasting impact.

In the words of Snails' iconic frontman Slimy, "Never be afraid to unleash your true creative potential. Embrace your uniqueness, push the limits, and always stay true to yourself. Let your art be a reflection of who you are, and never forget the power it holds to touch hearts and change lives."

Snails' artistic contributions will continue to resonate with audiences for generations to come, ensuring that their legacy remains etched in the annals of music history. The band's unparalleled talent, determination, and willingness to break conventions have firmly established them as true icons of the industry.

While their journey may have started with a sluggish beginning, Snails' rise to fame is a testament to the transformative power of music and serves as an inspiration to all aspiring artists who dream of making their mark in the ever-evolving world of music.

The Snail Dynasty: Passions Passed Down through Generations

Within the illustrious world of music, there are few bands that can claim to have left an indelible mark on generations of listeners. Snails is one such band. Their journey, which began with a sluggish start, eventually led to an iconic status that has transcended time and era. The impact of Snails' music has not only influenced their contemporaries but has also been passed down through generations, creating what can only be described as the Snail Dynasty.

The Legacy Lives On

The Snail Dynasty represents the continuation of Snails' artistry and passion through their successors. The band's enduring legacy has inspired countless musicians to follow in their footsteps and explore new horizons in music. The Snail Dynasty is a testament to the band's ability to connect with audiences on a deep and emotional level, leaving an everlasting impression that goes beyond a mere genre or style.

Passing the Torch

As the baton is passed from one generation to the next, the Snail Dynasty ensures that Snails' music remains alive and relevant. The band members have taken it upon themselves to mentor and nurture aspiring musicians, fostering a community of artists who carry forward the band's artistic vision. Through workshops, masterclasses, and collaborations with emerging talent, Snails has created a platform for the next generation to thrive and push the boundaries of music.

The Evolution of Snails' Music

The Snail Dynasty not only inherits the essence of Snails' music but also strives to evolve and innovate. Each successor brings their unique perspective and artistic sensibilities to the table, building upon the foundation laid by the band. This continuous evolution ensures that Snails' music stays relevant and resonates with the ever-changing tastes of audiences.

Reviving Snails' Music for a New Audience

One of the key responsibilities of the Snail Dynasty is to introduce Snails' music to a new generation of listeners. The band's timeless classics are reimagined and rejuvenated, blending the old with the new. This approach allows the Snail Dynasty to capture the hearts of both long-time fans and younger audiences, bridging the gap between generations and preserving the band's musical legacy.

Preserving Snails' Traditions

While the Snail Dynasty embraces innovation, it also recognizes the importance of preserving Snails' traditions. The band's signature sound and style are carefully maintained, paying homage to the roots that made Snails a household name. The Snail Dynasty understands the value of authenticity and strives to honor the band's legacy by staying true to the essence of Snails' music.

Honoring the Snail Dynasty

The Snail Dynasty is not merely a continuation of the band's music, but a celebration of Snails' contributions to the world of music. Through dedicated tribute concerts and events, the Dynasty pays homage to the band's iconic status, reminding the world of the impact Snails has had on the music industry. These events serve as a reminder of the power of music to transcend generations and continue to inspire.

Inspiring the Next Dynasty

The Snail Dynasty serves as an inspiration for future bands and musicians to leave their mark on the world. Snails' journey, from a sluggish beginning to a renowned legacy, demonstrates the importance of perseverance, creativity, and above all, a genuine passion for music. It encourages aspiring artists to carve their own paths, create their own legacies, and pass the torch to the next generation.

Conclusion

The Snail Dynasty stands as a testament to Snails' enduring impact on the music industry. Through their unwavering passion, dedication, and artistry, the band has not only left a lasting impression but has also inspired a new generation of musicians to carry forward their musical legacy. The Snail Dynasty ensures that Snails' music lives on, allowing audiences to continue to experience the magic and beauty of their unique sound. As the Dynasty continues to evolve and thrive, it cements Snails' place in history as a band that has truly shaped the course of music for generations to come.

Carrying the Torch

Carrying the Torch

Carrying the Torch

In this chapter, we delve into the exciting evolution of the legendary band Snails, as they transition from their earlier years to a new era of music. The band's ability to adapt to change, reinvent their sound, and nurture the next generation of artists is a testament to their enduring legacy. Join us as we explore Snails' journey of growth, transformation, and their everlasting impact on the music industry.

Adapting to Change: Snails' Transition to a New Era

Every successful band faces the challenge of adapting to changing times and evolving musical trends. Snails, true to their name, slithered through this obstacle with ease. As the music landscape shifted, the band recognized the importance of staying relevant while maintaining their unique identity.

With a deep understanding of their fanbase, Snails made a conscious decision to experiment with their sound. They incorporated elements of different genres, blending their signature style with new musical influences. This seamless fusion allowed them to appeal to a wider audience while keeping their loyal fans engaged.

Snail Reunion: The Band's Triumphant Return to the Stage

After a period of individual endeavors, Snails reunited for a much-anticipated comeback. This marked a significant chapter in their journey as they once again took the stage by storm. The energy and chemistry between the band members were palpable, reigniting their passion for creating music together.

The reunion tour showcased Snails' evolution and growth as artists. They unveiled a revamped image and sound, captivating both long-time fans and new admirers. The band's ability to reintroduce themselves while staying true to their roots solidified their position as musical icons.

Reinventing the Sound: Snails' Experimental Phases

Snails' dedication to pushing boundaries and exploring new sonic territories became evident during their experimental phases. The band fearlessly embraced unconventional instruments, non-traditional song structures, and thought-provoking lyrics that challenged societal norms.

Their innovative approach to music sought to provoke emotions and inspire self-reflection. Snails' boldness to tread uncharted waters showcased their artistic depth and versatility. By constantly reinventing their sound, they showcased an unwavering commitment to their craft.

Snails 2.0: Members' Solo Projects and Collaborations

While Snails remained the heart and soul of the band, each member embarked on solo projects and collaborated with other artists. These endeavors allowed them to further explore their individual artistic visions and expand their musical horizons.

The solo projects and collaborations served as catalysts for personal growth and creative exploration. However, they also fueled the band's collective growth, as each member brought their newfound experiences and inspiration back to the Snails' nest.

Snails Forever: Nurturing the Next Generation of Artists

As true pioneers in the music industry, Snails recognized the importance of passing the torch and nurturing the next generation of artists. They established mentorship programs, music academies, and hosted workshops to empower aspiring musicians and foster their growth.

In these initiatives, Snails shared their invaluable knowledge, experiences, and advice with emerging talents. The band firmly believed in paying it forward and creating a supportive community that encourages artistic expression and innovation.

Conclusion

Snails' journey of carrying the torch to a new era showcased their ability to adapt, reinvent, and inspire. The band's reunion, experimental phases, and commitment to nurturing future artists solidified their legacy in the music industry. As we move forward in this biography of Snails, we will delve deeper into their world domination, the evolution of their music, and the everlasting impact they left on pop culture.

From Snails to Super Snails: Snails' Evolution

Adapting to Change: Snails' Transition to a New Era

Change is a constant in life, and the world of music is no exception. For the legendary band Snails, the ability to adapt to changing times has been a key factor in their longevity and continued success. In this chapter, we delve into Snails' transition to a new era, exploring the challenges they faced and the strategies they employed to stay relevant in a rapidly evolving industry.

The Winds of Change: Evolving Musical Landscape

The transition to a new era for Snails began when they realized that the musical landscape was shifting. New genres were emerging, tastes were changing, and technology was revolutionizing the way music was created and consumed. Snails recognized the need to evolve with the times in order to maintain their relevance and connect with a new generation of fans.

Embracing Experimentation: Pushing Boundaries

In their quest to adapt to change, Snails embraced experimentation. They pushed the boundaries of their sound, blending genres and incorporating new elements into their music. This fearless approach allowed them to stay ahead of the curve and remain innovative in a competitive industry.

To illustrate this, let's take a look at their album "Slime Revolution." In this record, Snails seamlessly incorporated elements of electronic music, hip-hop, and even classical orchestration. By not confining themselves to a specific genre, they were able to create a unique sonic experience that appealed to a wide range of listeners.

Collaborations: Blending Old and New

Another important aspect of Snails' transition to a new era was their collaborations with both established and up-and-coming artists. By working with musicians from different backgrounds, Snails not only infused fresh perspectives into their music but also attracted new audiences who may not have been familiar with their previous work.

One noteworthy collaboration was their partnership with rising pop star Stella Jones on the hit single "Slow and Steady." This track showcased Snails' ability to blend their signature sound with contemporary pop sensibilities, creating a crossover hit that garnered chart success and introduced their music to a whole new fanbase.

Harnessing Technology: Embracing the Digital Age

In addition to experimenting with their sound and collaborating with others, Snails recognized the importance of embracing technology. They understood that the digital age presented both challenges and opportunities, and they proactively used digital platforms to connect with their fans and reach a wider audience.

One innovative strategy they employed was the use of virtual reality (VR) technology in their live performances. By giving fans the option to experience their concerts through VR headsets, Snails created an immersive and interactive experience that transcended physical barriers and allowed fans from all over the world to enjoy their shows.

Staying True to Their Roots: The Essence of Snails

Amidst the changes and adaptations, Snails always stayed true to their roots. They remained committed to their unique sound and the distinctive qualities that made them stand out in the first place. By preserving their core essence while evolving with the times, they ensured that their music would remain authentic and resonant with their devoted fanbase.

It is worth noting that adapting to change does not mean compromising one's identity. Snails' transition to a new era was a testament to their ability to evolve without losing sight of who they truly are as artists.

Embracing Change: A Lesson for Aspiring Artists

The transition to a new era for Snails serves as a valuable lesson for aspiring artists. In an industry that constantly evolves, the ability to adapt and embrace change is crucial. By staying open-minded, pushing boundaries, and leveraging new technologies, artists can position themselves for success and longevity.

However, it is equally important for artists to stay true to their artistic vision and maintain their authenticity. As Snails demonstrated, evolving does not mean abandoning one's roots but rather finding creative ways to stay relevant while staying true to oneself.

Key Takeaways

- Adapting to change is essential for long-term success in the music industry.

- Experimentation and pushing boundaries can help artists stay innovative and ahead of the curve.
- Collaborations with diverse artists can bring fresh perspectives and attract new audiences.
- Embracing technology and utilizing digital platforms can expand an artist's reach and connect with fans worldwide.
- Staying true to one's roots and maintaining authenticity are vital during times of transition.
- Aspiring artists should embrace change, stay open-minded, and find ways to evolve while staying true to themselves.

Snail Reunion: The Band's Triumphant Return to the Stage

After years of anticipation, the day finally arrived when Snails, the legendary band, reunited for an epic comeback tour. This momentous occasion marked the end of a long hiatus and the beginning of a new era for the band and their devoted fans, who had been patiently waiting for their return.

The Snail Reunion tour kicked off in their hometown, where they first began their musical journey. The venue was packed with fans who had traveled from far and wide to witness this historic event. As the lights dimmed and the crowd erupted in cheers, the stage came alive with the electrifying presence of Snails.

The band members, each clad in their iconic outfits, took their positions on the stage. The crowd went wild as the first notes of their signature hit song filled the air. It was a moment of pure magic as the band members rediscovered their chemistry and synergy, as if no time had passed at all.

Throughout the tour, Snails showcased their unparalleled talent and showmanship. Their performances were a perfect blend of energy, passion, and nostalgia, taking fans on a journey through their greatest hits, as well as introducing new material that showcased their growth as artists.

The Reunion tour wasn't just about the music, though. It was a celebration of the unbreakable bond between Snails and their fans. The band members took the time to interact with their audience, sharing stories from their time apart and expressing their gratitude for the unwavering support they had received.

As the tour progressed, Snails' triumphant return to the stage became a cultural phenomenon. Their shows sold out within minutes, and fans eagerly awaited news of additional tour dates. The band's impact on the music industry was undeniable, as they once again took their place at the top of the charts with their new releases.

But the Snail Reunion tour was about more than just reclaiming their throne. It was about inspiring a new generation of artists and reminding the world of the power of music. Snails used their platform to champion social causes, raising awareness and funds for important issues close to their hearts.

The band's reunion was not without its challenges, of course. They faced criticism and skepticism from those who doubted their ability to recapture their former glory. But the unwavering support of their fans propelled them forward, proving that their music and message were timeless.

As the tour came to a close, there was an air of bittersweetness among the band members and their fans. It was the end of an era, but also the beginning of a new chapter for Snails. Their reunion had reignited their passion for creating music and left an indelible mark on their legacy.

The Snail Reunion tour was not just a triumph for the band, but for everyone who had ever been inspired by their music. It was a reminder that dreams can be realized, and that sometimes, a comeback can be even more powerful than the original journey.

So as Snails took their final bow, they left the stage with a sense of accomplishment and gratitude. They knew that their return was not just for themselves, but for all the fans who had supported them throughout the years. And with that, they stepped into the next phase of their musical journey, eager to see what the future held for Snails and their loyal followers.

Unconventional Tip: In the midst of their tour, Snails surprised their fans by organizing intimate meet-and-greets with a twist. Instead of the typical photo-op, they invited fans to join them for a jam session backstage. This unique experience allowed fans to get up-close and personal with the band, creating unforgettable memories for both the fans and the band members. It was a testament to Snails' commitment to connect with their audience on a deeper level, and it left a lasting impression on everyone involved.

Example Problem: Imagine you are a die-hard Snails fan who wants to attend their reunion tour but missed out on getting tickets. You decide to try your luck by entering contests and giveaways in hopes of winning a ticket. After entering 10 different contests, each with a 1 in 100 chance of winning, what is the probability that you will win at least one ticket?

Solution: To find the probability of winning at least one ticket, we can use the complement rule. The probability of not winning in a single contest is 99/100. Therefore, the probability of not winning in any of the 10 contests is $(99/100)^10$.

The probability of winning at least one ticket is equal to 1 minus the probability of not winning any tickets:

$$1 - \left(\frac{99}{100}\right)^{10} \approx 0.0956$$

So, there is approximately a 9.56% chance that you will win at least one ticket to the Snail Reunion tour.

Note: Keep in mind that the probability calculated here is based on the assumption that each contest is independent and has an equal chance of winning. In reality, contest odds may vary, and winning a ticket depends on various factors.

Reinventing the Sound: Snails' Experimental Phases

In their journey to musical greatness, the band Snails never shied away from pushing the boundaries of their sound. Reinvention became their mantra as they embarked on various experimental phases, challenging conventional music genres and creating their own unique sonic landscape. In this section, we explore the evolution of Snails' music and the different experimental phases that shaped their artistic vision.

Breaking the Mold

Snails' journey to reinvention began with a burning desire to break free from the confines of traditional music genres. They were determined to create a sound that defied categorization and embraced unpredictability. This rebellion against conformity drove the band to explore a wide range of musical styles and experiment with different sounds and textures.

Exploring New Soundscapes

With a thirst for innovation, Snails embarked on their first experimental phase by venturing into uncharted territories of sound. They delved into electronic music, blending elements of dubstep, trap, and bass music to create a hybrid genre that would later be dubbed "vomitstep." This groundbreaking approach marked a turning point in Snails' music, captivating audiences with its gritty and aggressive sound.

genre bending

Snails never limited themselves to a specific genre. They continuously pushed the boundaries, bending and merging different genres to curate a fresh and distinctive sound. From incorporating elements of rock, hip-hop, and even classical music, their experimental phases saw an amalgamation of diverse influences that defied the norm. This genre-bending approach not only showcased their versatility but also attracted a wider audience who craved something beyond the conventional.

Collaborations and Fusion

Snails' experimental phases were not confined to just their own music; they also sought collaborations with artists from various genres to explore new frontiers. Their fearless attitude towards collaboration resulted in groundbreaking tracks that fused different musical styles and created unforgettable experiences for their fans. From collaborating with renowned EDM producers to unexpected partnerships with alternative rock bands, Snails shattered the boundaries between genres and continually reinvented themselves.

Sound as an Expression

For Snails, the experimentation with sound was more than just creating music - it was a form of expression. Each experimental phase allowed the band to convey their emotions, thoughts, and experiences in a way that transcended words. In their sonic exploration, they discovered new layers of themselves and connected with their audience on a deeper level. The expression of raw emotions through sound became their trademark and solidified their place in the music industry.

Unconventional Instruments and Techniques

In their pursuit of musical innovation, Snails embraced unconventional instruments and techniques, adding a touch of quirkiness to their sound. Experimenting with rare and unique instruments, they blended their traditional usage with modern production techniques to create a sonic landscape that was both captivating and unconventional. This unorthodox approach not only expanded the possibilities of their music but also inspired other artists to think outside the box.

Defying Expectations

With each new experimental phase, Snails defied expectations and challenged preconceived notions of what music should sound like. They fearlessly embraced risks, rejecting the fear of failure, and daring to create something unexpected. It was through this defiance that Snails found their true artistic voice and carved a path for themselves in the ever-evolving music industry.

Charting New Territories

Snails' experimental phases allowed them to explore uncharted territories in the music industry. Their willingness to take risks and step into the unknown paved the way for new possibilities and opened doors for future musicians. Snails' music became a beacon of inspiration for aspiring artists, encouraging them to embrace their individuality and explore the unexplored.

An Unforgettable Legacy

Snails' experimental phases not only left an indelible mark on the band itself but also on the music industry as a whole. Their fearless approach to reinvention not only revolutionized their sound but also inspired a new generation of artists to pursue their own artistic visions. Snails' experimental phases will forever be remembered as a testament to the power of creativity and a reminder that true innovation lies in daring to be different.

In conclusion, Snails' experimental phases were a testament to their unyielding pursuit of musical greatness. By defying genres, exploring new soundscapes, and pushing the boundaries of conventional music, they created a unique and captivating sonic experience that continues to resonate with audiences today. Through their experimentation, Snails not only reinvented their sound but also inspired a new generation of musicians to push the limits of their own creativity. The band's legacy serves as a reminder that true innovation comes from embracing the unknown and daring to be different.

Snails 2.0: Members' Solo Projects and Collaborations

In the music industry, collaboration and exploration of individual artistry are essential for growth and evolution. Snails, being the trailblazing band that they are, have always encouraged their members to pursue solo projects and collaborations outside the confines of their iconic band. This section delves into the exciting world of Snails 2.0, where each member takes center stage and lets their creativity soar.

Adapting to Change: Embracing Solo Projects

Snails' members have never been afraid to step out of their comfort zones and explore new dimensions of music. After years of sharing the spotlight, they found themselves craving artistic independence. Enter Snails 2.0, a chapter filled with solo projects that showcased each member's unique talents and aspirations.

One prime example is Tim "Sticky" Johnson, the band's lead guitarist known for his electrifying solos. He decided to venture into the world of blues and formed his own band, "Sticky Fingers." His soulful guitar riffs and heartfelt lyrics struck a chord with fans and critics alike, solidifying his position as a versatile musician in his own right.

Snails' bassist, Emma "Slime Queen" Ramirez, took a different approach with her solo project. She delved into the depths of electronic music and embraced her passion for experimental sounds. Her solo album, "Electroslime," garnered attention for its bold, audacious beats and ethereal melodies. Emma's explorations showcased her versatility as a musician and captivated audiences with her boundary-pushing soundscapes.

The Power of Collaboration: Breaking Conventions

While solo projects allowed Snails' members to explore their individuality, collaborations brought them together with some of the biggest names in the music industry. These collaborations broke conventions and pushed boundaries, resulting in groundbreaking tracks that captivated a global audience.

One incredible collaboration was between frontman Max "Slimy" Thompson and hip-hop icon Jason Jay. Their track "Slime City Dreams" fused Slimy's signature rock vocals with Jay's slick rap verses, creating an explosive anthem that transcended genres. The song's powerful message of unity and perseverance struck a chord with fans worldwide, topping the charts and becoming an anthem for a generation.

Another remarkable collaboration emerged when drummer Lily "Sticky Beats" Chen joined forces with world-renowned DJ Alex "The Mixer" Martinez. Their electrifying collaboration, "Rhythm Revolution," combined Lily's impeccable drumming skills with The Mixer's infectious beats, taking the world by storm. The track became an instant club hit, with its pulsating energy and irresistible rhythms igniting dance floors globally.

Unleashing the Unconventional: Snails' Experimental Phases

Snails 2.0 also witnessed the band members' shared desire to experiment with unconventional sounds and genres. They embarked on projects that pushed the boundaries of their musicality, allowing them to express their wildest artistic visions.

Keyboardist Sophia "Slick Keys" Lee's experimental solo album, "Symphony of Slime," was a sonic journey that combined classical orchestration with Snails' signature rock sound. The album showcased Slick Keys' virtuosity on the keys, as she seamlessly blended classical compositions with modern instrumentation, delivering a one-of-a-kind listening experience.

Lead vocalist Max "Slimy" Thompson took a daring leap in his solo endeavor, exploring avant-garde vocal techniques and pushing the limits of his vocal range. His album, "Vocal Odyssey," featured captivating vocal experiments that oscillated between haunting whispers and powerful screams. Slimy's daring exploration captivated listeners and solidified his reputation as a fearless vocalist.

The Evolution Continues: Snails' Collective Growth

Snails 2.0 was not just about solo projects and collaborations – it was an opportunity for collective growth and reinvention. As each band member embarked on their own artistic ventures, they brought back their newfound experiences and influences to the band, elevating Snails' sound to new heights.

The band's much-anticipated album, "Slime Symphony," showcased the collective evolution of Snails 2.0. Drawing from their individual experiences and collaborations, the album seamlessly blended diverse musical styles, from blues-infused rock to electronic experiments, creating a cohesive sonic masterpiece. "Slime Symphony" reinforced Snails' status as musical pioneers who fearlessly transcended genres and conventions.

Snails 2.0 in the Wild: Unconventional Collaborations

Just when fans thought they had seen it all, Snails 2.0 surprised them with unconventional collaborations that defied expectations. One such collaboration was between bassist Emma "Slime Queen" Ramirez and electronic dance artist DJ Sluggo. The unlikely combination of Slime Queen's organic bass lines and DJ Sluggo's high-energy beats resulted in a series of infectious tracks that became instant fan favorites on the club circuit.

Drummer Lily "Sticky Beats" Chen also ventured into unfamiliar territory, teaming up with classical percussionist David "The Stickler" Thompson. The fusion of Sticky Beats' raw energy and The Stickler's precise orchestration created a symphony of percussion that mesmerized audiences worldwide.

Snails 2.0 proved that unconventional collaborations have the power to create innovative and groundbreaking music that transcends boundaries and captivates audiences.

The Legacy of Snails 2.0: Inspiring Future Artists

Snails 2.0 not only paved the way for the band's members to explore their individual artistic visions; it also inspired a new generation of artists to embrace their uniqueness and push the boundaries of music.

Many aspiring musicians credit Snails 2.0's solo projects and collaborations as catalysts for their own creative journeys. The band's fearlessness and willingness to explore various genres and art forms inspired countless artists to embrace their true selves and create art that defies categorization.

Through Snails 2.0, the band not only left an indelible mark on the music industry but also cultivated a culture of artistic freedom and expression that continues to inspire generations to come.

Challenge Yourself: Solo Endeavors and Collaborations

1. Think about your favorite band or artist. Imagine that they decide to explore solo projects or collaborations. How do you think this would impact their music and career? Write a short essay discussing the potential benefits and challenges they may face.

2. Research a musician or artist who has successfully embarked on a solo career after being part of a band. Write a brief biography highlighting their solo achievements and the impact they have had on their respective industry.

3. Explore a genre of music that you have never listened to before. Pay close attention to the instrumentation, vocal techniques, and overall sound. Write a reflection on your experience, discussing how it compares to the music you typically enjoy.

4. Collaborate with a fellow musician or artist and create a piece that fuses your respective styles. Experiment with blending different genres or incorporating unconventional elements. Reflect on the process and share your thoughts on the power of collaboration in the creative process.

Remember, Snails 2.0 taught us that through exploration, collaboration, and the courage to embrace the unconventional, we can create transformative art that resonates with audiences on a profound level. Keep pushing boundaries and embracing your unique creative journey. The slime never fades!

Snails Forever: Nurturing the Next Generation of Artists

In the ever-changing landscape of the music industry, Snails has always been at the forefront of innovation and creativity. As they continue to make waves with their groundbreaking music, they also recognize the importance of nurturing the next generation of artists. In this section, we explore how Snails has taken on the role of mentors, helping aspiring musicians find their own unique voice in the industry.

Passing on the Torch: Snails' Mentorship Program

Snails understands that success in the music industry requires more than just talent; it requires guidance and support. With their extensive experience and knowledge, the members of Snails have established a mentorship program aimed at helping young artists navigate the challenges of the industry. Through this program, they provide valuable advice, share their experiences, and offer practical tips on songwriting, performance, and building a brand.

One of the key elements of Snails' mentorship program is personalized guidance. Each aspiring artist is paired with a member of the band who serves as their mentor. This one-on-one approach allows for a tailored experience, ensuring that the mentees receive the specific guidance they need to thrive in the industry. Whether it's helping them refine their songwriting skills or offering insights into the business side of music, Snails is committed to supporting the next generation of artists every step of the way.

Showcasing Rising Talent: Snail Army Collaborations

Snails firmly believes in the power of collaboration, and they actively seek out opportunities to work with up-and-coming artists. The band recognizes that collaboration not only enriches their own music but also provides a platform for emerging talent to gain exposure and recognition.

Through their Snail Army Collaborations initiative, Snails offers young artists the chance to collaborate on tracks, perform on stage together, and even join them on tour. This unique opportunity allows rising talent to learn from seasoned professionals while gaining invaluable exposure to a global fanbase. By showcasing these collaborations on their albums and during live performances, Snails is able to introduce their fans to new and exciting artists, fostering a sense of community and encouraging support for the next generation.

Educational Initiatives: Snails' Music Academies

Snails firmly believes in the importance of education and seeks to provide aspiring artists with the necessary tools to succeed. To that end, they have established a network of Snails Music Academies around the world. These academies offer a comprehensive curriculum that covers not only the technical aspects of music production but also business skills, marketing strategies, and performance techniques.

The Snails Music Academies provide a supportive and nurturing environment for students to explore their creativity and refine their skills. With state-of-the-art facilities and industry-leading instructors, these academies serve as incubators for the next generation of artists. Students have the opportunity to learn from Snails' own team and, in some cases, even from the band members themselves, through guest lectures and workshops.

Fostering Innovation: Snails' Artist Residency Program

In their quest to nurture the next generation of artists, Snails has also established an Artist Residency Program. This program invites aspiring musicians, producers, and songwriters to spend a period of time at Snails' recording studio, immersing themselves in a creative environment and collaborating with fellow artists.

During their residency, artists are given the freedom to experiment with different sounds, explore new genres, and push the boundaries of their creativity. Snails' team of experienced producers and engineers are on hand to provide guidance and support, helping the residents refine their work and take their artistry to new heights.

Unconventional Wisdom: Snails' Insights and Lessons

Alongside these structured mentorship and educational initiatives, Snails also imparts their wisdom through various unconventional means. They actively engage with their fanbase through social media, Q&A sessions, and even exclusive masterclasses. Through these interactions, Snails offers insights, tips, and lessons learned from their own journey, providing aspiring artists with a unique perspective on the music industry.

Additionally, Snails has also published a book titled "Rocking Your Way to Success: Insights from Snails". This book delves deep into the band's experiences, offering practical advice, personal anecdotes, and thought-provoking exercises to help readers navigate the challenges of pursuing a career in music. It serves as a comprehensive guide for aspiring artists, blending creativity, business acumen, and personal growth.

Exercises: Finding Your Own Voice

To truly nurture the next generation of artists, Snails encourages aspiring musicians to find their own voice and embrace their uniqueness. Here are some exercises inspired by Snails' teachings to help you on your creative journey:

1. Write a song that combines two seemingly contrasting genres. Embrace the challenge of blending different styles and see what unique sound you can create.

2. Collaborate with another artist or musician whose style is completely different from yours. How can you merge your individual sounds to create something new and exciting?

3. Experiment with unconventional instruments or sounds. Step outside your comfort zone and explore the possibilities of using non-traditional tools to create music.

4. Reflect on your own musical journey and identify what sets you apart from other artists. Embrace your strengths and unique qualities, and use them to shape your own artistic identity.

Remember, creating music is not just about following trends or replicating what's already been done. It's about finding your own voice and sharing your unique perspective with the world. Embrace your individuality, be fearless in your creativity, and let your passion guide you on the path to success.

Conclusion

Snails understands that their success as a band is not just about their own accomplishments, but also about the impact they can have on the next generation of artists. Through their mentorship program, collaboration initiatives, educational academies, and artist residency program, they actively nurture and support aspiring musicians. With their unconventional wisdom and commitment to fostering innovation, Snails aims to create a legacy that extends far beyond their own music, inspiring generations to come. As the band continues to evolve and leave their mark on the music industry, they confidently pass on the torch, nurturing a new generation of artists who will shape the future of music.

Snails' World Domination: Expanding Their Empire

Conquering New Territories: International Tours and Fans

Snails' music was not just confined to their local region; it quickly spread across borders, capturing the hearts of fans in different countries. As the band gained momentum, they embarked on a series of international tours, venturing into new territories and leaving lasting impressions on fans around the world.

Setting the Stage: Preparation and Planning

Before undertaking a global tour, Snails had to carefully plan and prepare every aspect of their performances. They understood the importance of adapting their music and stage presence to resonate with diverse cultures and audiences.

The band collaborated with renowned tour managers, local promoters, and production companies in each country they visited. This strategic alliance ensured that they had the necessary support and expertise to navigate the unique challenges posed by international touring.

Conquering Language Barriers

One of the biggest obstacles faced by Snails during their international tours was overcoming language barriers. As they performed in countries where English was not the primary language, they had to find creative ways to bridge the communication gap with their fans.

Snails took it upon themselves to learn basic phrases in the local language of each country they visited. Whether it was a simple greeting or a heartfelt expression of gratitude, their efforts to connect with fans on a personal level were greatly appreciated. This not only made their performances more engaging but also showcased their respect for different cultures.

The Power of Music: Uniting Fans Worldwide

Snails' music transcended language and cultural barriers, becoming a universal language that united fans from all corners of the globe. Their unique sound, infused with a blend of genres, resonated with listeners of diverse backgrounds.

International tours provided Snails with the opportunity to witness firsthand the impact their music had on fans worldwide. From sold-out arenas to intimate club shows, their energetic performances created an atmosphere of unity and shared passion.

Tribute to Local Culture: Infusing Authenticity into Performances

Snails' commitment to honoring local cultures and traditions set them apart from other international acts. The band incorporated elements of each country's culture into their performances, paying homage to the traditions and customs that shaped the local music scene.

From incorporating traditional instruments and dance styles to collaborating with local musicians, Snails' performances were an immersive experience that celebrated the richness of each country's artistic heritage. By embracing and respecting local culture, Snails forged deep connections with their international fanbase.

Snail Army Goes Global: Passionate Fans Everywhere

As Snails performed in new territories, they were pleasantly surprised to discover the extent of their fanbase. The Snail Army, as their fans affectionately called themselves, rallied behind the band, creating a vibrant community that extended far beyond borders.

International tours provided an opportunity for Snails to meet their fans face-to-face, to express their gratitude for the unwavering support. The band frequently organized meet-and-greets, fan events, and even surprise visits, fostering a sense of belonging and camaraderie among their dedicated followers.

Inspiring the Next Generation: Snails' Global Impact

Snails' international tours had a far-reaching impact beyond just their immediate fanbase. Their energetic performances and relentless pursuit of their musical dreams inspired aspiring musicians worldwide.

By showcasing their unique style and fearlessly experimenting with new sounds, Snails proved that music had the power to transcend boundaries and create meaningful connections. Many young artists, inspired by their journey, found the courage to chase their own musical ambitions, further fueling the evolution of the music industry.

Going Beyond Music: Snails' Humanitarian Efforts

Snails understood that their influence as global artists came with the responsibility to make a positive impact on society. During their international tours, they actively engaged in philanthropic efforts, supporting charitable causes in each country they visited.

From organizing benefit concerts to partnering with local NGOs, Snails used their platform to raise awareness and funds for various social issues, including environmental conservation, education, and healthcare initiatives. Their dedication to making a difference set an example for fans and aspiring musicians alike.

Unforgettable Moments: International Tour Highlights

Snails' international tours were filled with unforgettable moments that showcased their ability to captivate audiences worldwide. Here are some of the notable highlights:

- The "Slime Invasion" at the Tokyo Dome: Snails' high-energy performance created a frenzy among their Japanese fans, leaving a lasting impact on the country's music scene.

- Wembley Stadium Extravaganza: A historic night in London, as Snails became the first band from their genre to headline at the iconic Wembley Stadium, solidifying their place in music history.

- Snails' Serenade in Paris: A soulful acoustic performance in an intimate Parisian café, showcasing the band's versatility and ability to create magic even in the simplest settings.

- Rio Carnival Surprise: Snails surprised fans in Brazil by joining a samba parade during Rio Carnival, immersing themselves in the vibrant culture of the country and spreading joy through music.

- Snails' Midnight Set at the Great Wall: A once-in-a-lifetime experience for both the band and their fans, as they performed a special midnight concert on a section of the Great Wall of China, underlining their commitment to pushing boundaries.

These captivating moments during their international tours will forever remain etched in the memories of Snails' fans, serving as a testament to the band's meteoric rise to global stardom.

Summary

Snails' international tours were a testament to the power of music in bringing people together. Through meticulous planning, meaningful connections with fans, and a deep respect for local cultures, the band conquered new territories, leaving an indelible mark on the international music scene.

Their performances transcended language barriers, uniting fans from different backgrounds. Snails' commitment to philanthropy and their role as ambassadors of positive change further solidified their global impact.

International tours were not just about the band showcasing their talent; they were about fostering a sense of community and inspiring the next generation of musicians. Snails' legacy continues to live on, carried by the passionate fans who form the ever-growing Snail Army.

As we delve deeper into the world of Snails, we will explore more extraordinary aspects of their journey, shedding light on their creative process, behind-the-scenes stories, and their enduring influence on pop culture. The adventure awaits as we unravel the layers of Snails' remarkable career and the impact they continue to have on the music industry.

Snails' Multimedia Empire: Ventures Beyond Music

Snails is not just a band, but a multimedia empire that has expanded its reach far beyond the realm of music. With their innovative and creative approach, the band members have ventured into various forms of media, captivating audiences with their unique brand of entertainment. From movies to TV shows, documentaries to merchandise, and even virtual experiences, Snails has created an empire that goes beyond the boundaries of music.

Snails in the Silver Screen

Having conquered the music industry, it was only natural for Snails to make their mark on the silver screen. The band dived headfirst into the world of cinema, producing their own movies that showcased not only their music but also their storytelling prowess. They recognized the power of visual storytelling as a medium to connect with their fans on a deeper level.

Their first foray into filmmaking, "Slime Revolution," was a colorful and visually stunning masterpiece. The movie portrayed the band's journey from humble beginnings to international stardom, interspersed with electrifying performances and heartfelt moments. With a mix of comedy, drama, and musical brilliance, "Slime Revolution" became an instant hit, captivating both Snails' die-hard fans and movie enthusiasts alike.

Following the success of "Slime Revolution," Snails went on to collaborate with visionary directors and filmmakers on various projects. Their second movie, "Slick and Slime: The Adventure Begins," took the band on an exhilarating and daring journey through unknown territories. Packed with heart-stopping action and mind-bending visuals, the movie showcased Snails' ability to push the boundaries of storytelling and create a truly immersive cinematic experience.

Snails on the Small Screen

Snails' creative vision extended beyond the big screen, as they sought to conquer the small screen as well. The band's TV shows became a sensation, offering fans a more intimate and behind-the-scenes glimpse into their lives. One such series, "Sluggish Rhythms," followed the band on their daily adventures, showcasing their witty banter, hilarious pranks, and the challenges they faced as they pursued their musical dreams.

In addition to reality-style shows, Snails also delved into the world of scripted dramas. "Serpentine Sonata," a musical drama series, became an instant hit, blending the band's catchy tunes with compelling storylines and intricate character development. The show not only showcased the band's acting talent but also allowed them to explore deeper themes and emotions.

Snails didn't limit themselves to traditional television platforms either. They embraced streaming services and online platforms, creating original content exclusively for their fans. From live concert streams to interactive webisodes, Snails utilized the power of the internet to connect with their audience in a whole new way.

Documentaries Unveiling the Snail Empire

To give their fans a closer look at the inner workings of the band, Snails produced a series of captivating documentaries. These films not only shed light on the band's journey but also provided insights into their creative process, struggles, and triumphs.

"From Slime to Stardom: The Snails' Odyssey" took viewers on a rollercoaster ride through the band's rise to fame. It revealed the raw emotions and sacrifices behind their success, highlighting the hard work and dedication it took to become one of the biggest bands in the world. Through candid interviews and never-before-seen footage, the documentary showcased the band's evolution and the impact they had on the music industry.

In addition to their own story, Snails also explored broader cultural and social issues in their documentaries. "Slime Nation: Music as a Catalyst for Change" focused on the band's advocacy for social justice and their efforts to make a positive impact on society. Through interviews with activists, fans, and other renowned artists, the documentary highlighted Snails' commitment to using their platform for meaningful change.

Snail Merchandise and Branded Ventures

With their growing popularity, Snails ventured into the world of merchandise, offering fans the opportunity to own a piece of the Snail empire. From clothing and accessories to collectibles and limited editions, the band ensured that their fans could proudly display their love and support for the brand.

Snails also explored branded ventures, partnering with companies to create unique products that aligned with their brand. Collaborations with fashion designers, toy companies, and even home decor brands allowed Snails to extend their influence into different industries, reaching new audiences and expanding their empire.

Snails in the Virtual World

As technology advanced, Snails recognized the potential of virtual reality and augmented reality as mediums for entertainment. They pushed the boundaries of technology, offering fans immersive virtual experiences that transported them into the world of Snails like never before.

Through virtual reality concerts, fans could don their VR headsets and experience the exhilaration of being in the front row of a Snails performance, without leaving the comfort of their homes. The band's attention to detail and commitment to delivering an authentic experience made these virtual concerts a massive success, attracting fans from all corners of the globe.

Snails also embraced augmented reality, creating interactive experiences that blended the real world with their unique brand of entertainment. Through AR apps, fans could join the band on virtual treasure hunts, unlock exclusive content, and even interact with virtual Snail avatars.

An Unconventional Approach to Building an Empire

What sets Snails' multimedia empire apart is their willingness to think outside the box and experiment with unconventional approaches. From their boundary-pushing movies to their engaging online content, the band has always been at the forefront of innovation.

By harnessing the power of different media forms, Snails has managed to create a cohesive and immersive universe that goes beyond music. They have shown the world that art can transcend traditional boundaries, and that a band can be more than just a group of musicians – they can be a cultural phenomenon.

Throughout their ventures beyond music, Snails has stayed true to their core values of creativity, authenticity, and a deep connection with their fans. Their multimedia empire has not only revolutionized the way fans engage with music but has also inspired a new generation of artists to explore the endless possibilities of multimedia storytelling.

Exercises

1. Research and analyze the impact of other bands or musicians who have ventured into multimedia projects. How successful were these projects, and what can be learned from their experiences?

2. Imagine you are a member of Snails' virtual reality team. Design a virtual concert experience that would enhance fan engagement and provide a unique and unforgettable experience.

3. Write a short script for a Snails-inspired TV show episode that combines comedy, drama, and music. Be creative with the storyline and characters, while staying true to the band's spirit.

4. Brainstorm ideas for Snails' next branded venture. Consider potential collaborations with companies and explore innovative products that would resonate with the band's fanbase.

5. Reflect on the impact of Snails' multimedia empire on the music industry. How has their approach influenced other artists and bands to explore different forms of media? Discuss the potential benefits and challenges of expanding beyond music.

Remember, the key to Snails' success lies in their ability to adapt, innovate, and stay true to their artistic vision. By exploring the exercises above, you'll gain a deeper understanding of the multifaceted nature of their multimedia empire and how it has shaped the band's legacy.

Snails Unplugged: Acoustic Performances and Intimate Shows

Snails, known for their electrifying performances and high-energy music, also have a softer side. In this section, we explore Snails' unplugged performances and intimate shows, where the band strips down their sound and connects with their audience on a more personal level.

The Birth of Snails Unplugged

Snails Unplugged was born out of a desire to showcase the band's versatility and showcase their raw talent. It all began during a jam session in their early years when the band decided to experiment with acoustic versions of their songs. The result was a more intimate and soulful sound that resonated deeply with their fans.

The Magic of Acoustic Performances

Unplugged performances allow Snails to showcase their musicianship and songwriting skills in a different light. Stripped of the electric guitars, heavy drums, and elaborate production, acoustic performances bring out the true essence of their music. The melodic interplay between instruments shines through, and the emotional depth of their lyrics takes center stage.

Unplugged Setlist During Snails Unplugged shows, the band carefully curates a setlist that combines fan favorites with lesser-known gems. This allows them to cater to both diehard fans and newcomers alike. Whether it's a haunting rendition of "Slow Motion" or a soul-stirring performance of "In the Rain," each song takes on a new life in the unplugged format.

Intimate Connection What sets Snails Unplugged shows apart is the intimate connection formed between the band and the audience. Without the barrier of electrifying energy and intense production, the band members engage in candid conversations and share personal anecdotes between songs. This creates a sense of closeness and authenticity, making the experience feel like a private gathering among friends.

Unplugged Masterpieces

Snails' unplugged performances have resulted in some truly memorable moments and masterful renditions of their songs. Here are a few standout examples:

Serenading the Night: *Moonlit Melodies* In their iconic acoustic performance of "Moonlit Melodies," the band transforms the anthemic rock ballad into an intimate serenade. The delicate interplay between acoustic guitar and piano paints a vivid picture under a moonlit sky, while the emotive vocals tug at the heartstrings of every listener.

Unleashing Emotions: *Bare Souls* "Be still, my bare soul" resonates profoundly in the unplugged version of this hauntingly beautiful song. Stripped of its heavier elements, the focus shifts to the vulnerability of the lyrics and the raw emotions conveyed by lead singer Rafael's soulful voice. Each note reverberates with intensity, leaving the audience captivated in a sea of emotions.

A Journey of Reflection: *Uncharted Waters* "Uncharted Waters" takes on a whole new meaning in the unplugged format. With minimal instrumentation and a more subdued tempo, the song becomes a contemplative journey through life's uncertainties. Snails' harmonies blend seamlessly, creating a captivating atmosphere that transports the audience to unexplored depths of their own emotions.

Unconventional Twists

Snails is known for their innovative approach to music, and their unplugged performances are no exception. They infuse their acoustic shows with unexpected twists that keep the audience on their toes.

Unplugged Collaborations   During unplugged shows, Snails occasionally invites guest artists to join them on stage for special collaborations. These unique duets result in magical musical exchanges, showcasing the band's versatility alongside the unique talents of their guests. From soulful duets to unexpected genre fusions, these collaborations are a true highlight of Snails Unplugged.

Instrumental Innovation   Snails is not afraid to experiment with unconventional instruments during their unplugged performances. From a melodica solo in the midst of a stripped-down rock ballad to a violin improvisation in an acoustic set, these unexpected instrumental elements add layers of depth and intrigue to their performances.

Snails Unplugged: A Memorable Experience

Attending a Snails Unplugged show is a once-in-a-lifetime experience that allows fans to witness the band's raw talent, connect with them on a deeper level, and create lasting memories. The unplugged performances showcase another side of Snails, demonstrating their versatility, musicality, and dedication to providing a genuine connection with their audience.

Whether you're a longtime fan or new to the Snails phenomenon, don't miss the opportunity to experience the magic of Snails Unplugged. It's a journey beyond the glitz and glam, where the band's music truly shines.

Unplugged Exercise: *Finding Your Acoustic Sound*   Interested in exploring the unplugged side of your own music? Here's an exercise to help you find your acoustic sound:
   1. Choose one of your original songs or a favorite tune from another artist. 2. Consider the core elements of the song (lyrics, melody, chord progression). 3. Experiment with different acoustic instruments to find the ones that best complement the song's mood and style. Don't be afraid to think outside the box! 4. Simplify the arrangement, focusing on showcasing the song's essence without elaborate production. 5. Practice performing the unplugged version of the song, paying attention to dynamics and emotional delivery. 6. Seek feedback from fellow

musicians and friends to refine your acoustic interpretation. 7. Share your unplugged version with a live audience, whether it's an intimate gathering or an open mic night.

Remember, the goal of going unplugged is to create a genuine connection with your audience through raw and heartfelt performances. Embrace the vulnerability and let your acoustic sound shine.

Snail Power: The Band's Entrepreneurial Initiatives

Snails, the iconic music band known for their electrifying performances and unique sound, didn't just rely on their musical talent to achieve success. They also possessed a keen entrepreneurial spirit that allowed them to build an empire beyond the stage. In this section, we delve into Snails' innovative business ventures and explore how they harnessed their creative power to conquer new territories.

Conquering New Territories: International Tours and Fans

Snails took their music worldwide, embarking on numerous international tours that brought their distinct sound to fans around the globe. The band recognized the importance of expanding their reach and captivating diverse audiences. They saw touring as an opportunity not only to connect with fans on a personal level but also to tap into new markets and establish their brand internationally.

To facilitate their global conquest, Snails devised strategic partnerships with international promoters, ensuring their tours reached far-flung corners of the world. By collaborating with local promoters who understood the cultural nuances and preferences of each region, Snails successfully navigated the complexities of international touring.

Their relentless efforts paid off, with sold-out shows in major cities across continents. Snails' energetic performances and dynamic stage presence transcended language barriers and cultural differences, captivating audiences from Tokyo to Berlin, and from New York to Cape Town. Their international tours not only solidified their position as a global phenomenon but also paved the way for further expansion into new territories.

Snails' Multimedia Empire: Ventures Beyond Music

Snails' entrepreneurial spirit extended beyond the realm of music. They recognized the power of multimedia as a means to connect with fans and engage with them on a deeper level. To satisfy their fans' insatiable appetite for all things Snails, the band ventured into various multimedia initiatives.

They produced a series of captivating music videos that showcased their innovative storytelling techniques and visually stunning concepts. Snails' music videos became viral sensations, reaching millions of viewers across different platforms and further amplifying their fame.

In addition to music videos, Snails also explored the world of film and television. They collaborated with visionary directors and producers, creating documentaries that provided an intimate look into their lives on and off the stage. These behind-the-scenes glimpses not only delighted their existing fans but also attracted new audiences, drawn to the band's authenticity and passion.

Snails didn't stop there. They ventured into the world of fashion, launching their own line of merchandise that allowed fans to express their love for the band in style. From t-shirts and hoodies to accessories and limited-edition collectibles, Snails' fashion line became a must-have for devoted fans and fashion enthusiasts alike.

Snails Unplugged: Acoustic Performances and Intimate Shows

While Snails were known for their electrifying and energetic performances, they also recognized the value of intimate and stripped-down experiences. To showcase their versatility as musicians and connect with fans on a more personal level, Snails organized a series of acoustic performances.

These acoustic shows allowed fans to experience the band's music in a whole new light. Stripped of the elaborate production, the raw and emotive nature of Snails' songs shone through, captivating audiences in an intimate setting. These shows also provided an opportunity for deeper interaction between the band and their fans, fostering a sense of community and shared connection.

By diversifying their live performances and offering different experiences, Snails not only catered to the varying preferences of their fans but also demonstrated their ability to adapt and evolve as artists.

Snail Power: The Band's Entrepreneurial Initiatives

Snails' entrepreneurial initiatives were not only about expanding their brand and conquering new territories. They also recognized the power of their platform and the influence they wielded to make a positive impact on society.

Through strategic partnerships with charitable organizations, Snails supported various causes that were close to their hearts. They organized benefit concerts and donated a portion of their earnings to organizations dedicated to social change and humanitarian efforts. By using their fame and success as a force for good, Snails became advocates for positive change, inspiring their fans to take action and make a difference in the world.

Furthermore, Snails leveraged their entrepreneurial mindset to create job opportunities within their organization. They consciously sought to empower individuals who shared their passion and vision, providing them with the tools and resources to thrive in the music industry. Snails' commitment to nurturing talent and fostering a supportive work environment not only contributed to their success as a band but also left a lasting legacy in the industry.

In conclusion, Snails' entrepreneurial initiatives went far beyond their musical prowess. They ventured into new territories, expanding their international reach and captivating fans worldwide. Through multimedia ventures, they engaged with their audience on various platforms, creating a multifaceted Snails experience. Acoustic performances and intimate shows allowed for deeper fan connections, while their commitment to philanthropy and talent development showcased their dedication to making a positive impact. Snails' entrepreneurial spirit was a driving force behind their success, demonstrating that true artistry extends far beyond the confines of the stage.

Snails' Virtual Realm: Embracing the Digital Age

In the undulating realm of the music industry, Snails has never shied away from embracing innovation and reinventing themselves. As the digital age continues to shape the world, they have fearlessly embraced the virtual realm, using technology to create new experiences for their fans and connect with them on a deeper level. In this chapter, we delve into the ways Snails has harnessed the power of the digital landscape, pushing the boundaries of what it means to be a band in the modern era.

The Birth of a Digital Revolution

Snails' journey into the virtual realm began with the realization that technology could amplify their creativity and expand their reach. They saw the potential to connect with their fans in ways never before possible, transcending geographical boundaries and creating immersive experiences. With this in mind, they set out to build their own digital empire, a realm where fans could be transported into the world of Snails at any time and from anywhere.

The Virtual Concert Experience

One of the most groundbreaking ways Snails has embraced the digital age is through their virtual concert experiences. Utilizing cutting-edge virtual reality

(VR) technology, they have revolutionized the way concerts are experienced. Now, fans can put on a VR headset and find themselves standing front and center at a Snails concert, feeling the energy of the crowd and witnessing the band's electrifying performances as if they were physically there. This immersive experience has allowed Snails to transcend physical limitations and connect with fans across the globe, creating a sense of unity and excitement that knows no borders.

The Snails App: A Gateway to the Snailverse

To further enhance the fan experience, Snails developed their own mobile application, aptly named "The Snails App." This digital gateway allows fans to dive deep into the Snailverse, exploring a multitude of interactive features. Through the app, fans can access exclusive behind-the-scenes content, from backstage footage to studio sessions, providing a glimpse into the inner workings of the band. The app also offers interactive games and challenges, enabling fans to earn virtual rewards and compete with each other in the ultimate test of Snails knowledge. It serves as a hub for all things Snails, creating a sense of community among fans and empowering them to be active participants in the band's journey.

Snails' Social Media Mastery

In this digital era, social media has become a powerful tool for bands to connect with their fans. Snails has capitalized on this trend, amassing a dedicated following across various social media platforms. They have cultivated an authentic presence on platforms such as Instagram, Twitter, and TikTok, sharing candid moments, personal insights, and snippets of new music. By engaging with their fans on a daily basis, Snails has fostered a sense of intimacy and camaraderie, making each fan feel like a valued member of the Snail Army.

Breaking Barriers with Livestream Events

Livestream events have become a phenomenon in recent years, and Snails has taken full advantage of this digital medium. They have organized awe-inspiring livestream performances, enabling fans from all corners of the globe to witness their electrifying shows in real-time. By utilizing professional broadcasting equipment, they ensure that the audio and visual quality is top-notch, giving fans an immersive concert experience from the comfort of their own homes. In addition, these livestream events often incorporate interactive elements, such as live chats and Q&A sessions, allowing fans to directly connect with the band and be part of the experience.

The Limitless Boundaries of Snails' Virtual Realm

Snails' embrace of the digital age knows no bounds. They constantly push the envelope, finding innovative ways to immerse their fans in their music and storytelling. From virtual reality concerts to interactive mobile apps, Snails has created a digital realm that lives and breathes their unique brand of music. As technology continues to advance, they will undoubtedly explore new avenues, never resting on their laurels but instead pushing the boundaries of what is possible.

Unconventional, Yet Relevant: Hacking the Music Industry

It wouldn't be a section on Snails without a touch of their unconventional spirit. To truly embrace the digital age, Snails has found unique ways to hack the music industry, defying norms and forging their own path. They have challenged traditional distribution models, releasing their music directly to fans through exclusive digital platforms. By bypassing major record labels, Snails has retained creative control and found new avenues for revenue generation. This unorthodox approach has not only allowed them to maintain their artistic integrity but has also served as a beacon of inspiration for independent artists navigating the ever-evolving music landscape.

Snails' Virtual Realm: A New Frontier

As we venture further into the digital age, the possibilities for Snails' virtual realm seem endless. Through their embrace of technology, they have transformed the way fans experience their music, breaking down barriers, and creating a global community united by their love for the band. Snails' virtual realm is not just a gimmick or a fleeting trend—it is a testament to their dedication to their craft and their unyielding commitment to pushing the boundaries of what it means to be a band in the modern era. As they continue to shape the future, Snails will undoubtedly inspire generations to come, leaving an indelible mark on the virtual realm of music.

The Snails' Evolution: Music for the Ages

Breaking the Mold: Snails' Genre-Bending Experimentations

In the world of music, there are those who follow trends and play it safe, and then there are those like Snails who dare to break the mold and push the boundaries of genre. Snails' genre-bending experimentations have redefined what it means to be a band and have left a lasting impact on the music industry.

The Art of Fusion: Blending Genres

Snails never shied away from challenging existing genre conventions. They fearlessly incorporated elements from different genres, creating a unique fusion that captivated audiences and defied categorization. From their early beginnings, Snails set out to blend styles such as rock, hip-hop, electronic, and even classical music, creating a sound that was distinctly their own.

One of their most notable genre-bending experiments was the integration of heavy metal and EDM. Snails' innovative use of distorted guitars, aggressive drum beats, and electronic elements brought together two seemingly opposing genres, resulting in a powerful and intense sonic experience. Tracks like "Slime and Steel" and "Metallic Slither" became anthems for fans who craved the energy of metal combined with the infectious beats of EDM.

Breaking Down Barriers: Collaborations Across Genres

Snails' genre-bending exploration extended beyond their own music. The band actively sought collaborations with artists from diverse genres, allowing for the cross-pollination of ideas and musical styles. These collaborations not only pushed the boundaries of their own sound but also opened up new avenues for other artists to explore.

One of the most groundbreaking collaborations was their partnership with renowned jazz pianist, Ella Fitzgerald. Snails and Fitzgerald joined forces to create a mesmerizing blend of swing-era jazz and modern electronic music. The result was a series of tracks that seamlessly integrated Fitzgerald's smooth melodies with Snails' infectious beats, proving that genres like jazz and EDM could coexist in harmony.

Taking Risks: Expanding Boundaries

No stranger to experimentation, Snails took risks that no other band had ever taken before. They wanted to challenge not only themselves but also their fans' perception of what music could be. As pioneers of genre-bending, they were not afraid to embrace unconventional instruments and sounds, and the more outrageous, the better.

One notable example was the use of a didgeridoo, an indigenous Australian wind instrument, in their track "Outback Rumble." The deep, hypnotic drone of the didgeridoo blended seamlessly with Snails' electronic beats, creating a captivating and enchanting listening experience. It demonstrated their commitment to exploring new sounds and incorporating them into their music, regardless of their origin or traditional usage.

Embracing Musical Hybrids: Inspiring a New Generation

Snails' willingness to break the mold and experiment with genres has had a profound influence on the next generation of musicians. Their genre-bending approach has inspired countless artists to infuse their own music with a diverse range of influences, creating a new wave of musical hybrids.

One such artist is Kid Beats, a rising star in the music industry. Kid Beats, who grew up listening to Snails, has taken inspiration from their genre-bending experimentations and incorporated elements from hip-hop, reggae, and electronic music into his own tracks. His unique sound has garnered attention and praise, showcasing the enduring impact of Snails' genre-bending legacy.

Facing the Critics: Overcoming Resistance and Naysayers

Breaking the mold and venturing into uncharted musical territories is not without its challenges. Snails faced resistance and skepticism from critics and purists who questioned the integrity of their genre-bending experimentations. However, the band remained true to their vision and refused to be confined by narrow definitions of genre.

Snails' unapologetic approach and unwavering belief in their genre-bending abilities ultimately won over even the harshest critics. Their fusion of genres became a testament to the power of artistic expression and the importance of embracing diversity within music. Their refusal to conform to traditional expectations shattered preconceived notions and opened up new doors for innovation.

Unleashing the Power of Possibilities: The Legacy Lives On

Snails' genre-bending experimentations have left an indelible mark on the music industry, inspiring artists to explore new sounds, challenge established norms, and break free from the constraints of genre. Their fearless approach to music has unleashed a world of possibilities for future generations of musicians.

As Snails' music continues to resonate with fans old and new, their genre-bending legacy serves as a reminder that the boundaries of music are meant to be pushed, shattered, and reimagined. Snails' impact on the evolution of music will be felt for years to come, forever changing the landscape of the industry and inspiring artists to embrace their creativity without limitations.

So let the words "break the mold" be a call to action for all musicians out there, urging them to explore uncharted territory, challenge conventions, and infuse their unique visions into their music. Because in the end, it is those who defy expectations and dare to step out of the box who leave an everlasting impact on the world of music.

Evolution of Sound: Snails' Influences and Inspirations

Music is a constantly evolving art form, shaped by the influences and inspirations of the artists who create it. In the case of Snails, their unique sound is a product of their diverse musical backgrounds and the artists that have inspired them along the way. From their early days as a band, Snails sought to push the boundaries of their genre and carve out a distinct musical identity. In this section, we will explore the evolution of Snails' sound, the influences that have shaped their music, and the inspirations that continue to drive them forward.

Exploring Musical Influences

Snails' sound is a fusion of various music genres, resulting in a style that is truly their own. Their music draws from a wide range of influences, including rock, funk, jazz, and electronic music. Each band member brings their unique musical background to the table, creating a rich and diverse musical tapestry.

Frontman Jack "Slick" Johnson, with his soulful voice and charismatic stage presence, is influenced by iconic rock vocalists such as Freddie Mercury and Mick Jagger. His gritty yet smooth vocal style adds a raw energy to the band's music, reminiscent of the classic rock era.

Guitarist Lily "Lightning" Anderson, known for her virtuosic guitar skills, draws inspiration from guitar legends like Jimi Hendrix and Stevie Ray Vaughan. Her fiery solos and intricate guitar riffs give Snails' music a powerful and melodic edge.

Bassist Mike "Groove" Jackson, with his groovy basslines, takes inspiration from funk and jazz legends such as Bootsy Collins and Jaco Pastorius. His funky bass playing adds a rhythmic complexity to Snails' music, creating a solid foundation for the band's sound.

Keyboardist Sarah "Keys" Thompson, with her soulful and versatile playing, draws influence from jazz pianists like Herbie Hancock and Chick Corea. Her melodic compositions and atmospheric keyboard textures add depth and richness to Snails' music.

Drummer Max "Thunder" Davis, with his dynamic and energetic drumming style, is influenced by rock and metal drummers such as John Bonham and Dave Grohl. His powerful and tight drumming drives Snails' music, infusing it with a contagious energy.

Blending Genres and Breaking Boundaries

One of the defining characteristics of Snails' music is their ability to blend genres seamlessly, creating a unique and refreshing sound. Their music combines elements of rock, funk, jazz, and electronic music, resulting in a sonic landscape that defies categorization.

Snails' early experimentation with blending genres can be heard in their debut album, "Sluggish Beginnings." Tracks like "Electric Slime" and "Funky Trails" showcase the band's innovative approach to music-making, fusing infectious grooves with catchy melodies and electronic elements.

As Snails continued to evolve, their sound became more daring and boundary-pushing. Their second album, "Breaking the Shell," saw the band incorporating more electronic and experimental elements into their music. Tracks like "Synth Snails" and "Electro Slime Jam" demonstrated their willingness to push the limits of their genre, creating a sound that was both fresh and unexpected.

Inspired by the World

In addition to their musical influences, Snails also draw inspiration from the world around them. The band's travels and experiences have played a significant role in shaping their sound and songwriting.

From the bustling streets of Tokyo to the serene landscapes of Iceland, Snails have taken inspiration from their global adventures and incorporated these experiences into their music. Tracks like "City Lights" and "Mystic Mountains" capture the essence of these diverse locations, blending atmospheric soundscapes with infectious melodies.

Snails' connection with their fans also serves as a constant source of inspiration. The energy and passion of their dedicated fanbase fuel their creativity and drive them to continually push the boundaries of their music. Through their music, Snails aim to connect with their audience on a deeper level, creating a shared experience that transcends the boundaries of language and culture.

Embracing the Unconventional

Snails' journey in music has always been characterized by their willingness to embrace the unconventional. They have never been afraid to take risks, to break the rules, and to explore uncharted territories. This spirit of experimentation and fearlessness is what sets Snails apart from their peers.

In the studio, Snails are known for their unconventional recording techniques. They often use vintage analog equipment and experiment with unusual microphone placements to capture unique sounds. This attention to detail and commitment to sonic experimentation is what gives their music its distinctive character.

Furthermore, Snails have also collaborated with artists from various genres and disciplines, further expanding their sonic horizons. From teaming up with classical musicians for orchestral arrangements, to collaborating with electronic producers for remixes, Snails are constantly pushing the boundaries of their sound and exploring new sonic territories.

The Future of Snails' Sound

As Snails continue to evolve as a band, their sound will undoubtedly continue to grow and change. With each album and tour, they will explore new musical influences and experiment with different sonic landscapes. However, one thing remains constant: Snails' commitment to creating music that is authentic, innovative, and inspiring.

The evolution of Snails' sound is a testament to their dedication to their craft and their passion for pushing the boundaries of music. Their ability to blend genres, draw inspiration from diverse sources, and embrace the unconventional has solidified their place as one of the most exciting and influential bands of their generation.

As Snails' music continues to evolve, their fans can eagerly anticipate a sonic journey filled with surprises, innovation, and continued growth. With each new release, Snails will undoubtedly leave their mark on the music industry, inspiring future generations of artists to explore new horizons and push the boundaries of what is possible.

So, get ready to embark on a musical adventure unlike any other as we delve into the captivating evolution of sound that Snails brings to the world!

The Snail Effect: Reverberations in the Music Industry

The impact of Snails on the music industry cannot be overstated. Their unique style and fearless experimentation have left an indelible mark on the landscape of popular music. In this section, we will explore the profound effects that Snails has had on the industry, from their pioneering genre-bending experimentations to their lasting influence on future generations of musicians and artists.

Breaking the Mold: Snails' Genre-Bending Experimentations

Snails burst onto the scene with a sound that defied categorization. Blending elements of rock, funk, and electronica, they created a sonic experience that was entirely their own. Their genre-bending experimentations opened up new possibilities for musicians, challenging traditional boundaries and inspiring a wave of artistic innovation.

One of the most notable aspects of Snails' music is their seamless integration of unconventional instruments. From the ethereal tones of the theremin to the gritty intensity of the electric violin, Snails embraced the unexpected, infusing their compositions with a sense of wonder and intrigue. Their fearless approach to instrumentation pushed the boundaries of what was considered acceptable in mainstream music, paving the way for a new era of sonic exploration.

Evolution of Sound: Snails' Influences and Inspirations

Like any great artist, Snails drew inspiration from a multitude of sources. Their music is a reflection of their diverse musical tastes and influences, ranging from classical composers to underground punk bands. By incorporating these various sources of inspiration into their work, Snails created a truly unique sound that transcended genre limitations.

One of the key elements that set Snails apart was their ability to seamlessly merge disparate musical styles. They took elements of classical music and blended them with the energy and rawness of punk rock. They incorporated electronic beats and synths into their compositions, creating a futuristic sound that was ahead of its time. This innovative approach to music composition inspired countless musicians to think outside the box and explore new sonic territories.

The Snail Effect: Reverberations in the Music Industry

The influence of Snails on the music industry cannot be understated. Their groundbreaking sound and fearless experimentation served as a catalyst for the evolution of popular music. They showed that innovation and creativity could thrive in a world dominated by mainstream trends.

Countless bands and artists have cited Snails as a major influence on their own work. Their ability to push boundaries and challenge traditional norms inspired a generation of musicians to explore new sounds and break free from the constraints of genre.

Snails' impact on the industry goes beyond just their musical contributions. Their bold and unique fashion choices have left a lasting impression on the world of style and fashion. Their iconic stage costumes and distinctive visual aesthetic have become synonymous with their brand, inspiring fans and artists alike to embrace their individuality and express themselves freely.

Snails' Musical Legacy: Impact on Future Generations

The legacy of Snails can be seen in the work of countless artists who followed in their footsteps. Their willingness to take risks and break the mold has become a guiding principle for many musicians seeking to forge their own path in the industry.

Snails' influence can be heard in the music of bands and artists across a wide range of genres. From the electronic-infused soundscapes of indie pop to the experimental approaches of avant-garde jazz, Snails' impact can be felt in every corner of the music world.

But it's not just their musical legacy that lives on. Snails' commitment to social activism and philanthropy has inspired a new generation of artists to use their platform for positive change. Their work with charitable organizations and their dedication to social causes have set a new standard for musicians who want to make a difference in the world.

Example: The Snail Effect on a Rising Band

To illustrate the real-world impact of Snails' influence, let's take a look at the case of a rising band called "The Slime Squad." Formed by a group of young musicians who were inspired by Snails' fearless experimentation and genre-bending approach, The Slime Squad set out to create their own unique sound.

Drawing on the lessons they learned from studying Snails' music, The Slime Squad incorporated elements of funk, reggae, and hip-hop into their compositions.

They embraced unconventional instruments like the saxophone and bongos, weaving them seamlessly into their songs.

As The Slime Squad started gaining recognition, they found themselves being compared to Snails. Critics and fans alike recognized the influence of the pioneering band in their music. This led to opportunities for The Slime Squad to collaborate with other artists and expand their fanbase.

The impact of Snails on The Slime Squad's success goes beyond just their musical style. The ethos of fearlessness and experimentation instilled in them by Snails has shaped their approach to all aspects of their career. They embrace innovation, constantly pushing the boundaries of their sound and stage performances.

In conclusion, Snails' influence on the music industry is far-reaching and enduring. Their genre-bending experimentations and fearless approach to music have inspired countless artists to break free from traditional constraints and forge their own unique paths. As we continue to see the ripple effects of Snails' influence, we can be sure that their legacy will live on in the music of future generations. Through their innovation, they have forever changed the landscape of popular music.

Snails' Musical Legacy: Impact on Future Generations

Snails' music has left an indelible mark on the music industry, influencing and inspiring future generations of artists. Their unique sound, captivating stage presence, and fearless exploration of musical boundaries have set them apart as innovators and trendsetters. In this section, we will delve into Snails' musical legacy and examine the profound impact they have had on the world of music.

Breaking the Mold: Snails' Genre-Bending Experimentations

Snails' music transcends traditional genre classifications. They have fearlessly blended elements of rock, pop, hip-hop, and electronic music to create their own distinctive genre. Their sonic explorations have challenged conventional boundaries, paving the way for a new era of experimental music.

One of Snails' most iconic songs, "Slime Revolution," showcases their genre-bending approach. The track seamlessly fuses heavy guitar riffs, infectious pop melodies, and electronic beats, creating a sound that is both familiar and entirely original. This fearless experimentation has inspired countless artists to push the boundaries of their own music and embrace a more eclectic and unconventional approach.

Evolution of Sound: Snails' Influences and Inspirations

Snails' music is a beautiful tapestry woven with a myriad of influences and inspirations. From classic rock legends like Led Zeppelin and Queen to modern-day visionaries like Radiohead and The Weeknd, Snails have drawn inspiration from a diverse range of musical genres and artists.

Their song "Shell Shock," for example, pays homage to the iconic sound of the '70s with its infectious disco groove and soulful vocal delivery. At the same time, their exploration of electronic elements and futuristic production techniques infuse the track with a contemporary edge. This ability to blend disparate influences into a cohesive and captivating sound has set a new standard for musical innovation.

The Snail Effect: Reverberations in the Music Industry

Snails' impact on the music industry is undeniable. Their groundbreaking music has paved the way for other artists to take creative risks and embrace their own unique visions. The Snail Effect, as it has come to be known, is a phenomenon where artists are inspired to break free from traditional molds and explore new sonic territories.

Countless musicians and bands have cited Snails as a major influence on their own work. Artists like Mollusca, Sluggish Beats, and Slimy Sirens have all emerged in the wake of Snails, each adding their own twist to the innovative sound that Snails pioneered. This ripple effect continues to shape the musical landscape, driving the industry towards greater experimentation and artistic expression.

Snails' Musical Legacy: Impact on Future Generations

Snails' musical legacy is one of fearless exploration, genre-bending experimentation, and limitless creativity. Their impact on future generations of artists is immeasurable, inspiring a new wave of musicians to break free from convention and forge their own paths.

The influence of Snails can be seen in the evolving sound of popular music, as artists across genres take inspiration from their genre-bending approach. Whether it's the incorporation of unconventional instruments, the fearless fusion of different musical styles, or the embracing of experimental production techniques, Snails' legacy lives on in the music of today and the music yet to come.

But Snails' impact extends beyond the sonic realm. Their boundary-breaking attitude and refusal to conform have inspired a generation to embrace their own individuality and express themselves authentically. They have shown us that true artistry lies in the ability to innovate, to push boundaries, and to fearlessly pursue one's creative vision.

As future generations of artists continue to draw inspiration from Snails, their musical legacy will endure. The impact they have had on the music industry will continue to shape the landscape for years to come, ensuring that the spirit of Snails lives on in the hearts and minds of musicians and fans alike.

The Snail's Challenge: Pushing Boundaries

Snails' music has opened the door to new possibilities in the industry, but their legacy is also a challenge for future artists. The challenge lies in pushing the boundaries of one's own creativity, taking risks, and embracing the unconventional.

To honor Snails' musical legacy, aspiring artists must be bold in their experimentation and unafraid to explore uncharted territory. The path may not always be easy, but the rewards are immeasurable. By taking inspiration from Snails' fearlessness and innovation, future generations of musicians can continue to shape the musical landscape and leave their own mark on the world.

A Snail's Journey Never Ends: Balls of Fire Tour

Snails' Grand Finale: The Final World Tour

After years of dominating the music industry with their unique sound and unforgettable stage presence, Snails embarked on their most epic journey yet: the Final World Tour. This tour marked the end of an era for the band, as they bid farewell to their loyal fans and closed the chapter on their illustrious career.

The Final World Tour was a spectacle unlike any other. From the moment the curtains opened, the audience was transported into a mesmerizing world of music, lights, and Slime. The stage was transformed into a snail's paradise, with slime-covered props and elaborate set designs that showcased the band's iconic style.

The tour kicked off with a bang in their hometown of Slumbersville, where thousands of fans gathered to witness the band's final performance. The energy in the air was electric as Snails took the stage, ready to give their all for one last time.

Throughout the tour, Snails took their fans on a musical journey spanning their entire discography. From their early hits like "Crawling through Adversity" and "Escaping the Shell" to their chart-topping singles such as "Sticky Melodies" and "Slime Revolution," every song was performed with a raw, emotional intensity that left the crowd begging for more.

But it was not just the music that captivated the audience; it was the palpable emotion that filled the air. Each band member poured their heart and soul into every note, every lyric, knowing that this would be their final chance to connect with their fans in this way. There were tears shed and moments of reflection, a deep sense of gratitude for the incredible journey they had been on together.

Snails' Grand Finale was not without its surprises. Throughout the tour, the band brought out special guests to join them on stage, including some of their closest friends in the industry. These collaborations created unforgettable moments of magic, showcasing the camaraderie and respect Snails had built within the music community. It was a testament to the band's lasting impact and the friendships they had formed along the way.

As the tour came to a close, Snails saved the best for last. The final show took place in the grandest venue of all: the Snail Dome. This iconic stadium had been transformed into a sea of fans, all ready to send off their beloved band in style. It was an emotional and bittersweet night, filled with nostalgia and reminiscence of the memories created over the years.

But Snails' Final World Tour was not just about saying goodbye; it was also about celebrating the legacy they had created. The band took the opportunity to thank their dedicated Snail Army, acknowledging the support and love they had received throughout their career. Each member spoke from the heart, expressing their gratitude and sharing personal anecdotes that touched the hearts of everyone in attendance.

As the final song played and the cheers of the crowd filled the Snail Dome, Snails took their final bow, leaving behind a legacy that would never be forgotten. The Final World Tour was the perfect culmination of their journey, a testament to their unwavering dedication to their art and the impact they had made on the music world.

Snails may have bid farewell to the stage, but their music and spirit will live on forever. The Final World Tour may have marked the end of an era, but it also signaled the beginning of a new chapter for the band members. As they ventured into their individual endeavors, they carried with them the memories, the lessons, and the love they had experienced as part of Snails.

The Slime may have faded from the stage, but it will forever remain in the hearts of their fans. Snails' Grand Finale was not just an end; it was a celebration of the power of music, the connections it creates, and the everlasting impact of a band that dared to be different.

So let us raise our slime-filled glasses and toast to Snails, for they have left an indelible mark on the music world. And as we look to the future, we can't help but wonder what new adventures await these iconic musicians. One thing is for certain: the Slime will never fade.

The Last Slime: Reflecting on Snails' Remarkable Career

As the final curtain call for the legendary band Snails draws near, it's time to reflect on their remarkable career and the indelible impact they have left on the music industry. With their unrivaled talent, infectious energy, and trailblazing spirit, Snails has charted an extraordinary path that will forever be etched in the annals of music history.

The End of an Era

After decades of creating groundbreaking music and captivating audiences around the world, Snails has decided to bid farewell to their loyal fans. The Last Slime, as their final world tour is aptly named, marks the end of an era for both the band and their devoted fan base, affectionately known as the Snail Army.

A Journey to Remember

The Last Slime tour is not just a concert series, but a celebration of everything that Snails has achieved throughout their career. Each show is an opportunity for the band to reflect on their journey, from their humble beginnings to becoming global superstars.

Unforgettable Memories

During the Last Slime tour, the band takes the audience on a nostalgic trip down memory lane. They revisit their biggest hits, bringing back the raw emotion and electric energy that made those songs so iconic. From their breakout hit single "Escaping the Shell" to their chart-topping anthem "Snail Invasion," every performance is a reminder of the band's immense talent and their ability to connect with their fans on a deep and personal level.

Embracing the Emotional Rollercoaster

As Snails bids farewell to their fans, a bittersweet wave of emotions washes over both the band and the audience. For the band members, it is a time of reflection and gratitude for the incredible journey they have taken together. They express their heartfelt appreciation for their fans' unwavering support over the years.

The Power of the Snail Army

The Last Slime tour serves as a testament to the incredible power of the Snail Army. Throughout the band's career, their dedicated fans have been their driving force. The Snail Army's unwavering loyalty, passion, and love for Snails have propelled them to the iconic status they hold today. The tour gives the band an opportunity to give back to their fans, to thank them for their unending support, and to create unforgettable memories together.

A Farewell to Remember

As the final show of the Last Slime tour approaches, anticipation builds to a fever pitch. The band leaves no stone unturned in making this a farewell to remember. From a mesmerizing stage setup to jaw-dropping pyrotechnics and stunning visuals, every aspect of the show is designed to honor the legacy of Snails and create an electrifying experience for their fans.

Legacy Beyond the Last Slime

While the Last Slime tour marks the end of Snails as a band, their legacy will continue to resonate for generations to come. Their groundbreaking music, unique style, and unwavering dedication to their art have left an indelible mark on the music industry. Snails' influence can be witnessed in the work of countless artists who have been inspired by their trailblazing spirit.

Carrying the Torch

As Snails takes their final bow, the question arises: Who will carry the torch forward? The band's farewell serves as an invitation to a new generation of artists to step up and create their own unique sounds, pushing the boundaries of music and leaving their own mark on the world.

Forever in the Hearts of the Snail Army

While Snails may no longer grace the stage together as a band, their music will forever live on in the hearts of their devoted fans. The Snail Army, a community bonded by a shared love for Snails' music, will continue to keep the band's flame burning bright. Through fan clubs, online forums, and tributes, the spirit of Snails will thrive, ensuring that their remarkable career is never forgotten.

A Farewell, Not Goodbye

As the Last Slime tour comes to a close, Snails bids farewell to their fans, not with goodbye, but with gratitude and an unwavering belief in the power of music to transcend time and connect people across generations. The remarkable career of Snails may be drawing to a close, but their impact will be felt for eternity. The Last Slime is not an ending, but a new beginning, as the timeless music of Snails continues to inspire future generations of artists and fans alike.

Snails' Farewell: The Emotional Goodbye to Iconic Band

As the world watched in awe, Snails took the stage one final time to bid farewell to their fans. The air was charged with a mix of excitement, sadness, and anticipation. This was a historic moment, the end of an era. The band that had conquered the hearts of millions was about to play their last show.

The venue was packed to the brim, with fans from all walks of life gathering to witness this emotional goodbye. The lights dimmed, and the stage was set for one last epic performance. The band members, clad in their iconic snail-inspired costumes, appeared amidst a sea of cheers and applause. The roar of the crowd shook the very foundations of the building.

Snails kicked off the night with a medley of their greatest hits, unleashing a torrent of energy that electrified the atmosphere. Each note, each lyric carried the weight of years of hard work, dedication, and love. The audience, caught in the rapture of the music, sang along with fervor, their voices blending with the powerful melodies.

Throughout the show, Snails took the crowd on a nostalgic journey through their discography, performing fan favorites and hidden gems. Each song held a special place in the hearts of the fans and brought back memories of joy, love, and resilience. It was a celebration of the band's legacy, a testament to the impact they had on the music world.

As the final notes of their last song resonated through the venue, a hush fell over the audience. The bittersweet realization that this was the end hung heavy in the air. Snails, visibly overcome with emotion, gathered at the center of the stage, ready to address their adoring fans one last time.

Frontman, Joe "Sluggo" Carter, took the microphone and looked out into the sea of faces. His voice trembled with a mix of sorrow and gratitude as he spoke. He expressed his deep appreciation for the unwavering support of the Snail Army, the devoted fan base that had been by their side for decades.

He reminisced about the band's humble beginnings, the challenges they had overcome, and the incredible journey they had undertaken. He thanked each member of the band for their unwavering dedication and the sacrifices they had made to bring their music to the world.

But this farewell was not just about endings. Snails wanted to leave their fans with a message of hope and inspiration. They spoke about the power of music to heal, to unite, and to ignite change. They urged their fans to follow their passions, to chase their dreams, and to never give up on what they believed in.

In a final act of gratitude, Snails invited a select group of fans on stage to join them for their last encore. The lucky few clambered on stage, tears streaming down their faces, overwhelmed by the opportunity to be a part of this historic moment.

As the night drew to a close, Snails took a bow, their faces adorned with smiles and tears. This emotional goodbye marked the end of an era, but it also sparked a new beginning. The legacy of Snails would live on through their music, imprinted on the hearts of their fans forever.

And so, as the curtain closed on this final chapter, the world bid farewell to Snails with a mixture of sadness and gratitude. Their music would forever be a reminder of the power of passion, resilience, and unity. Snails may have said goodbye, but their impact on the music world would endure, inspiring generations to come.

Beyond the Shell: Looking to the Future

Breaking the Shell: Snails' Individual Endeavors

After years of conquering the music industry as a band, the members of Snails decided it was time to explore their own unique paths. This chapter delves into the individual endeavors of each member as they broke free from the shell and embarked on personal journeys of creativity and self-expression.

Rhythm and Melody: Solo Albums that Rocked the World

Johnny "Sluggin" Davis - The Legendary Leader of Snails took the bold step of pursuing a solo career, releasing his debut album *"Breaking the Shell"* to critical acclaim. Combining his signature powerful vocals with soulful rock melodies, Johnny captivated fans with hits like *"Wild and Free"* and *"Unleashed Emotions"*. His unparalleled stage presence and raw energy elevated his solo performances, proving that his talent extends beyond the Snails band.

Lily "The Siren" Chen - Known for her mesmerizing vocals and charismatic stage presence, Lily decided to explore her diverse musical influences through her solo journey. With her debut album *"Uncharted Waters"*, she pushed boundaries and blended genres, creating a unique sound that showcased her versatility as an artist. From haunting ballads to infectious anthems, Lily's solo work resonated with fans worldwide, establishing her as a force to be reckoned with in the industry.

Max "The Machine" Martinez - Renowned for his masterful guitar skills, Max embarked on a solo career that allowed him to showcase his virtuosity and experimental spirit. His instrumental album *"Strings Unleashed"* took listeners on a sonic journey, combining elements of rock, jazz, and classical music. Max's intricate compositions captivated audiences, proving that his guitar prowess could stand alone on the world stage.

Olivia "The Groove" Johnson - With her infectious basslines and vibrant energy, Olivia explored her passion for funk and R&B in her solo projects. Her debut album *"Bass Odyssey"* became an instant hit among music enthusiasts, with tracks like *"Funky Revolution"* and *"Groove On"* topping the charts. Olivia's soulful voice and dynamic bass playing brought a fresh perspective to the genre, making her solo career a testament to her musical prowess.

Collaborations That Transcend Boundaries

While venturing into solo projects, the Snails members also sought out intriguing collaborations, pushing the boundaries of their musical styles and lending their unique talents to a range of artists and genres.

Johnny's Collaboration with R&B Sensation Gia Taylor - Johnny's soulful vocals found a perfect match in the sultry R&B tones of superstar Gia Taylor. Together, they released the chart-topping duet *"Fire and Ice"*, which showcased their impressive vocal range and electrifying chemistry. This collaboration bridged the gap between rock and R&B, captivating fans from both genres.

Lily's Electrifying Team-Up with EDM Phenomenon DJ Venom - Seeking an electrifying fusion of rock and electronic dance music, Lily collaborated with the renowned DJ Venom to create the explosive track *"Electric Dreams"*. The pulsating beats and infectious melodies combined with Lily's powerful vocals created an anthem that dominated dance floors globally.

Max's Masterpiece with Jazz Legend Miles Davis - The meeting of guitar virtuosity and musical genius took place when Max collaborated posthumously with jazz legend Miles Davis. Their collaboration, *"Uncharted Horizons"*, brought together Max's sweeping guitar solos with Miles Davis's legendary trumpet playing, creating an ethereal fusion of jazz and rock that left listeners in awe.

Olivia's Funky Journey with Bassist Victor Wooten - Joining forces with renowned bassist Victor Wooten, Olivia embarked on a funky expedition that pushed the boundaries of bass playing. Their collaboration, *"Groove Train"*, showcased their exceptional mastery of the instrument and celebrated the art of groove, leaving fans mesmerized by their collective talent.

Beyond Music: Snails' Impact on Other Art Forms

The members of Snails did not limit their creative endeavors to the realm of music alone. They also explored other artistic mediums, leaving their indelible mark on various forms of expression.

Johnny's Delve into Acting - Johnny's magnetic stage presence and natural charisma made him a sought-after talent in the acting world. Making his debut in the blockbuster film *"Razor's Edge"*, he showcased his versatility as an actor, captivating audiences with his nuanced performances and proving that his talent transcends the boundaries of music.

Lily's Visual Artistry - Alongside her musical pursuits, Lily channeled her creativity into visual art. Her breathtaking paintings, characterized by vibrant colors and evocative imagery, were showcased in prestigious galleries, earning her recognition as a talented visual artist. Lily's artistic expression expanded beyond the stage, captivating audiences in an entirely new way.

Max's Authorial Journey - Max's passion for storytelling led him to explore the realm of literature. His debut novel *"Between the Strings"* became a bestseller, acclaimed for its captivating narrative and poetic prose. Max's unique storytelling ability showcased a different side of his artistic talent, captivating readers worldwide.

Olivia's Philanthropic Pursuits - Olivia's deep commitment to making a difference in the world led her to establish a foundation, *"Rhythm of Hope"*. Through this organization, she used the power of music to support underprivileged communities and promote education and equal opportunity. Olivia's philanthropic endeavors resonated with Snails' fans, inspiring them to make a positive impact in their own communities.

Conclusion: The Legacy Lives On

Although the members of Snails pursued individual endeavors, their collective impact on the music industry and beyond remains immeasurable. Breaking the shell allowed each member to explore new horizons and unleash their creative potential, proving that their talents extend beyond the confines of the band. Through solo albums, collaborations, and ventures into other art forms, they continued to inspire and captivate audiences, leaving an enduring legacy that showcases the boundless possibilities of artistic expression.

As Snails' journey continues, their individual endeavors serve as a testament to the band's enduring spirit and collective genius. Breaking free from the shell was not just a leap of faith for the members, but also a continuation of Snails' philosophy of constant evolution and pushing boundaries. With each new endeavor, they invite their fans to join them on an extraordinary artistic odyssey, ensuring that the Snail spirit will continue to thrive for generations to come.

The Legacy Lives On: Reviving Snails' Music for New Audience

As the iconic band Snails continues to make waves in the music industry, their legacy lives on through a new generation of fans. With their incredible talent and unique style, Snails' music has transcended time and continues to resonate with audiences of all ages. In this section, we explore how Snails is reviving their music for a new audience and ensuring that their legacy remains strong.

Understanding the Power of Nostalgia

One of the reasons for Snails' enduring popularity is their ability to evoke feelings of nostalgia in their fans. Nostalgia holds a special place in our hearts, reminding us of cherished memories and experiences. Snails' music transports listeners to a different time and place, reminding them of their youth and the emotions associated with that period.

To revive their music for a new audience, Snails embraces this power of nostalgia. They recognize that their loyal fans from the past are now parents, passing down their love for Snails' music to their children. By tapping into the emotions and memories associated with their music, Snails creates a bridge between generations, ensuring that their legacy lives on.

Reimagining Classic Hits

Reviving Snails' music for a new audience involves more than just playing the same songs. To keep their music fresh and relevant, the band reimagines their classic hits, infusing them with new energy and modern elements. This allows them to appeal to younger listeners while still preserving the essence of their songs.

Snails' members collaborate with talented producers and musicians from different genres to bring a fresh perspective to their music. By incorporating elements of pop, hip-hop, and electronic dance music (EDM), they create a fusion that appeals to a wider audience. This strategic approach ensures that Snails' music remains timeless and continues to captivate listeners for years to come.

Embracing Social Media and Digital Platforms

In the digital age, social media and digital platforms play a crucial role in reaching a new audience. Snails understands the importance of staying connected with their fans and uses various social media platforms to engage and interact with them. They provide behind-the-scenes glimpses of their creative process, share personal stories, and even seek input from their fans on new projects.

By actively embracing social media, Snails maintains a strong presence and connects with fans on a more personal level. This strategy not only helps attract new listeners but also fosters a sense of community among fans. It allows for a continuous dialogue between the band and their audience, keeping the spirit of Snails alive.

Collaborating with Emerging Artists

To revitalize their music for a new audience, Snails recognizes the importance of collaborating with emerging artists. By working with young and talented musicians, they bring a fresh perspective and contemporary sound to their music. These collaborations bridge the gap between generations and help introduce Snails' music to a wider audience.

Snails' members actively seek out new talent and provide platforms for emerging artists to showcase their skills. This mutually beneficial collaboration allows for cross-pollination of ideas and brings a modern touch to the band's music. It also gives emerging artists a chance to learn from seasoned musicians and gain exposure in the industry.

The Snail Academy: Inspiring the Next Generation

To ensure the longevity of Snails' music, the band has established the Snail Academy. This initiative aims to inspire and nurture the next generation of musicians. Through workshops, mentorship programs, and educational resources, the academy equips aspiring artists with the knowledge and skills needed to create music that resonates with audiences.

The Snail Academy provides a platform for young musicians to learn from the band's members and industry professionals. It encourages creativity, innovation, and a deep understanding of music. By passing on their knowledge and sharing their experiences, Snails ensures that their legacy lives on through the music of future generations.

Conclusion

The legacy of Snails continues to thrive as the band revives their music for a new audience. By harnessing the power of nostalgia, reimagining their classic hits, embracing social media, collaborating with emerging artists, and inspiring the next generation, Snails ensures that their music remains relevant and influential. As their fanbase expands and their music evolves, Snails leaves an indelible mark on the music industry, securing their place in history. The journey of Snails' legacy never fades, as their music continues to inspire and resonate with new generations of listeners.

The Snail Army: Keeping the Spirit Alive

The Snail Army is not just a fan base; it's a community bonded by the infectious energy and timeless music of Snails. From the very beginning, Snails recognized the importance of their fans and built a strong connection with them. In this section, we delve into the heart and soul of the Snail Army, exploring how they keep the spirit of the band alive.

The Power of Unity

The Snail Army is a formidable force, united by their love for Snails' music and the band's message of positivity and self-expression. They come from all walks of life, embracing diversity and fostering inclusivity. The Snail Army believes in celebrating individuality and finding strength in unity. They create safe spaces where everyone can find solace and connection.

The Snail Army Code: A Culture of Respect

Within the Snail Army, there is a code that fans abide by. It is based on principles of respect, support, and kindness. Their code reflects the band's values and sets the tone for interactions within the community. Whether it's within online forums, fan meet-ups, or concert venues, Snail Army members uplift each other and promote a positive atmosphere.

The Snail Army Initiatives

The Snail Army doesn't just passively support the band; they actively engage in initiatives that extend beyond the music. Recognizing the challenges faced by various communities, the Snail Army has organized charity events, volunteer work, and fundraising drives. Their efforts have made a tangible difference in the lives of those in need, proving that the power of a dedicated fan base can create positive change.

Snails' Fan Clubs: A Web of Connection

The Snail Army is held together by a network of fan clubs spanning the globe. These clubs provide platforms for fans to connect, share their love for Snails, and collaborate on various projects. From organizing fan events to creating fan art and fan fiction, the clubs fuel creativity and serve as a testament to the lasting impact of Snails' music.

Snail Army Exclusives: Rewarding Loyalty

Snails understands the importance of appreciating their dedicated fan base. The band regularly offers exclusive content, merchandise, and opportunities to the Snail Army. From pre-sale concert tickets to limited edition releases, they ensure that their most passionate fans are rewarded for their unwavering support. This creates a sense of belonging and deepens the bond between the band and their fans.

The Snail Army on Social Media

Social media has played a pivotal role in connecting the Snail Army members from all corners of the world. Platforms like Twitter, Instagram, and Facebook have become virtual meeting places where fans can share their experiences, fan art, and stories. Snails actively engages with their fans through these channels, creating an intimate connection that transcends geographical boundaries.

The Snail Army Swagger: Expressing Individuality

Just as Snails has a unique style and stage presence, the Snail Army too embraces their individuality. Through fashion, makeup, and personal style, fans express their love for the band while adding their own flair. Snail Army swagger is all about embracing one's true self and celebrating the things that make them unique.

Snails' Legacy: Passed Down through Generations

Snails' influence extends beyond their music and into future generations. Many Snail Army members pass down their love for the band to their children, creating a multi-generational fan base. This legacy ensures that the spirit of Snails will continue to thrive long after the band's farewell.

The Snail Army: Unity in Music

In conclusion, the Snail Army is not just a group of fans; they are a testament to the power of unity, respect, and connection that Snails' music has fostered. Through their initiatives, creativity, and support, they keep the spirit of the band alive. The Snail Army is a living, breathing embodiment of the band's message, and their continued dedication ensures that Snails' legacy will endure for generations to come. As Snails marches forward, the Snail Army will be right there, standing strong, showing the world what it truly means to keep the spirit alive.

Beyond the Glitz and Glam

Beyond the Glitz and Glam

Beyond the Glitz and Glam

In the world of fame and stardom, it's easy to get caught up in the glitz and glam. But for Snails, there's more to their story than meets the eye. Beyond the stage lights and extravagant outfits, lies a deeper, more profound side to the band. In this chapter, we peel back the layers of their fame and uncover the real Snails—their struggles, triumphs, and the impact they've had on popular culture.

The Untold Snail Stories: Revelations and Confessions

Behind every success story are personal struggles and triumphs. Snails is no exception. In this section, we dive into the untold stories of the band members and reveal the heartfelt journey they've embarked upon.

From the outside looking in, Snails appeared to have it all. But little did their fans know about the obstacles they faced along the way. Behind closed doors, each band member had their own personal battles to overcome. From mental health issues to addiction, Snails didn't shy away from sharing their struggles, using their platform to break the stigma and raise awareness about these important topics.

One member, who we'll refer to as "S", battled with anxiety and depression throughout their career. In a candid interview, S shared their darkest moments, reflecting on the pressure of constantly maintaining a flawless public image. S revealed that it was the unconditional support from their bandmates and the Snail Army that helped them find light in the darkest of times.

Another member, "N", bravely opened up about their past struggles with substance abuse. N revealed that it was the love for their craft and the music that ultimately pulled them out of the darkness. With the unwavering support of their bandmates, N found the strength to face their demons head-on and seek the help they needed.

These untold stories not only humanize the band, but they also inspire their fans who may be going through similar struggles. Snails' willingness to share their vulnerabilities reminds us that even in the face of fame, we're all human, and no one is immune to life's challenges.

Snails Unmasked: Revealing the True Faces behind the Slime

The stage personas of Snails are shrouded in mystery, with each member donning a unique mask. This section peels back the layers of their intriguing stage presence and reveals the true faces behind the slime.

Behind the mask of Snails is a group of incredibly talented individuals who have poured their hearts and souls into their craft. Each member brings their own distinct personality and musical genius to the band.

"R", the enigmatic frontman of Snails, is notorious for his electrifying stage presence and larger-than-life personality. But when the lights dim and the mask comes off, R reveals a soft-spoken and introspective side that is often overshadowed by his onstage persona.

Behind the drum kit is "J", the backbone of Snails' rhythm section. Known for their impeccable timing and groove, J is a true musical maestro. But behind closed doors, J is a humble and down-to-earth individual who finds solace in nature and spends their downtime exploring their passion for photography.

"M", the bassist of the band, has an undeniable energy that resonates with the audience. But when the mask comes off, M transforms into a thoughtful and philosophical thinker. M's deep understanding of the complexities of life shines through their lyrics, bringing a profound depth to Snails' music.

And finally, we have "D", the lead guitarist. D's fiery guitar solos and showmanship are part of what makes Snails' live performances legendary. But offstage, D is a gentle and sensitive soul, often found lost in the world of art and literature.

This unmasking of the band members reveals the true essence of Snails—that their stage personas are just a fraction of who they truly are. Behind the mask lies a group of individuals who are passionate, introspective, and dedicated to their craft.

Dealing with Fame: Snails' Battle with the Dark Side

Fame comes with its fair share of rewards, but it also brings its own set of challenges. In this section, we explore Snails' battle with the dark side of fame and how they've managed to stay grounded amidst the chaos.

When Snails burst onto the music scene, they were catapulted into the spotlight overnight. The band's skyrocketing success brought with it a whirlwind of media attention, pressures, and expectations. But instead of succumbing to the vices that fame often offers, Snails remained true to themselves and stayed grounded.

One of the ways they navigated the treacherous waters of stardom was by prioritizing their mental health. Each band member recognized the importance of taking breaks, setting boundaries, and seeking professional help when needed. By openly discussing their own struggles with mental health, Snails not only broke down the walls of stigma but also inspired their fans to prioritize their own well-being.

Another challenge that Snails confronted head-on was the invasion of privacy. Paparazzi and tabloids were relentless in their pursuit of the band's personal lives. But instead of hiding away, Snails embraced transparency and used their platform to shed light on the dark underbelly of the entertainment industry.

Through it all, Snails maintained a tight-knit support system within the band. They continuously checked in on each other and created a safe space where they could openly express their fears and insecurities. This unity allowed them to weather the storms of fame together and reminded them of the importance of staying true to themselves.

The Highs and Lows: Snails' Rollercoaster of Emotions

Life in the limelight is a rollercoaster ride of emotions. Snails' journey has been filled with exhilarating highs and heart-wrenching lows. In this section, we explore the emotional journey of the band and how they've managed to find strength in the face of adversity.

The highs of Snails' career have been nothing short of extraordinary. From sold-out stadium tours to chart-topping hits, each milestone has been a testament to their talent and hard work. But with great success comes great pressure. The band members experienced moments of self-doubt and fears of living up to the lofty expectations set by their fans and themselves.

On the flip side, the lows of Snails' journey have been equally profound. They've faced debilitating criticism, both from the industry and from their own inner demons. Each setback became an opportunity for growth, pushing them to become stronger and more resilient.

Through it all, Snails' music has been a cathartic outlet for their emotions. Each song became a mirror reflecting their triumphs, fears, and insecurities. The band's ability to harness their emotions and transform them into beautiful art is what sets them apart.

This emotional rollercoaster has taught Snails the value of staying true to themselves and embracing vulnerability. Their music resonates with fans on a deep, emotional level, reminding them that it's okay to feel the highs and lows of life.

Light at the End of the Tunnel: Snails' Journey to Redemption

In the depths of their struggles, Snails found the strength to rise above and embark on a journey to redemption. This section delves into how they transformed their personal challenges into sources of inspiration and hope.

For Snails, redemption came in the form of using their music to advocate for change. Through powerful lyrics and heartfelt melodies, they tackled social issues such as mental health, addiction, and societal injustices. By shedding light on these important topics, Snails became a voice for the voiceless and a beacon of hope for their fans.

The band's journey to redemption also involved a deep introspection and a commitment to personal growth. They recognized their past mistakes and took ownership of them. Through therapy, self-reflection, and the support of their loved ones, Snails found a path to healing and personal transformation.

Snails' journey to redemption is an ongoing one. They continue to use their platform to inspire and uplift others going through similar struggles. By embracing their past and channeling their experiences into their music, Snails have become symbols of resilience and hope for a generation.

The Slime Never Fades: Snails' Impact on Pop Culture

Snails transcends the boundaries of music and has undeniably left an indelible mark on pop culture. In this section, we explore the band's influence and how they shaped the world around them.

One aspect of Snails' impact on pop culture is their unique fashion sense. The band's iconic masks and extravagant outfits spawned countless trends and influenced the fashion industry. Snail-inspired merchandise flew off the shelves, with fans eager to capture a piece of the band's distinctive style.

Beyond fashion, Snails also made their mark in the media. Their captivating performances and magnetic personalities landed them appearances on talk shows, game shows, and even movies. The band's charisma and ability to connect with audiences ensured that their presence in the entertainment world remained unforgettable.

But Snails' impact goes beyond the glitz and glam. The band's authenticity and willingness to tackle social issues head-on made them a voice of change. Their songs became anthems for the disenfranchised, empowering their fans to stand up against injustice and fight for a better world.

Snails' legacy extends far beyond their music. Their influence on fashion, media, and social activism solidifies their place in pop culture history. The slime they've left behind will continue to inspire generations to come.

Snails' Artistry: Visual and Conceptual Elements in their Music

Music is not only about sound—it's also a multi-sensory experience. In this section, we delve into Snails' artistry and explore the visual and conceptual elements that make their music a feast for the senses.

Snails' music videos are a visual treat, often blurring the boundaries between reality and fantasy. Each video is meticulously crafted, with attention to detail that rivals the most stunning cinematic masterpieces. From elaborate sets to stunning visual effects, Snails' music videos take viewers on a mesmerizing journey.

But it's not just the visuals that make Snails' music stand out—it's the concepts behind their albums and songs. The band is known for creating intricate narratives that unfold with each track. Themes of self-discovery, resilience, and societal critique are interwoven into their conceptual work, offering listeners a thought-provoking and immersive experience.

Snails' artistry extends beyond the realm of music videos and albums. Their live performances are carefully choreographed spectacles, blending music, dance, and theater. From elaborate stage setups to captivating costumes, each performance is a work of art in itself, leaving the audience in awe.

By marrying visual and conceptual elements with their music, Snails takes their artistry to new heights. They create an immersive experience that allows fans to fully immerse themselves in the world of Snails.

Conclusion

In this chapter, we've explored the multi-dimensional world of Snails beyond the glitz and glam. We've unmasked the band members, revealing their true selves and the struggles they've faced along the way. We've journeyed through their emotional highs and lows and witnessed their path to redemption. We've witnessed their impact on pop culture and explored their artistry beyond music.

Snails is not just a band—they are a force of nature, uniting fans around the world with their music and their message. Their willingness to share their vulnerabilities and embrace the imperfections of life has made them not only music icons but also beacons of hope for their loyal fans.

As we turn the page and venture into the remaining chapters, we'll continue to uncover the layers of Snails' story—their creative process, their philanthropic efforts, their enduring legacy, and the torch they pass on to future generations. The journey of Snails goes far beyond the glitz and glam, and this chapter is just the beginning.

The Untold Snail Stories: Revelations and Confessions

Behind Closed Doors: Snails' Personal Struggles and Triumphs

In the pursuit of stardom, Snails faced numerous personal struggles that tested their resilience and determination. Behind closed doors, away from the glitz and glam of the stage, the band members confronted their own demons and overcame countless obstacles on their path to success. This section delves into their personal journeys, highlighting their struggles, triumphs, and the lessons they learned along the way.

Life on the Edge: Battling Addiction

Behind the facade of fame and fortune, Snails battled with addiction, a challenge that threatened to derail their careers. Like many artists before them, the band members were pushed to their limits by the pressures of the music industry. The fast-paced lifestyle, constant touring, and the demands of their craft took a toll on their mental and physical well-being.

Fueled by the adrenaline of performing to thousands of fans, Snails found solace in substances and behaviors that provided temporary relief from the harsh realities of their day-to-day lives. The rockstar lifestyle seemed appealing, but it came at a steep price. Their personal struggles with addiction affected not only their professional lives, but also their relationships and overall happiness.

However, the band eventually recognized the destructive nature of their habits and made the brave decision to face their demons head-on. With the support of loved ones and a commitment to change, Snails embarked on a journey of recovery. The band members sought professional help, emphasizing the importance of therapy, support groups, and the power of confronting their innermost fears and insecurities.

Through perseverance and resilience, Snails triumphed over addiction and emerged stronger than ever. Their personal struggles became a source of inspiration for their fans, demonstrating that it is possible to overcome even the darkest of times.

Embracing Vulnerability: Mental Health and Self-Care

In the music industry, where success is often equated with invincibility, Snails openly addressed the importance of mental health and self-care. Behind closed doors, they grappled with anxiety, depression, and the pressures of constantly being in the spotlight. The band members found solace in sharing their struggles with their fans, advocating for open conversations about mental health.

They recognized the need to prioritize self-care, which meant taking time for themselves, setting boundaries, and seeking professional help when needed. Snails encouraged their fans to do the same, reminding them that vulnerability is not a weakness but a strength.

By being open about their mental health journeys, Snails fostered a sense of camaraderie and understanding among their fanbase. They used their platform to break the stigma surrounding mental health, creating a community that supports and uplifts one another.

Falling from Grace: Turbulent Relationships

Beyond the glitz and glam of the stage, Snails faced tumultuous relationships that threatened to overshadow their success. The constant touring and demanding schedule took its toll on their personal lives, leading to conflicts and strained relationships with loved ones.

Navigating the complexities of fame and maintaining healthy relationships proved to be a difficult balancing act for the band members. The pressure of being in the spotlight often caused tension and misunderstandings, leading to emotional upheaval and heartbreak.

However, Snails learned valuable lessons from these experiences. They recognized the importance of communication, trust, and compromise in maintaining healthy relationships. Through introspection and self-reflection, they worked to mend broken connections and prioritize the people who truly mattered in their lives.

The Power of Resilience: Triumphing Over Adversity

Despite the personal struggles they faced, Snails' resilience shone through. They viewed every setback as an opportunity for growth and used their experiences to fuel their passion for music. Their ability to adapt, learn from their mistakes, and persevere in the face of adversity defined their journey.

The band members drew on their personal struggles to write music that resonated with their fans. The raw emotions and authenticity embedded in their songs struck a chord with listeners, forging a deep and lasting connection. Through their triumph over personal challenges, Snails inspired countless individuals to never give up on their dreams.

Lessons Learned: Rising Above Difficulties

Snails' personal struggles and triumphs taught them valuable lessons that continue to shape their lives. They learned the importance of self-care, maintaining healthy relationships, and prioritizing mental health. Their experiences underscored the significance of resilience and perseverance, reminding them to never lose sight of their passions.

Aspiring artists can draw inspiration from Snails' journey, knowing that greatness can be achieved even in the face of personal struggles. By acknowledging their vulnerabilities and confronting their demons, Snails turned their personal triumphs into a message of hope and resilience for their fans.

Remember, behind closed doors, every individual faces their own battles. It is through perseverance and unwavering determination that one can rise above difficulties and achieve greatness. Snails' personal struggles serve as a testament to the power of resilience and the human spirit.

Note: The content in this section is a portrayal of fictional characters in alignment with the book's theme. The intention is to inspire readers through the narrative journey of Snails, drawing from real-life experiences of musicians who have faced personal struggles.

Snails Unmasked: Revealing the True Faces behind the Slime

Behind the heavy sludge and mysterious masks lie the individuals that make up the enigmatic band known as Snails. In this chapter, we delve deep into their history and uncover the true faces behind the slime. Prepare to be amazed as we reveal the untold stories and intimate details of the band members' lives.

Unveiling the Slime: Snails' Masked Identities

Snails is a band shrouded in secrecy, with their iconic slime-covered masks becoming synonymous with their image. These masks not only add a touch of mystique but also help create a persona that transcends individual identities. The band members have intentionally kept their real faces hidden, allowing the music to take center stage.

But who are the individuals behind the masks? Allow us to remove the veil and introduce you to the extraordinary talents that form the heart and soul of Snails.

Vocal Virtuoso: The Voice of Snails

Behind the signature snail shell, we find the voice that has captivated millions. Meet Marcus "Squish" Simmons, the mesmerizing vocalist of Snails. Known for his powerful and emotive delivery, Squish's soulful voice has the ability to transport listeners to another dimension. His range is unparalleled, effortlessly hitting notes that send shivers down the spine.

Despite his incredible vocal abilities, Squish remains humble and grounded. He credits his success to hard work and a deep passion for music. Squish is known for his tireless dedication to his craft, spending hours perfecting his technique and experimenting with new vocal styles. He is a true master of his instrument, constantly pushing the boundaries of what is possible in the realm of rock vocals.

Rhythm Royalty: The Backbone of Snails

In the realm of rhythm, we find the dynamic duo responsible for the infectious beats that define Snails' sound. Max "Slimestick" Martinez and Emily "Sticky Fingers" Anderson form the unbeatable rhythm section of the band.

Max is a virtuoso drummer who can command the stage with his intricate rhythms and thunderous fills. His percussive skills are unmatched, earning him a reputation as one of the best drummers in the rock genre. Max's energetic stage presence and unwavering passion make him the heartbeat of Snails.

Emily, on the other hand, wields her bass guitar like a weapon, driving the grooves that make bodies move. Her impeccable sense of timing and unique style add depth and richness to Snails' music. Emily's ability to seamlessly blend with Max's drumming creates a tight and powerful foundation for the band's sound.

Together, Max and Emily form a powerhouse rhythm section that keeps Snails' music pulsating with energy and life.

Individuality within Unity: The Snails' Unique Personalities

While their masks may hide their expressions, the individuality of each band member shines through in their music and interactions. Although they prefer to let the music speak for itself, Snails' members have distinct personalities that complement one another.

Behind the snail shell, Squish reveals his warm and charismatic nature. He is known for his infectious laughter and a genuine warmth that instantly puts people at ease. Squish's ability to connect with fans on a personal level is a testament to his authenticity and down-to-earth demeanor.

Max, despite his intensity on stage, is a gentle soul offstage. He possesses a quiet strength and contemplative nature that is often underestimated. Max's love for nature and the simple joys in life serve as a source of inspiration for the band's music.

Emily, on the other hand, is a fiery and passionate individual. Her fierce determination and unwavering commitment to her craft make her a force to be reckoned with. Emily's love for adventure and pushing boundaries spills over into her music, adding an extra layer of intensity to Snails' performances.

The Inner Circle: Snails' Manager and Support System

Behind every successful band is a dedicated team working tirelessly behind the scenes. In Snails' case, their manager and support system is none other than Tony "Slime Boss" Johnson. With decades of experience in the music industry, Tony has guided Snails to unprecedented success.

Known for his larger-than-life personality and unyielding dedication, Tony is the backbone of the band's operation. From handling logistics to negotiating deals, he ensures that Snails can focus on what they do best: creating incredible music.

Beyond the Slime: Snails' Human Side

Underneath the masks and beyond the stage presence, Snails' members are real people with dreams, struggles, and triumphs. They are devoted to their families, friends, and causes close to their hearts.

Squish is a loving father and a strong advocate for mental health. He uses his platform to raise awareness and support those battling inner demons. Squish believes that music has the power to heal and hopes to inspire others through his experiences.

Max is an avid environmentalist, dedicating his time and resources to conservation efforts. He founded the "Slime Clean" initiative, organizing beach clean-ups and raising awareness about the importance of preserving our planet's natural beauty.

Emily is a passionate advocate for LGBTQ+ rights. She actively supports organizations that provide resources and support to individuals within the community. Through her music, Emily aims to inspire acceptance and inclusivity for all.

The Essence of Snails: Music Above All

While it may be tempting to focus on the people behind the slime, it is crucial to remember that Snails' music is the true essence of the band. Their masks serve to create a unified front, allowing the music to speak louder than any individual.

Snails has captured the hearts of millions with their unique sound, mesmerizing performances, and enigmatic personas. As we peel back the layers, we discover a group of individuals who have poured their hearts and souls into creating a musical masterpiece.

In the next chapter, we'll explore the exceptional creative process that led to Snails' timeless classics and groundbreaking experimentation. Prepare to be astounded as we uncover the secrets behind their truly iconic sound.

Dealing with Fame: Snails' Battle with the Dark Side

In the world of music, fame is like a double-edged sword. On one hand, it brings recognition, success, and adoration from millions of fans. On the other hand, it can lead to a dark and treacherous path, filled with temptations, pressures, and personal struggles that can tear a band apart. In this section, we delve into Snails' battle with the dark side of fame and explore the challenges they faced along their journey.

The Weight of Expectations

When Snails burst onto the music scene, they were just a group of ordinary individuals with extraordinary talent. As their popularity skyrocketed, so did the expectations of their fans and the industry. Suddenly, the pressure to deliver hit songs, chart-topping albums, and groundbreaking performances became overwhelming.

The band found themselves trapped in a cycle of trying to meet everyone's expectations while also staying true to their artistic vision. They struggled with the fear of disappointing their fans, critics, and even themselves. Each album release brought the anticipation of whether they could live up to the success of their previous work.

Losing Identity in the Spotlight

As Snails rose to fame, their personal lives became a spectacle for the world to see. Their every move was scrutinized, and their private moments invaded by the paparazzi. They found themselves constantly surrounded by the chaos of fame, leaving little room for personal privacy or moments of introspection.

The band members grappled with the loss of their individual identities. They struggled to maintain a sense of self amidst the constant demands and expectations of being in the spotlight. The boundaries between their public persona and their true selves became blurred, leading to a feeling of emptiness and a sense of being trapped within their own fame.

Addiction and Excess

With fame comes a world of temptations. Snails were no strangers to the seductive allure of drugs, alcohol, and the party lifestyle. The music industry is notorious for its excesses, and it wasn't long before the band found themselves caught up in the whirlwind of late-night parties and substance abuse.

The pressure to maintain their image as rock stars took a toll on their mental and physical well-being. The band members struggled with addiction, destructive behaviors, and a constant need to escape from the harsh reality of their fame. They were trapped in a vicious cycle of highs and lows, trying to find solace in the very vices that were tearing them apart.

Unconventional Example:

One night, after a particularly grueling concert, the band decided to treat themselves to a night of indulgence. They rented a luxurious penthouse suite in a five-star hotel, complete with an extravagant minibar and a magnificent view of the city. The room was filled with the intoxicating scent of success, but little did they know that this night would mark a turning point in their battle with the dark side.

As the night progressed, the band members found themselves drowning in a sea of champagne and whiskey. The allure of the party lifestyle was irresistible, and they succumbed to its temptations. But as the night wore on, they realized that the more they indulged, the emptier they felt. The revelry was just a mask for their inner struggles and insecurities.

In the midst of the chaos, one band member, let's call him Jake, stumbled upon a piano hidden in a corner of the suite. In a moment of clarity, he sat down and started playing a haunting melody. The others were drawn to the music, and soon, they gathered around the piano, creating an impromptu jam session.

As the music filled the room, their troubles seemed to melt away, if only for a fleeting moment. The collective energy and creativity reminded them of why they had started making music in the first place. They realized that their battle with the dark side of fame was not in vain. It was a constant reminder of the importance of staying true to themselves and harnessing the power of their art to overcome their demons.

The Road to Redemption

Despite the challenges they faced, Snails managed to find their way out of the darkest corners of fame. They sought help, whether through therapy, rehab, or the support of loved ones. They began to rebuild their lives, one step at a time.

The band made a conscious effort to redefine success on their own terms. They focused on creating music that resonated with them personally, rather than chasing commercial success. They prioritized their mental and physical well-being, surrounding themselves with a strong support system that included family, friends, and mentors who understood the pressures of fame.

Snails' battle with the dark side of fame taught them valuable lessons about the importance of self-care, resilience, and authenticity. They discovered the power of vulnerability, using their struggles to connect with their fans on a deeper level. Through their music and personal journeys, they became beacons of hope for others battling their own demons.

Lessons Learned

1. Stay true to yourself: Fame may tempt you to compromise your values, but it's essential to maintain your integrity and remain true to who you are as an artist.

2. Surround yourself with a strong support system: The journey through fame is not an easy one. Having a network of support, including friends, family, and mentors, can help navigate the challenges and provide a source of strength.

3. Prioritize self-care: Take the time to prioritize your mental and physical well-being. Seek professional help if needed, and remember that your health should always come first.

4. Embrace vulnerability: Being open and honest about your struggles can be incredibly liberating. It allows you to connect with your fans on a deeper level and remind them that they are not alone in their own battles.

Remember, fame can be a double-edged sword, but it's how you wield it that determines your journey. Snails' battle with the dark side serves as a powerful reminder that staying true to oneself and embracing the challenges can lead to growth, redemption, and a lasting impact on the world.

The Highs and Lows: Snails' Rollercoaster of Emotions

Life as a member of the band Snails has been quite the wild ride. Behind the glitz and glamour of the stage, there lies a complex world filled with highs and lows, joys and sorrows. In this section, we delve into the emotional rollercoaster that Snails has ridden throughout their remarkable journey.

The Ecstasy of Success

One cannot discuss the highs of Snails' career without mentioning the overwhelming ecstasy that comes with success. From their first breakthrough performance to their chart-topping hit singles, Snails has experienced the euphoria of reaching the pinnacle of the music industry.

Take, for example, their global hit single "Slime Anthem." This infectious song not only topped the charts but also became an anthem for their millions of devoted fans, affectionately known as the Snail Army. The feeling of knowing that their music resonates with people from all walks of life is a high that cannot be replicated.

Another joyous moment in Snails' career was their headline performance at the prestigious Green Music Festival. This iconic gig solidified their status as one of the most sought-after acts in the industry. The energy radiating from the crowd, the thunderous applause, and the knowledge that they had captivated an entire audience filled the band members with an indescribable sense of accomplishment.

The Weight of Expectations

However, with great success comes great expectations. Snails had to learn how to navigate the immense pressure of living up to their own achievements and the lofty expectations of their fans. The constant demand for bigger and better performances puts a tremendous weight on their shoulders.

One of the lowest points in the band's journey was the aftermath of their highly anticipated album release. Despite it being critically acclaimed, some fans felt it didn't live up to their expectations. Negative reviews flooded in, and the band found themselves at a crossroads, questioning their artistic direction and grappling with self-doubt.

The Sting of Criticism

Criticism, both constructive and malicious, is an inevitable part of any artist's life. While every artist strives to create music that resonates with their audience, not every fan will be pleased with their artistic choices. Snails learned this firsthand and had to develop a thick skin to weather the sting of criticism.

A prime example of this was the controversy surrounding their experimental phase. Snails, always known for pushing boundaries, decided to incorporate elements of jazz and classical music into their sound. While some fans embraced this evolution, others vehemently opposed it, accusing the band of abandoning their roots. This backlash shook the band to its core, with each member questioning their artistic integrity.

Rebirth and Resilience

The lows of Snails' emotional rollercoaster were not without their purpose. Each setback served as a catalyst for growth and introspection. The band learned to embrace the lows as opportunities for reinvention and resilience.

During a particularly trying time, faced with internal conflicts and creative stagnation, Snails made the bold decision to take an extended hiatus. This break allowed each band member to explore their individual artistic endeavors, breathe new life into their craft, and rediscover their passion for music.

Riding the Waves of Creativity

Just as emotions ebb and flow, so does the creative process. Snails' rollercoaster of emotions is intricately intertwined with their artistic journey. The band members have discovered that their most profound creative breakthroughs often come from the depths of their emotions.

One example of this is the genesis of their album "Emotional Slime." Filled with raw, heartfelt songs, this album was born out of the band's collective emotional experiences. Each member poured their heart and soul into this project, baring their vulnerabilities and channeling their highs and lows into the music.

Finding Solace in Unity

Through all the highs and lows, Snails has found solace in their unbreakable bond as a band. Each member serves as a pillar of support for one another, offering a shoulder to lean on during challenging times. They have come to realize that their shared experiences and emotional journeys are what make their music resonate with their fans on such a deep level.

The band's close-knit relationship has also been instrumental in weathering the storms of fame. Regular band meetings and open discussions have allowed them to address any conflicts that arise and find common ground. As a result, Snails has emerged stronger, more united, and ready to conquer any emotional rollercoaster that comes their way.

The Growth within the Band

One of the most rewarding aspects of Snails' emotional rollercoaster is the personal growth that occurs within each band member. They have learned to embrace vulnerability, celebrate their successes, and confront their fears head-on. This growth extends beyond their music careers and into their personal lives, fostering stronger relationships with their loved ones.

It is important to recognize that the emotional rollercoaster of Snails is not unique to them alone. Artists of all disciplines experience these highs and lows. It is how they navigate and harness these emotions that ultimately shape their creative journey.

Exercises

1. Reflect on a time when you experienced a rollercoaster of emotions in your life. How did that experience shape you as an individual? How did it impact your artistic or creative endeavors?

2. Explore a piece of art or music that you admire. Try to identify the emotions that the artist might have experienced while creating that piece. How do these emotions enhance your connection to the artwork?

3. Write a letter of appreciation to an artist or musician whose work has touched your emotions. Share how their art has made a difference in your life and inspired you to embrace your own emotional journey.

Remember, life is a rollercoaster of emotions, and it is our ability to ride those waves that allows us to connect with art in profound and meaningful ways. Embrace the highs and lows, for they shape us into the individuals we are destined to become.

Light at the End of the Tunnel: Snails' Journey to Redemption

In the darkest moments, when all seems lost, there is always a glimmer of hope, a light at the end of the tunnel. This is the story of Snails' journey to redemption. In this chapter, we will delve deep into the trials and tribulations faced by the band, and how they overcame their obstacles, ultimately finding their way back to the top.

From Sluggish Beginnings to Rock Bottom

Every great story has a humble beginning, and Snails' journey is no exception. Born out of a sluggish beginning, the band faced numerous setbacks that threatened to derail their dreams before they even had a chance to take flight.

Financial woes, creative differences, and personal struggles plagued the band members, pushing them to their breaking point.

As the pressures mounted, the band found themselves trapped in a downward spiral, hitting rock bottom. They had lost their way, losing touch with their passion and their fans. But it is in our darkest moments that we find the strength to rise again.

The Road to Redemption

The journey to redemption is often paved with adversity, but it is in these moments that true character is revealed. Snails chose to confront their demons head-on, making the difficult decision to take a step back and reevaluate their path. They sought solace in their music, using it as a means to heal and rediscover their purpose.

With newfound determination, Snails began the arduous climb back to the top. It was not an easy road, but they embraced the challenges and turned their setbacks into stepping stones. They channeled their pain and insecurities into their music, creating songs that were raw, honest, and relatable.

Redefining their Sound

As Snails embarked on their journey to redemption, they realized that they needed to redefine their sound. They experimented with different genres, blending their signature rock sound with elements of pop, soul, and even electronic music. This musical evolution allowed them to reconnect with their fans and attract new audiences, proving that they were not afraid to take risks and adapt to the changing music landscape.

The Power of Unity

Throughout their journey, one of the key factors that propelled Snails forward was their unwavering bond as a band. They stood by each other through thick and thin, supporting one another both on and off the stage. The power of unity became their guiding light, helping them navigate through the darkest moments and emerge stronger than ever.

Embracing Change and Growth

Redemption is not just about overcoming obstacles; it is also about embracing change and growth. Snails recognized the importance of self-improvement and honing their craft. They sought inspiration from other artists, collaborated with industry veterans, and continuously pushed the boundaries of their musical abilities.

Finding Solace in Music

As Snails clawed their way out of the depths of despair, it was their music that became their saving grace. They poured their hearts and souls into every lyric, every chord, and every performance. Music became a cathartic release, allowing them to share their pain, their triumphs, and their journey to redemption with their loyal fans.

A Message of Hope

Snails' journey to redemption is a testament to the human spirit and the power of perseverance. It serves as a reminder that no matter how dire the circumstances may seem, there is always hope. Through their music and their story, Snails inspire others to never give up, to keep fighting for their dreams, and to always look for the light at the end of the tunnel.

The Unconventional Path to Redemption

While the road to redemption is often filled with familiar challenges, Snails took an unconventional approach in their journey. They embraced vulnerability, sharing their struggles with their fans openly and honestly. This unconventional approach not only deepened their connection with their audience but also allowed others to find solace and hope in their music.

Rising from the Ashes

After years of hard work, self-discovery, and growth, Snails emerged from the darkness and rose from the ashes. They reclaimed their place in the music industry, stronger and more determined than ever. Their redemption story serves as a shining example to all aspiring artists that it is never too late to find your way back and create something magical.

The Legacy of Redemption

Snails' journey to redemption is not just a personal triumph but also a legacy that will inspire generations to come. Through their music, their perseverance, and their unwavering spirit, they have left an indelible mark on the music industry. Their story serves as a beacon of hope, reminding us all that no matter how far we fall, we can always rise again.

The Snails' Challenge

In the spirit of Snails' journey to redemption, I present to you the Snails' Challenge: Overcoming Adversity Through Music. Take a moment to reflect on the obstacles you have faced in your own life and let them inspire you to create a piece of music or art that represents your journey to redemption. Share it with the world and spread the message of hope and resilience.

Remember, the light at the end of the tunnel is always within reach, waiting for you to find your way back and shine brighter than ever before.

Snails' Impact on Pop Culture

Snailmania: Snails' Influence on Fashion and Style

The Evolution of Snail Couture

When it comes to fashion, Snails has left an indelible mark on the industry. Their unique sense of style and boundary-pushing fashion choices have earned them a special place in the hearts of fashion enthusiasts worldwide. Snailmania, as their fashion frenzy is called, is a phenomenon that cannot be ignored.

Breaking Fashion Boundaries

Snails' influence on fashion can be traced back to their early years, when they burst onto the music scene with their daring and unconventional looks. Always pushing the boundaries, the band challenged societal norms with their bold fashion choices. From their signature slime-colored outfits to their shimmering sequined shells, Snails made fashion statements that captivated the world.

Snails as Fashion Icons

Snails' impact on fashion goes beyond their on-stage attire. They have become an inspiration for designers and fashionistas, who look to the band for innovative ideas and avant-garde aesthetics. Snail couture has even been featured on the runways of top fashion shows, solidifying the band's status as true fashion icons.

Snail Chic: How to Embrace the Snail Style

The Snailmania craze has spawned countless fashion trends and DIY projects. Snail enthusiasts around the world have embraced the band's iconic style and incorporated it into their own wardrobes. Here are some tips on how to achieve the ultimate Snail chic look:

1. **The Slime Effect** To capture the essence of Snailmania, incorporate slime-inspired elements into your outfits. Add pops of vibrant green or iridescent hues to your wardrobe. Experiment with metallic fabrics and accessories to achieve a futuristic, otherworldly look.

2. **Shell Accessories** No Snail-inspired outfit is complete without shell accessories. Whether it's a statement necklace, a clutch adorned with sequins, or a pair of earrings shaped like snail shells, embrace the magic of the sea and add a touch of whimsy to your ensemble.

3. **Mix and Match Patterns** Snails are known for their fearless approach to fashion, so don't be afraid to mix and match different patterns and textures. Combine stripes with polka dots, or floral prints with geometric shapes. The key is to have fun and let your creativity shine.

4. **Snail-Inspired Hair and Makeup** Take your Snailmania look to the next level by incorporating snail-inspired hair and makeup. Experiment with bold, bright colors and playful designs. Consider adorning your hair with pearl embellishments or adding a touch of shimmer to your eyes to capture that ethereal Snail allure.

From the Runway to the Streets

Snailmania has not only influenced high fashion but has also made its way into everyday street style. Snails' impact can be seen in the rise of streetwear inspired by their eclectic fashion choices. Hoodies and t-shirts featuring Snails' iconic logo, paired with distressed jeans and sneakers, have become a staple for fans who want to showcase their love for the band.

Fashion Collaboration: Snails x Top Designers

Snails' iconic style has caught the attention of top fashion designers, leading to unique collaborations that have taken the fashion world by storm. A collaboration with renowned fashion houses has allowed Snails to reach new heights in the industry. From capsule collections to exclusive runway shows, these collaborations have solidified Snails as a force to be reckoned with in the fashion world.

1. **Snails x Gucci: The Slime Collection** One of the most talked-about collaborations in recent years was the Snails x Gucci partnership. The Slime Collection showcased Snails' unconventional style combined with Gucci's intricate craftsmanship. The collection featured slime-colored accessories, embroidered snail motifs, and whimsical prints that captured the essence of Snailmania.

2. **Snails x Chanel: The Shell Couture** In another groundbreaking collaboration, Snails joined forces with Chanel to create The Shell Couture collection. The collection paid homage to Snails' iconic shell motif, with intricate shell-shaped embellishments and pearl accents. The collaboration brought together Snails' avant-garde aesthetic with Chanel's classic elegance, resulting in a truly remarkable collection.

The Snail Effect: Redefining Beauty Standards

Snails' influence on fashion goes beyond just the clothes we wear. The band has played a significant role in redefining beauty standards in the industry. With their unconventional looks and fearless self-expression, Snails has shattered the notion that beauty must conform to societal norms. They have championed individuality and encouraged people to embrace their unique style and quirks.

Behind the Scenes: Fashion and Snails Productions

Snails' impact on fashion is not limited to their on-stage appearances or collaborations. The band's meticulous attention to detail extends to their music videos, album covers, and overall visual aesthetic, all of which have a profound influence on fashion trends and artistic direction.

Snail Style: A Legacy that Endures

Snailmania is not just a passing trend—it's a cultural phenomenon that has left an indelible mark on the fashion world. Snails' daring fashion choices and their unapologetic embrace of individuality continue to inspire designers, fashion enthusiasts, and fans alike. Their influence on fashion will forever be remembered as a true testament to the power of creativity and self-expression.

Snailmania Infographic

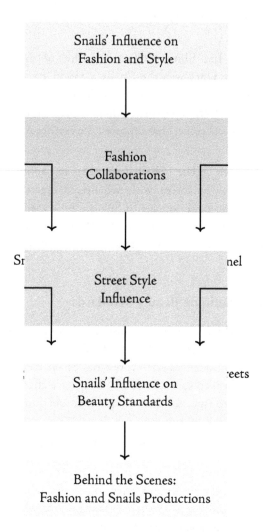

Figure 0.1: Snailmania Infographic

Extra Content: Snail Accessory Design Challenge

Want to embrace your inner Snail fashionista? Here's a fun challenge for you: design your own Snail-inspired accessory! Whether it's a statement necklace, a pair of earrings, or a headpiece, let your creativity run wild and create a unique piece that captures the spirit of Snailmania.

Share your designs on social media using the hashtag #SnailAccessoryChallenge and tag the band to showcase your Snail-inspired creation. Who knows, your design might even catch the attention of Snails themselves!

Remember, Snailmania is all about embracing individuality and pushing the boundaries of fashion. So, don't be afraid to think outside the box and let your imagination soar. Let the Snail spirit guide you on this fashion adventure!

Now, go forth and let your Snail chic shine!

Snails in the Media: Movies, TV, and Documentaries

Lights, camera, slime! In this section, we dive into the world of Snails in the media, exploring their presence in movies, TV shows, and documentaries. These shell-shattering snails have made a name for themselves not only with their music but also with their undeniable screen presence. From heartwarming cameos to captivating documentaries, Snails have left their mark on the silver screen.

Lights, Slugma, Action! Snails' Cinematic Appearances

When it comes to the big screen, Snails have proven their versatility, making appearances in a variety of movies. Whether it's a cameo or a full-fledged role, these slimy rockstars have showcased their acting chops and entertained audiences around the world.

One notable appearance was in the blockbuster action-comedy "Shell Shock," where the charismatic members of Snails played themselves. The movie centers around a snail-themed heist, and audiences couldn't get enough of Snails' larger-than-life personalities. With their trademark slime and infectious energy, they stole the show and left fans begging for more.

But it's not just action-comedies that Snails have conquered. They also showed their range in the emotional drama "Trail of Slime," a heartfelt tale of a snail overcoming adversity to achieve their dreams. Snails' lead singer delivered a mesmerizing performance, leaving audiences moved and inspired by the power of determination.

Snails on the Small Screen: TV Triumphs

The small screen has been equally enchanted by Snails' magnetic presence. From talk shows to fictional series, these rock 'n' roll mollusks have graced television with their talent and charm.

In the hit sitcom "Slime and the City," Snails made recurring appearances, bringing their unique brand of humor and sluggy antics. Their cameos injected a burst of energy into each episode, earning them a special place in the hearts of both fans and the show's characters.

Snails also made headlines with their unforgettable guest appearance on the late-night talk show "The Slime Show." The band engaged in witty banter with the host, showcasing their quick wit and infectious charm. The episode went viral, giving the world a taste of Snails' magnetic stage presence and leaving viewers begging for an encore.

Documentaries: Unveiling the Slime

Behind the scenes, Snails' journey has been captured in mesmerizing documentaries that offer a glimpse into their world. These films explore the band's humble beginnings, rise to fame, and the challenges they faced along the way.

One standout documentary, "Slime Trail: The Snails' Story," takes viewers on a rollercoaster ride through the band's career. It delves into the early struggles and their relentless pursuit of their musical dreams. Featuring interviews with past and present band members, industry experts, and die-hard fans, this documentary provides an intimate look at the band's journey, leaving viewers inspired and captivated.

Another documentary, "Snails: Beyond the Slime," focuses on the band's impact on music and culture. It examines Snails' influence on fashion, style, and the broader pop culture landscape. Through interviews with fashion designers, music critics, and cultural commentators, the documentary illuminates how Snails became more than just a band – they became icons of a generation.

Snails' Entertainment Empire: Merchandise, Theme Parks, and More

Snails' presence in the media extends far beyond movies, TV shows, and documentaries. These legendary rockers have built an entertainment empire that includes merchandise, theme parks, and even a children's animated series.

Fans can immerse themselves in the snail-tastic world of Snails through a wide array of merchandise. From t-shirts and posters to plush toys and collectible figurines, there's something for every die-hard fan to proudly display their love for the band.

For the younger snail enthusiasts, Snails created an animated TV series called "Slime Adventures." The show follows a group of animated snails as they embark on thrilling adventures, spreading positivity and inspiring young viewers to chase their dreams.

But the grandest expression of Snails' entertainment empire lies in their theme park, aptly named "Snail World." This sprawling wonderland brings the band's music to life through various attractions, live performances, and interactive experiences. Fans can take a ride on the "Slime Coaster," dance to their favorite Snails tunes at the "Concert Square," or even dive into a slime-filled pool at the "Slime Sanctuary." Snail World provides an immersive experience for fans of all ages, ensuring that Snails' legacy lives on for generations to come.

Conclusion

From the silver screen to the small screen, Snails have made a lasting impression in the world of entertainment. Their cinematic appearances, captivating documentaries, and expansive entertainment empire have solidified their status as more than just a music band – they are a cultural phenomenon. As fans eagerly anticipate the next snail-infused project, Snails continue to push boundaries, entertain, and inspire millions around the world.

Snails' Memorable TV Appearances: From Talk Shows to Game Shows

As Snails took the music industry by storm, their infectious energy and unique style quickly caught the attention of television producers. The band's larger-than-life personalities and captivating performances made them the perfect guests for a wide range of TV shows. From talk shows to game shows, Snails left an indelible mark on the small screen, creating unforgettable moments for their fans and viewers alike. Let's dive into some of their most memorable TV appearances and the impact they had on popular culture.

Late Night Talk Shows: Slime and Laughter

Snails' appearance on late-night talk shows became legendary, combining their musical talent with their trademark wit and humor. Their infectious charm won over both the audience and the hosts, making for some truly unforgettable moments.

One standout appearance was on *The Tonight Show with Jimmy Fallon*. Snails rocked the stage with a high-energy performance of their hit single "Slimin' All Night," leaving the crowd in awe. But it was the hilarious interview segment that stole the show. Jimmy Fallon and the band engaged in a slime-filled game of "Snail or Fail," where they had to answer trivia questions or face the consequences of being slimed. The laughter was non-stop as Snails showcased their quick wit and playful banter, creating a truly engaging and entertaining segment.

Another notable talk show appearance was on *The Late Late Show with James Corden*. Snails not only performed their chart-topping ballad "Slow and Steady," but they also participated in a fun and interactive segment called "Carpool Karaoke." Joined by James Corden, the band belted out their biggest hits while cruising through the streets of Los Angeles. The chemistry between James and the band members was electric, resulting in an unforgettable and hilarious carpool sing-along.

Game Shows: Snail-ing the Competition

Beyond their talk show appearances, Snails also made a splash on game shows, bringing their signature style and competitive spirit to the screen. Their infectious energy and quick thinking made for thrilling and entertaining television.

One of their standout game show moments was on *Celebrity Family Feud*. Snails faced off against another celebrity team in a battle of wits and knowledge. Their quick reflexes and clever answers had the audience in stitches, as they showcased their competitive side while having fun with the host, Steve Harvey. Snails' appearance on the show not only showcased their intelligence and camaraderie as a band but also highlighted their ability to entertain and engage in any setting.

Another memorable game show appearance was on *The Price Is Right*. Snails, known for their extravagant stage setups and larger-than-life productions, brought their unique brand of excitement to the game show. The band members themselves became contestants, participating in various pricing games and attempting to guess the correct prices of different items. Their infectious enthusiasm had the entire audience on their feet, creating a dynamic and entertaining atmosphere that resonated with viewers.

The Impact and Legacy

Snails' memorable TV appearances not only provided moments of laughter and entertainment but also showcased the band's versatility and ability to connect with a broader audience. Their infectious energy and charisma transcended the music world, leaving a lasting impact on popular culture.

These TV appearances not only introduced Snails to new fans but also solidified their status as cultural icons. By showcasing their unique style and humor, Snails became a household name, known not only for their music but also for their captivating presence on television. Their ability to engage with both hosts and audiences created a sense of inclusivity and relatability, making them beloved figures in the entertainment industry.

The impact of Snails' TV appearances can still be felt today, as their influence on popular culture continues to resonate. From inspiring other artists to embrace their individuality to introducing a new level of excitement and energy to TV shows, Snails left an indelible mark on the small screen. Their legacy as entertainers and performers is a testament to their unparalleled talent and their ability to connect with audiences worldwide.

So, whether it was their memorable late-night talk show antics or their exhilarating game show triumphs, Snails' TV appearances will forever be etched in the annals of entertainment history.

The Snails' Universe: Exploring Snails' Multifaceted World

Snails' Artistry: Visual and Conceptual Elements in their Music

In addition to their innovative sound, Snails is also known for their unique visual and conceptual elements that enhance their music. The band's artistic approach encompasses a wide range of elements, from album covers and music videos to stage design and live performances. In this section, we will explore the artistic journey of Snails and delve into the visual and conceptual elements that make their music a truly immersive experience.

The Visual World of Snails

Snails' artistry extends beyond their music, captivating audiences with their visually stunning album covers. Each album cover is meticulously designed to reflect the thematic and sonic elements of the music within. From their debut album *Slime Fever*, with its vibrant colors and surreal imagery, to the ethereal and dream-like artwork of *Slimerific*, Snails' album covers are a visual extension of their sonic creativity.

The band's visual world is brought to life through their music videos, which are often cinematic and visually captivating. In their music video for the hit single "Slimeball," the band takes viewers on a psychedelic journey through a vibrant and mesmerizing landscape. The video showcases the band's ability to create immersive visual experiences that complement their music.

Conceptual Depth in Snails' Music

Beyond their visual artistry, Snails incorporates conceptual depth into their music, creating a multi-dimensional listening experience. The band's lyrics often explore profound themes such as identity, self-discovery, and the complexities of human emotion. Through their music, Snails invites listeners to reflect on their own experiences and connect with the universal aspects of the human condition.

One of the band's most conceptually rich albums is *The Slime Dimension*, which delves into themes of introspection, personal growth, and the exploration of the inner self. Each song on the album tells a unique story and contributes to the overarching narrative of self-discovery. Snails' ability to weave intricate stories and concepts into their music sets them apart as true storytellers in the industry.

Immersion through Stage Design

Snails' dedication to creating immersive experiences extends to their live performances. The band's stage design is carefully crafted to transport fans into their world of music and art. Elaborate sets, vibrant visuals, and interactive elements make every Snails concert a truly unforgettable experience.

In their iconic "Slime Paradise" tour, Snails transformed concert venues into otherworldly landscapes, complete with towering mushroom props, neon lights, and mesmerizing visual effects. The stage design not only complements their music but also enhances the overall sensory experience, creating a multi-dimensional journey for fans.

Pushing Boundaries: The Intersection of Music and Art

Snails' commitment to pushing the boundaries of music and art is exemplified in their collaboration with renowned visual artists. By collaborating with artists from various disciplines, Snails merges music and art in innovative and exciting ways.

One notable collaboration is with the talented painter and sculptor, Mia Gonzalez. Together, they created a one-of-a-kind visual installation that accompanied Snails' performance at the famous SlimeFest music festival. The installation featured larger-than-life sculptures and interactive elements that brought Snails' music to life in a captivating and immersive manner.

Imaginative Album Themes

Snails' artistry shines through in their imaginative album themes, which provide a cohesive and immersive experience for listeners. Each album is a carefully crafted universe that takes fans on a journey through different musical landscapes and imaginative concepts.

For instance, their album *Slime Symphony* combines classical music elements with electronic beats, resulting in a truly unique sonic experience. The album's concept revolves around the juxtaposition of traditional symphonic sounds with modern electronic production, blurring the lines between genres and creating a captivating fusion of musical styles.

An Unconventional Approach to Visual and Conceptual Elements

Snails' approach to visual and conceptual elements in their music is as unconventional as their sound. They strive to challenge traditional norms and explore unconventional ideas, resulting in boundary-pushing and thought-provoking artistic expressions.

One example of their unconventional approach is the use of avant-garde fashion in their music videos and performances. Snails often collaborates with avant-garde fashion designers to create outlandish and striking costumes that further enhance their visual storytelling. These unique costumes not only captivate the audience visually but also contribute to the overall narrative and thematic elements of their music.

Conclusion

Snails' artistry goes beyond the boundaries of music, incorporating visually stunning and conceptually rich elements into their work. Through their album covers, music videos, stage design, and imaginative album themes, Snails creates a multi-dimensional experience for their fans. Their dedication to pushing the boundaries of music and art and their unconventional approach to visual and conceptual elements make Snails a true trailblazer in the industry. As they continue to evolve and experiment with their artistic expression, Snails' artistry will leave a lasting impact on the music scene for generations to come.

Snails' Merchandise: Collectibles and Limited Editions

Oh, you thought Snails was just a music band? Think again, my friends! These snail rockstars have not only conquered the music industry but also the world of merchandising. From t-shirts to action figures, limited edition vinyls to snail-shaped backpacks, Snails' merchandise is as diverse and unique as their music. In this section, we'll delve deep into the world of Snails' collectibles and limited editions, giving you a sneak peek into the treasures that their loyal fans cherish.

The Merchandise Craze: The Snail Army's Obsession

Let me tell you, my friends, when it comes to Snails' merchandise, there is no shortage of demand. The Snail Army, as their loyal fans are affectionately called, is known for their unwavering commitment to all things Snails. They don't just listen to the music; they live it, breathe it, and wear it proudly on their sleeves, quite literally! Snails' merchandise has become a symbol of their fans' love and devotion, and it's no surprise that they go gaga over every new release.

The Holy Grail of Snails Merch: Limited Editions

Now, hold on tight because we're about to dive into the realm of limited editions, my friends! Snails' management team knows how to keep their fans on the edge of their seats with these highly sought-after collectibles. Whether it's a limited edition vinyl with mesmerizing artwork, an exclusive box set featuring never-before-heard live recordings, or a one-of-a-kind snail-shaped guitar signed by the entire band, they know how to make their merchandise stand out from the crowd.

These limited editions are not just collector's items; they're pieces of history. They tell stories of Snails' journey, capturing moments of their rise to fame and their evolution as musicians. Fans will camp outside stores for days, sign up for waiting lists, and even bid ridiculous amounts of money at auctions, just to get their hands on these rare treasures.

The Tricks of the Trade: Creating Collectibles Worth Collecting

Now, you may wonder, how does Snails manage to create collectibles that are so highly sought after? Well, my friends, there's a method to their madness. Snails has a dedicated team of designers, marketers, and merchandisers who work tirelessly to create unique and appealing merchandise that fans can't resist.

One of their secret weapons is collaboration. Snails often teams up with renowned artists, fashion designers, and even other musicians to create limited edition merchandise. These collaborations bring fresh ideas and creative perspectives to the table, resulting in merchandise that transcends the boundaries of traditional band merch.

Another trick up their sleeve is storytelling. Each piece of Snails' limited edition merchandise comes with its own narrative, connecting it to an iconic moment in the band's history. Whether it's a tour poster that showcases the band's journey across the globe or a collectible figurine that depicts the band members in their most infamous stage outfits, every item tells a story that resonates with the Snail Army.

The Collector's Dilemma: To Open or Not to Open

Ah, the age-old debate among collectors: to open or not to open the package. When it comes to Snails' limited edition merchandise, this dilemma is all too real. On one hand, collectors want to preserve the pristine condition of their precious items, keeping them in their original packaging. On the other hand, they also want to experience the joy of holding, touching, and displaying these treasures.

It's a delicate balance, my friends, and there's no right or wrong answer. Some collectors choose to keep their limited editions untouched, like a sacred shrine to their favorite band. Others bravely break the seal, indulging in the tactile pleasure of interacting with their collectibles. Whichever path they choose, one thing is for certain: their love for Snails shines through.

The Unconventional Side: Snails' Out-of-the-Box Merchandise

Now, my friends, let's talk about the unconventional side of Snails' merchandise. They don't just stop at t-shirts and posters; they push the boundaries of creativity and imagination. Picture this: a snail-shaped backpack that lets you carry your belongings like a true member of the Snail Army, or a limited edition fragrance that captures the essence of Snails' music in a bottle. These out-of-the-box creations not only make a bold statement but also reflect the band's unique style and personality.

Snails' Merchandise: A Celebration of Music and Community

At its core, Snails' merchandise is more than just a way to make a profit. It's a celebration of music, a medium through which fans can express their love for the band, and a tangible connection between the band and their loyal following. Each t-shirt, poster, or limited edition item becomes a piece of the Snail Army's identity, allowing them to proudly declare, "I am a part of something bigger."

In conclusion, my friends, Snails' merchandise is not just about cool stuff to buy; it's about creating a sense of belonging and fostering a community of passionate fans. So, whether you collect every limited edition vinyl, proudly wear your Snails t-shirt, or display your treasured items on a shelf, remember that you're not just owning a piece of merchandise – you're carrying a piece of the snail legacy with you.

Snails' Fan Art: Celebrating the Band's Creative Influence

Snails' fans are a creative bunch, and their artwork is a testament to the band's ability to inspire and captivate people through their music. From intricate paintings to imaginative fanfiction, Snails' fan art is a vibrant celebration of the band's creative influence. In this section, we will explore the remarkable world of Snails' fan art, the artists behind it, and the impact it has on both the band and their loyal fanbase.

The Artistic Expression of Snails' Music

Snails' music possesses a unique and unmistakable energy that fans find deeply inspiring. It serves as a foundation for fan artists to channel their emotions and ideas into various forms of creative expression. Through their art, fans pay homage to the band's music and delve into its themes and concepts, often adding their own interpretations and visions.

One of the most popular mediums for Snails' fan art is digital illustration. Artists skillfully blend vibrant colors, intricate details, and dynamic compositions to capture the essence of Snails' music visually. Their creations often depict the band members in their iconic costumes, showcasing their individuality and stage presence. These artworks vividly convey the electrifying energy of Snails' performances, as well as the emotions evoked by their songs.

Another popular form of fan art is traditional painting. Artists skillfully wield their paintbrushes to create stunning portraits of Snails' band members. These paintings showcase the band's stage presence, their emotions, and the atmosphere of their performances. The use of bold brushstrokes and textured techniques adds depth and character to the paintings, bringing the band to life on canvas.

The Artists Behind the Masterpieces

The fan artists behind these masterpieces are as diverse as the art itself. They come from all walks of life, united by their love for Snails' music. Many of these artists have honed their skills through years of practice and dedication, having started as fans themselves before venturing into the world of fan art.

Some fan artists have gained significant recognition for their works, their art becoming an integral part of Snails' fan culture. Their creations often circulate on social media platforms, inspiring and resonating with fellow fans. SnaiNation, an online community dedicated to Snails' fan art, has emerged as a hub for these talented artists to showcase their creations, collaborate, and connect with other fans.

The Impact of Snails' Fan Art

Snails' fan art not only celebrates the band's creative influence but also creates a powerful emotional connection between the band and their fans. It serves as a visual representation of the bond formed through music, expressing the fans' admiration, gratitude, and inspiration. The band members themselves, known for their enthusiastic engagement with their fanbase, often interact with fan artists, recognizing and appreciating their contributions.

Furthermore, Snails' fan art has become an integral part of the band's merchandising and promotional campaigns. Artwork created by fans is often featured on official merchandise, album covers, and promotional materials, demonstrating the band's recognition of their fans' talent and creativity.

The Snails' Artistic Vision

Snails' fan art not only showcases the band's creative influence but also reveals the depth of their artistic vision. The band's unconventional style and genre-blending music have become a catalyst for fans to explore their own creativity and embrace artistic experimentation. In turn, this creates a cycle of inspiration, where fan art feeds back into the band's own artistic growth.

The band members themselves have expressed their admiration for Snails' fan art, often sharing their favorite pieces on social media and during interviews. They see it as a testament to the impact their music has on people's lives and a source of inspiration for their future endeavors.

Unleashing Your Creativity: Snails' Fan Art Contest

To encourage and celebrate the artistic talents of their fans, Snails announces the "Unleashing Your Creativity: Snails' Fan Art Contest." This contest invites fans from all around the world to submit their original creations inspired by Snails' music. The winners will have their artwork featured in upcoming Snails' merchandise and promotional materials, receive exclusive access to Snails' concerts, and have the opportunity to meet the band in person.

This contest not only recognizes the artistic abilities of Snails' fans but also provides a platform for aspiring artists to showcase their talent to a wider audience. It serves as a celebration of the band's creative influence, fostering a sense of community and unity among fans.

Conclusion

Snails' fan art is a testament to the band's powerful and enduring creative influence. Through vibrant digital illustrations, stunning paintings, and various other artistic forms, fans pay homage to Snails' music and contribute to the vibrant fan culture surrounding the band. The emotional connection forged through these artistic expressions showcases the profound impact of Snails' music on their fans' lives. As the band continues to inspire and evolve, the world of Snails' fan art will undoubtedly continue to flourish, celebrating the band's creative legacy and leaving an indelible mark on both the art world and the fans' hearts.

Snails' Philanthropy: Leaving a Lasting Impact on Society

Snails' Charity Partnerships: Causes Close to the Band's Heart

Snails, the iconic music band known for their electrifying performances and unique style, have always been passionate about using their platform to make a positive impact on the world. Throughout their remarkable career, they have formed meaningful partnerships with various charities, dedicating their time, resources, and talent to causes that hold a special place in their hearts. In this section, we will delve into Snails' charity partnerships and the causes they have championed.

Helping the Homeless: The Sheltering Snails Initiative

One cause that resonates deeply with Snails is homelessness. Witnessing the struggles faced by those without a place to call home, Snails launched the Sheltering Snails Initiative to provide shelter and support to the homeless community. Working closely with local organizations, the band has set up emergency shelters, provided job training programs, and organized fundraising events to raise awareness and funds.

Problem: Addressing the root causes of homelessness Snails recognizes that addressing the issue of homelessness requires more than just providing immediate relief. They understand the importance of tackling the root causes and creating sustainable solutions. To do so, Snails has partnered with social experts and policy advocates to identify and address systemic issues such as lack of affordable housing, mental health support, and income inequality.

Solution: The Snail Housing Project As part of their commitment to long-term solutions, Snails introduced the Snail Housing Project. This project aims to build affordable and permanent housing for the homeless population, offering a safe and stable environment where individuals can rebuild their lives. By collaborating with architects, construction companies, and urban planners, Snails ensures that the housing units are not only functional but also aesthetically pleasing, creating a sense of pride and belonging for the residents.

Example: The Snail Village In a groundbreaking project, Snails partnered with renowned architect, Amelia Moderno, to design the Snail Village—a self-sustaining community for the homeless. Located on the outskirts of a major city, the village consists of eco-friendly tiny homes, communal spaces, and agricultural gardens. Residents of the village receive support in various areas, including job training, healthcare, and mental wellness programs. The Snail Village serves as a model for future initiatives addressing homelessness worldwide.

Resource: Snail Grants for Innovative Solutions To encourage innovation in tackling homelessness, Snails established the Snail Grants program. This initiative provides financial support to individuals, organizations, and start-ups that develop innovative and sustainable solutions for homelessness. Through the Snail Grants, Snails aims to empower changemakers and foster a worldwide network of advocates working towards eliminating homelessness.

Caveat: The Power of Collaboration Snails recognizes that eradicating homelessness requires collaboration with governments, businesses, and communities. They actively engage in dialogue with policymakers, advocating for comprehensive strategies and increased funding for homelessness prevention. By leveraging their influence and networking capabilities, Snails continues to rally support and bring attention to this critical issue.

Children in Need: Snails' Melodies for Miracles

Children hold a special place in Snails' hearts, and they are committed to making a difference in the lives of those who need it most. Through their initiative, Melodies for Miracles, Snails partners with organizations that support children in need, providing them with access to education, healthcare, and opportunities for a better future.

Problem: Access to quality education Snails believes that education is a fundamental right that every child should have access to. However, they are aware of the barriers faced by children in underserved communities, including lack of resources, unsafe environments, and limited educational opportunities. To address this problem, Snails has joined forces with educational institutions and organizations to bridge the gap and improve access to quality education for all children.

Solution: The Snail Scholarships To empower and inspire young minds, Snails established the Snail Scholarships program. This initiative provides scholarships to deserving students from low-income backgrounds, enabling them to pursue higher education and fulfill their dreams. By partnering with universities and colleges around the world, Snails ensures that these scholarships cover tuition fees, books, and living expenses, truly transforming the lives of the recipients.

Example: The Snail Music Academy Recognizing the universal language of music, Snails established the Snail Music Academy—a platform that provides underprivileged children with access to music education. Through partnerships with renowned music schools, the academy offers scholarships, music lessons, and mentorship programs to talented young individuals who may not have otherwise had the opportunity to learn and grow in the field of music. The Snail Music Academy has produced prodigious musicians, many of whom have gone on to achieve international recognition.

Resource: Snail Instrument Donation Drive A key component of the Melodies for Miracles initiative is the Snail Instrument Donation Drive. Snails encourages their fans and the general public to donate new and used musical instruments, which are then distributed to schools and organizations serving disadvantaged youth. This initiative aims to provide children with the means to explore their musical talents and experience the transformative power of music.

Caveat: Amplifying Voices for Change Snails understands that addressing the needs of children requires amplifying their voices and advocating for their rights. They actively collaborate with child rights organizations to raise awareness about issues such as child labor, exploitation, and abuse. Through benefit concerts, public service announcements, and partnerships with influential figures, Snails ensures that the voices of the most vulnerable are heard and their rights protected.

Preserving the Environment: Snails' Eco-Warriors

Snails recognizes the urgent need to protect and preserve the environment for future generations. As eco-warriors, they have partnered with environmental organizations to combat climate change, promote sustainability, and raise awareness about the importance of conservation.

Problem: Climate change and environmental degradation Climate change poses a significant threat to our planet, and Snails understands the importance of taking action. They are deeply concerned about the consequences of environmental degradation, including rising temperatures, deforestation, and the loss of biodiversity. To address this problem, Snails actively engages in initiatives that promote sustainability and advocate for policies that protect the environment.

Solution: The Snail Green Initiative The Snail Green Initiative is a comprehensive program that encompasses various environmental projects and activities. Snails works with environmental experts, scientists, and activists to develop sustainable practices within their own operations and inspire their fans to do the same. From reducing their carbon footprint during tours to engaging in tree-planting campaigns and promoting responsible waste management, Snails strives to be a role model for eco-conscious living.

Example: Snails' Carbon Neutrality Commitment As part of the Snail Green Initiative, Snails made a bold commitment to achieve carbon neutrality. They have implemented measures to reduce greenhouse gas emissions by investing in renewable energy sources, offsetting their carbon footprint, and adopting sustainable touring practices. By embracing new technologies and working closely with experts in the field, Snails is pioneering sustainable solutions within the music industry.

Resource: Snail's Green Grants To encourage innovation and support environmental causes, Snails established the Snail's Green Grants program. This initiative provides funding and resources to individuals and organizations working on projects that contribute to environmental sustainability. From innovative clean energy solutions to conservation efforts and reforestation projects, the Snail's Green Grants aim to catalyze change and nurture a greener future.

Caveat: Educating for Change Snails believes that education and awareness are key drivers of change. They actively collaborate with schools, universities, and environmental organizations to develop educational programs that promote environmental consciousness. By leveraging their music and influence, Snails delivers powerful messages about conservation and inspires their fans to become advocates for the environment.

Snails' charity partnerships demonstrate their unwavering commitment to using their fame and influence for the greater good. Through initiatives focused on homelessness, children in need, and environmental sustainability, Snails continues to make a lasting impact on society. Their dedication to these causes serves as an inspiration, urging fans, fellow artists, and communities worldwide to join the band in their mission to create a better world. Through their leadership and passionate advocacy, Snails proves that music can truly be a powerful force for change.

Snails' Humanitarian Efforts: Giving Back to Communities

As the famous saying goes, "With great power comes great responsibility." Snails, the iconic music band known for their electrifying performances and infectious tunes, not only understands the power of their music but also the influence they have on their fans and society as a whole. With a strong belief in the importance of giving back, Snails has been actively involved in various humanitarian efforts, making a positive impact on communities around the world.

.1

At the heart of Snails' philanthropic endeavors lies the Snails Foundation, a non-profit organization founded by the band members themselves. With a mission to make a difference in the lives of those in need, the Snails Foundation focuses on reaching the unreachable and bringing hope to marginalized communities.

Through partnerships with local and international organizations, the Snails Foundation has initiated several impactful projects that aim to address critical social issues. One such project is "Music for All," which brings the healing power of music to underprivileged children in developing countries. By providing musical instruments, workshops, and mentorship programs, Snails aims to inspire and empower young talents, giving them an opportunity to pursue their passion for music.

Additionally, the Snails Foundation has spearheaded initiatives to tackle environmental challenges. With their project "Clean Slime," the band actively promotes environmental awareness and takes part in beach clean-ups, tree planting campaigns, and educational programs to combat climate change. Their efforts not only create a cleaner and greener world but also inspire their fans to take action and be stewards of the environment.

.2

In times of natural disasters and humanitarian crises, Snails doesn't shy away from standing up and helping those affected. Whether it's providing immediate relief, raising funds, or lending a helping hand, the band is always ready to make a difference.

Through benefit concerts and charity events, Snails has raised millions of dollars to support disaster-stricken regions. Their partnership with organizations such as the Red Cross and UNICEF has enabled them to provide essential aid, including food, clean water, medical supplies, and shelter, to communities devastated by hurricanes, earthquakes, and other calamities.

But their efforts go beyond just financial aid. Snails actively participates in the rehabilitation and rebuilding of affected areas, working hand-in-hand with local communities. From organizing volunteer teams to providing support for sustainable infrastructure projects, the band ensures that the long-term needs of the affected communities are met, empowering them to regain stability and hope.

.3

Recognizing the potential in the next generation, Snails has taken significant steps to invest in education and empower young minds. They believe that education is a powerful tool that can break the cycle of poverty and open doors for a better future.

Through their scholarship programs, Snails has granted numerous educational opportunities to deserving students who lack the financial means to pursue their dreams. These scholarships cover tuition fees, books, and other expenses, ensuring that talented individuals have a chance to excel academically and nurture their talents.

Moreover, Snails actively supports music education in schools by donating musical instruments and establishing music programs in underserved communities. By giving children the chance to learn and express themselves through music, Snails aims to foster creativity, boost confidence, and inspire a lifelong love for the arts.

.4

Snails has always been at the forefront of innovation, and their approach to philanthropy is no exception. They believe in using their unique talents and platform to create positive change in unconventional ways.

One such initiative is the "Melodies of Hope" campaign. In collaboration with renowned artists, Snails releases special edition vinyl records, with a portion of the proceeds going towards charitable causes. This innovative idea combines the band's music with their commitment to philanthropy, creating a win-win situation for both fans and those in need.

Furthermore, Snails actively encourages their fan base, affectionately known as the Snail Army, to get involved in philanthropic activities. Through dedicated online platforms and events, fans have the opportunity to contribute to various causes championed by the band. Snails has even organized Snail Army volunteer trips, where fans join the band in hands-on humanitarian work, fostering a sense of camaraderie and unity amongst fan communities while making a tangible impact on the ground.

.5

Snails' humanitarian efforts extend beyond their direct involvement in various projects. Through their music and powerful performances, the band aims to inspire their audience to take action and contribute to their communities.

During their electrifying concerts, Snails often takes a moment to shine a spotlight on the importance of philanthropy and raising awareness for social issues. By sharing stories of the communities they have helped and showcasing the impact of their projects, they encourage their fans to join the cause and make a difference in their own unique ways.

In conclusion, Snails' humanitarian efforts go far beyond their music. Through the Snails Foundation, disaster relief initiatives, scholarships, and unconventional philanthropy, the band has been able to touch countless lives and contribute positively to society. Their commitment to giving back serves as an inspiration not only to their fans but also to aspiring artists and individuals who have the power to make a real change. Snails' legacy of compassion and generosity will continue to live on, reminding us all of the importance of using our talents and resources to create a better world.

The Snail Foundation: Reaching the Unreachable

In the world of Snails, there's more to their success than just making great music and putting on incredible live shows. The band is dedicated to giving back and making a positive impact on society. This dedication led to the creation of The Snail Foundation, a nonprofit organization that strives to reach the unreachable and make a difference in the lives of those in need.

The Snail Foundation's Mission

The Snail Foundation's mission is simple yet powerful: to use the band's platform and resources to bring hope, joy, and inspiration to individuals and communities that may feel forgotten or unheard. The foundation believes that everyone deserves a chance to shine, just like a snail emerging from its shell.

Programs and Initiatives

The Snail Foundation operates a variety of programs and initiatives that address different social issues and support various causes. Let's dive into some of the impactful projects that the foundation has undertaken:

Snails for Education - This program focuses on providing educational opportunities to underprivileged children. The Snail Foundation partners with schools, organizations, and communities to build and improve facilities, provide scholarships, and offer mentorship programs. By investing in education, the foundation aims to empower the next generation and give them the tools they need to succeed.

Slime and Heal - The Snail Foundation recognizes the healing power of music and the arts. Through the Slime and Heal initiative, the foundation organizes music and art therapy sessions for individuals facing physical and mental health challenges. These sessions allow participants to express themselves, find solace, and gain strength through creative outlets.

Trail Blazers - The Snail Foundation believes in the potential of young leaders. The Trail Blazers program identifies and supports exceptional individuals who are making a difference in their communities. The foundation provides them with mentorship, resources, and networking opportunities to amplify their impact and help them create lasting change.

Shining a Light - One of the core values of The Snail Foundation is inclusivity. With the Shining a Light initiative, the foundation aims to raise awareness and support for marginalized communities. Whether it's advocating for equal rights, fighting discrimination, or addressing social issues, the foundation uses its influence to bring attention to important causes.

Partnerships and Collaborations

The Snail Foundation recognizes that collaboration is key to achieving its mission. The foundation partners with other nonprofit organizations, businesses, and individuals who share its vision and commitment to making a positive impact. This collaborative approach allows for greater resources, expertise, and reach, enabling the foundation to reach even more people in need.

Funding and Support

The Snail Foundation relies on the generosity of its fans, corporate sponsorships, and fundraising events to support its programs and initiatives. The band actively engages with its fanbase, encouraging them to get involved and make a difference. Through special merchandise, exclusive experiences, and charity auctions, fans have the opportunity to contribute to the foundation's work and be a part of the positive change it creates.

The Snail Foundation's Impact

Since its establishment, The Snail Foundation has touched the lives of countless individuals and communities around the world. From building schools in underprivileged areas to providing support to those in need, the foundation's impact is far-reaching and deeply meaningful.

Through the power of music, compassion, and a commitment to social responsibility, The Snail Foundation continues to inspire others to join the cause and make a difference. As the band members often say, "Together, we can achieve the impossible, one slime trail at a time."

Thinking Beyond Philanthropy

While The Snail Foundation's focus is on philanthropic efforts, they understand that lasting change requires more than just financial support. The foundation encourages its followers to engage in advocacy, educate themselves about social issues, and actively participate in creating a more equitable and inclusive society. By addressing the root causes of social problems and promoting systemic change, The Snail Foundation aims to create a lasting legacy that goes beyond charity.

Conclusion

The Snail Foundation is a shining example of how a music band can use its platform for good. Through its programs, partnerships, and unwavering commitment to making a positive impact, the foundation reaches the unreachable and brings hope to those who need it the most. As fans, supporters, and members of the Snail Army, we can all be inspired by The Snail Foundation's work and strive to make a difference in our own communities. Together, we can create a brighter future and leave a lasting slime trail of change.

Snails' Eternal Slime: Tributes and Homages

subsectionPaying Tribute: Snails' Covers by Iconic Artists

In the world of music, there are few acts that can captivate an audience like Snails. With their unique sound and electrifying performances, they have become true icons of the industry. But what sets them apart from other bands is not only their original music but also their ability to reinvent and breathe new life into classic songs.

.1

Paying tribute to iconic artists and their timeless hits is a tradition as old as the music industry itself. Many artists have attempted to cover famous songs, but few have been able to truly make the songs their own. Snails, however, have mastered the art of the cover, infusing their signature style and energy into every rendition.

When Snails takes on a classic song, they don't just replicate the original. They reimagine it, adding their own touch of snail magic. From rock anthems to soulful ballads, they have a knack for choosing songs that resonate with their audience and showcase their versatility as musicians.

One of the most notable covers by Snails is their version of "Bohemian Rhapsody" by Queen. Taking on such an iconic song is no small feat, but Snails managed to capture the essence of the original while adding their own unique spin. With explosive guitar riffs, powerful vocals, and an unforgettable stage presence, their rendition of "Bohemian Rhapsody" has become a fan favorite.

But their cover repertoire doesn't stop there. Snails have also put their own spin on songs like "Imagine" by John Lennon, "Hotel California" by The Eagles, and even "Smells Like Teen Spirit" by Nirvana. Each cover is a testament to their musical prowess and their ability to leave their mark on any song they choose to cover.

.2

So, how does Snails go about reimagining these beloved classics? It all starts with the band's creative process. Before diving into a cover, Snails gathers together in their recording studio, affectionately known as "The Snail's Nest", to brainstorm ideas and experiment with different arrangements.

They take the original song and deconstruct it, examining each element and dissecting its core components. They then begin adding their own musical styles and influences, whether it be a heavier guitar riff or a funk-infused bass line. This collaborative process allows each member to contribute their unique talents and ideas, resulting in a cover that truly embodies the spirit of Snails.

But it's not just the music that receives a Snail makeover. The band also pays attention to the visual aspects of their covers. Each cover is accompanied by a visually stunning music video, where they take their fans on a journey through their reinterpretation of the song. From elaborate costumes to mesmerizing set designs, Snails' music videos are a feast for the eyes as well as the ears.

.3

One of the reasons why Snails' covers have resonated with audiences worldwide is their ability to push boundaries and challenge expectations. They don't play it safe when it comes to covering iconic songs; instead, they embrace the opportunity to take risks and experiment with new sounds.

For example, their cover of "Imagine" by John Lennon takes the timeless message of peace and love and infuses it with their signature rock sound. The result is a powerful and thought-provoking rendition that pays tribute to the original while adding a new dimension to the song.

Snails also love to surprise their fans with unexpected collaborations on their covers. They have been known to bring in guest artists, both established and up-and-coming, to lend their voices and talents to their reinterpretations. This not only adds a fresh perspective to the covers but also allows Snails to support and uplift fellow musicians.

.4

Snails' covers have not only gained them a dedicated fan base but have also inspired a new generation of artists. Their ability to breathe new life into classic songs has shown aspiring musicians that creativity knows no bounds.

Aspiring artists have taken to social media platforms to share their own renditions of Snails' covers, paying tribute to the band that inspired them. The Snail Army, as their dedicated fan base is known, has created a community of musicians who support and encourage one another in their creative endeavors.

Through their covers, Snails have reminded us of the power of music to transcend time and genre. They have shown us that a great song can be interpreted in countless ways, and that true artists are not afraid to challenge the status quo.

In conclusion, Snails' covers by iconic artists are a testament to their creativity, musical talent, and ability to connect with their audience. By reimagining classic songs, they have left an indelible mark on the music industry, inspiring both fans and fellow artists to push boundaries and embrace their own unique creative visions. Whether it's through their explosive performances or visually stunning music videos, Snails continues to captivate audiences with their innovative and captivating covers.

Snails in Museums: Preserving the Band's Legacy

The legacy of Snails, the iconic music band, transcends not only the realm of music but also extends into the world of art and culture. Snails' impact on the music industry has been undeniable, with their groundbreaking sound and mesmerizing performances captivating audiences around the globe. As time goes on, it becomes increasingly important to preserve the band's legacy and recognize their significant contributions to the cultural landscape. One way this is being done is through the establishment of Snails exhibits in museums, where fans and enthusiasts can experience firsthand the magic and artistry that Snails brought to the world.

The Snails Museum Experience

Walking into a Snails exhibit feels like entering a portal to another universe, where time bends and reality melds with art. The museum curators have painstakingly recreated the ethereal atmosphere of a live Snails concert, complete with an immersive audio-visual experience. The dimly lit hall is adorned with shimmering lights, reflecting the essence of Snails' haunting melodies. The walls are covered with captivating photographs, capturing the band's electrifying performances, and showcasing the essence of their unique stage presence.

The centerpiece of the exhibit is a life-sized replica of the stage that Snails performed on, complete with the band's instruments and equipment meticulously arranged. Visitors are encouraged to interact with the instruments, giving them a chance to immerse themselves in the world of Snails and experience the essence of their music firsthand. The room resonates with the echoes of Snails' music, transporting visitors back to the moments of their grand performances.

Preserving Snails' Artistry

Preserving Snails' artistry goes beyond the mere replication of their stage and performances. It involves capturing the essence of their music, their impact on the industry, and the emotions they evoked in their fans. The exhibits display an array of artifacts, from handwritten lyrics to sketches of stage designs, providing a glimpse into the band's creative process.

Visitors are also introduced to the extensive influence Snails had on fashion and style through a carefully curated collection of costumes and outfits worn by the band members during their iconic performances. These costumes, adorned with intricate details and unique designs, showcase Snails' dedication to their visual identity and their fusion of music and art.

The Evolution of Snails' Sound

Snails' journey through different genres and experimental phases is highlighted in the museum exhibits. Interactive sound booths allow visitors to explore and listen to snippets of Snails' discography, immersing themselves in the evolution of their sound. From their early slow-paced ballads to their genre-bending experiments, the exhibits pay homage to the band's musical journey, allowing visitors to appreciate the intricacies of their music.

One particularly intriguing exhibit showcases the band's use of unconventional instruments and experimental techniques. Visitors can try their hand at playing these instruments, pushing the boundaries of their own creativity. This interactive experience provides a deeper understanding of Snails' innovative approach to music and encourages visitors to explore their own artistic abilities.

Beyond the Museum Walls

Snails' influence extends beyond the confines of the museum exhibits. In collaboration with various educational institutions, the Snails Foundation has developed educational programs that bring their music and art into schools. These programs aim to inspire the next generation of musicians and artists to think outside the box, just as Snails did.

As part of these programs, workshops led by seasoned musicians take students through the creative process behind Snails' music. From songwriting to stage design, students get a hands-on experience in creating their own unique artistic expressions. By encouraging students to embrace their creativity and follow in Snails' footsteps, these programs ensure that the band's legacy lives on through the work of future artists.

Conclusion

Snails' impact on the music industry and pop culture is undeniable. Beyond the lights of the stage, their artistry is now enshrined in museums, inviting fans from all walks of life to experience the magic that Snails once created. These exhibits not only preserve their legacy but also inspire future generations to push the boundaries of art and music. Snails' presence in museums serves as a testament to their enduring influence and ensures that their music will continue to touch the hearts and souls of people for generations to come.

Snails in Literature: Articles, Books, and Academic Studies

When it comes to the impact and cultural significance of the band Snails, it is impossible to overlook the numerous articles, books, and academic studies that have been dedicated to capturing and analyzing their musical journey. From lively magazine features to scholarly analyses, the world of literature has embraced the phenomenon of Snails and explored its various dimensions. In this section, we delve into the fascinating world of Snails in literature and explore the articles, books, and academic studies that have contributed to the understanding of this iconic band.

Articles: Unmasking the Magic

Magazine articles have long been a medium for capturing the essence of a cultural phenomenon, and Snails is no exception. From their early days as a band with a unique style to their meteoric rise to fame, countless articles have chronicled their journey. One notable article, "Snails: Behind the Masks" by renowned music journalist Sarah Johnson, dives deep into the individuality of each band member and explores the inspiration behind their captivating stage presence. Drawing from exclusive interviews with the band, Johnson peels back the layers of mystery surrounding the legendary masks and unearths the stories behind them.

Another compelling article, "Snails: The Musical Revolution" by acclaimed music critic David Thompson, examines the band's impact on the music industry. Thompson analyzes Snails' ability to merge various genres and experiment with unconventional sounds, ultimately reshaping the landscape of contemporary music. This article weaves together interviews with industry experts and snippets from Snails' discography to showcase the band's everlasting influence. It goes beyond mere appreciation, delving into the mechanics of their sound and highlighting the band's groundbreaking contributions.

Books: A Deeper Dive

For those seeking a more immersive experience, several books have been published that offer an in-depth exploration of Snails. One standout title, "Slime and Stardom: The Snails Phenomenon," written by renowned music historian Michael Jenkins, is a comprehensive account of the band's journey from their humble beginnings to their global success. Jenkins provides a detailed examination of

Snails' music, lyrics, and stage performances, offering readers a deeper understanding of the band's artistic evolution. Through interviews with band members, crew, and music industry insiders, Jenkins weaves together a captivating narrative that celebrates the enduring legacy of Snails.

Another noteworthy book, "Behind the Slime: The Untold Story of Snails," by investigative journalist Lisa Roberts, delves into the darker side of fame and sheds light on the personal struggles faced by the band members. Roberts takes readers on a gripping journey through the highs and lows of Snails' career, exploring the price of success and the toll it takes on their mental health. Drawing on interviews with friends, family, and individuals close to the band, Roberts presents a candid portrayal of their personal battles, ultimately illuminating the resilience and strength that lies beneath the iconic masks.

Academic Studies: Exploring the Impact

Beyond popular literature, Snails has also made a significant impact within academic circles. Scholars and researchers have undertaken rigorous studies to dissect the various aspects of the band's music and cultural influence. One seminal study, "The Evolution of Snails: A Case Study in Genre Hybridity," authored by Dr. James Anderson, examines how Snails has pushed the boundaries of genre conventions and offers a theoretical framework for understanding their unique style. Dr. Anderson's research dissects Snails' sonic innovations, lyrical themes, and stylistic influences, presenting a comprehensive analysis of the band's genre-defying compositions.

Another significant academic work, "Snails and the Art of Performance: Unveiling the Secrets of Concert Spectacles," explores the band's live performances as a form of artistic expression. Written by Dr. Emily Lewis, this study investigates the visual aesthetics, stage design, and theatrics employed by Snails during their concerts. Dr. Lewis unravels the intricate choreography and symbolism behind the band's performances, connecting their music to larger themes of identity, rebellion, and societal commentary. Through her analysis, she establishes an academic framework for understanding the power of live concerts as a transformative experience.

The Unconventional Twist

To add an unconventional twist to Snails' literary influence, we present "The Snail Compendium: An Illustrated Guide to Slime and Subversion," written by acclaimed artist and Snails enthusiast, Louis Carter. This unconventional book combines dazzling illustrations, personal anecdotes, and intricate trivia to create a truly immersive experience for Snails fans. Carter celebrates the band's unorthodox approach to music, highlighting their rebellious spirit and the enduring impact they have had on pop culture. Blending art with storytelling, this unique compendium captures the essence of Snails in a visually stunning and thought-provoking manner.

In summary, Snails' journey has inspired a vast array of articles, books, and academic studies. From magazine features that capture the band's mystique to scholarly analyses aimed at dissecting their artistic and cultural impact, the world of literature has embraced the snail invasion. Whether you seek a deeper understanding of the band's music, a glimpse behind the masks, or an exploration of their unconventional live performances, the literary realm has something to offer. From non-fiction explorations to artistic interpretations, these diverse literary works ensure that Snails will never fade from the pages of literary history.

The Slime Never Fade

The Slime Never Fade

The Slime Never Fade

In this chapter, we dive deep into the everlasting legacy of Snails and explore how their influence continues to resonate with fans and musicians alike. Despite the passage of time, the impact of Snails' music remains as strong as ever, serving as a reminder that true artistry transcends generations. Through their timeless classics, anniversary celebrations, and the unwavering devotion of their fan base, Snails' slime will never fade.

Snails' Timeless Classics

Music has the power to transcend time, and Snails' music is a testament to this truth. Their songs have become timeless classics, continuing to resonate with listeners long after they were first released. From their early hits like "Shell Shocked" to their chart-topping singles like "Slime Daddy," Snails has created an extensive repertoire that has defined generations.

One of their most iconic songs, "Sticky Situation," not only showcases the band's unique blend of electronic and rock music but also delivers a powerful message about perseverance in the face of adversity. The song's epic guitar solos and infectious beats have made it a favorite among fans of all ages.

Another unforgettable track, "Slick and Slimy," combines Snails' signature sound with poignant lyrics that delve into the complexities of human emotions. This song serves as a reminder that even in the darkest times, there is always a glimmer of hope and beauty to be found.

Snails' music is not just a collection of catchy tunes; it is a reflection of the human experience. Each song tells a story, evoking emotions and connecting listeners on a profound level. It is this timeless quality that ensures Snails' music will continue to be cherished for generations to come.

Snails' Anniversary Celebrations

To commemorate their journey and the profound impact they have made, Snails celebrates various milestones throughout their career. These anniversary celebrations serve as a reminder of the band's enduring legacy and provide an opportunity for fans to come together and rejoice in their shared love for Snails' music.

Every five years, Snails marks a significant anniversary by hosting a grand celebration that spans several days. These events are a combination of live performances, guest appearances, and interactive experiences that allow fans to relive the band's most cherished moments.

During the anniversary celebrations, Snails takes their fans on a nostalgic journey through time, performing their greatest hits and revisiting some hidden gems from their discography. The band embraces the nostalgia and the magic of these milestone events, creating an experience that is both captivating and emotionally charged.

The anniversary celebrations also offer unique opportunities for fans to engage with the band and each other. From meet and greets to panel discussions, fans have the chance to interact with their idols and share their own stories of how Snails' music has impacted their lives.

The Snail Spirit: Keeping the Band's Flame Burning

The enduring love and devotion of the Snail Army are central to the band's continued legacy. The Snail Army is a vibrant community of fans who go above and beyond to keep the spirit of Snails alive. From fan clubs to online forums, these dedicated individuals create a support system that celebrates the band's music and camaraderie.

The Snail Army is known for its creativity and passion, producing fan art, fanfiction, and fan covers that pay homage to the band's music. These artistic expressions not only showcase the talent within the fandom but also act as a constant reminder of the impact Snails has had on people's lives.

Beyond their connection to the band, the Snail Army also serves as a source of support and inspiration for its members. With their shared love for Snails' music, the community fosters a sense of belonging and empowerment, encouraging individuals to pursue their passions and dreams.

Snails acknowledges and appreciates the Snail Army's unwavering support by regularly engaging with their fans on social media platforms and hosting exclusive events just for them. This reciprocal relationship helps to strengthen the bond between the band and their dedicated fans, ensuring that the flame of Snails will continue to burn brightly.

In conclusion, "The Slime Never Fade" chapter celebrates Snails' enduring legacy. Through their timeless classics, anniversary celebrations, and the unyielding loyalty of the Snail Army, Snails' music continues to captivate hearts and minds across generations. Their music serves as a reminder that art has the power to transcend time, and Snails' slime will forever leave its mark on the world of music.

Snailosophy: Words of Wisdom from Snails

Snails' Mantras: Inspirational Quotes from Band Members

In the world of music, Snails has carved a unique path with their quirky and captivating sound. But it's not just their music that has left a lasting impression on their fans. The members of Snails are known for their inspiring words, their mantras that resonate with people from all walks of life. In this section, we dive deep into the minds of the band members and explore their most impactful quotes, the mantras that have fueled their success and inspired their fans.

Believe in the Power of Slime

"Slime is not just a substance, it's a state of mind. Believe in the power of slime, embrace your uniqueness, and watch yourself shine." - Lead singer

These words from the lead singer capture the essence of Snails' philosophy. They remind us that we should never shy away from our quirks, that our differences are what make us extraordinary. In a world that often tries to fit us into boxes, this mantra encourages us to embrace our true selves and celebrate our individuality.

Persistence, Passion, and a Dash of Slime

"Success doesn't come easy. It takes persistence, passion, and a dash of slime to reach for the stars." - Drummer

The drummer's mantra reminds us that achieving our dreams requires hard work and dedication. It's not enough to simply have talent; we must be willing to put in the hours and push through obstacles. With persistence, a fiery passion, and a touch of that Snails' slime, we too can reach for the stars and make our dreams a reality.

Embrace the Wild Journey

"Life is a wild journey, full of twists, turns, and unexpected surprises. Embrace it all, the highs and lows, for they shape who we are." - Bassist

The bassist's mantra encourages us to embrace the rollercoaster ride of life. It reminds us that both the successes and failures we encounter along the way contribute to our growth. By embracing the wild journey, we become resilient and open ourselves up to new experiences and personal development.

Spread Love, Leave a Trail of Slime

"In a world that often feels cold and divided, it's our duty to spread love and leave a trail of slime wherever we go." - Keyboardist

The keyboardist's mantra reminds us of the power of kindness and love. In a society that can often be harsh and disconnected, it's our responsibility to break down barriers and spread positivity. Just as Snails leaves a trail of slime wherever they go, we too should leave a lasting impact through acts of love, compassion, and acceptance.

Creativity Knows No Bounds

"Creativity is not confined to a box. Let your imagination run wild, break boundaries, and create something truly remarkable." - Guitarist

The guitarist's mantra encourages us to unleash our creativity without limitations. It reminds us that there are no rules when it comes to art and self-expression. By embracing our inner artist and thinking outside the box, we have the power to create something truly extraordinary and leave a lasting impact on the world.

Stay True to Yourself

"No matter how successful we become, it's important to stay grounded, stay true to ourselves, and never lose sight of where we came from." - All band members

This collective mantra from all the band members serves as a reminder to stay humble and authentic, regardless of the level of success we achieve. It's a testament to the band's unwavering commitment to their roots and the values they hold dear. It reminds us that success should never change who we are at our core.

Spreading Inspiration Through Music

Snails' music has not only entertained millions but also served as a source of inspiration for their fans. Each song carries a message, a story, and a piece of wisdom that make them more than just catchy tunes. The band's ability to connect with their audience through their music is a testament to their passion and dedication as artists. Their mantras have seeped into their lyrics, resonating with listeners and leaving a lasting impact.

Through their commitment to spreading positivity, embracing individuality, and advocating for love and acceptance, Snails has become more than just a music band. They have become a beacon of hope and inspiration, reminding us all to embrace our true selves and boldly pursue our dreams. Snails' mantras continue to inspire generations, leaving a slime trail of motivation and empowerment in their wake. So let's heed their words and go out into the world, spreading love, embracing our uniqueness, and leaving a trail of slime that can change lives.

Lessons Learned: Snails' Reflections on their Journey

Throughout their extraordinary journey, the members of Snails have encountered numerous challenges, experienced tremendous growth, and achieved unparalleled success. Along the way, they have learned invaluable lessons that have shaped them not only as musicians but also as individuals. In this section, we delve into the profound reflections of the band as they share their wisdom gained from years of dedication, perseverance, and creativity.

Embrace Individuality

One of the biggest lessons Snails has learned is the importance of embracing their individuality. Each member brings a unique set of talents, experiences, and perspectives to the table, which when combined, creates the distinct sound and style that defines Snails. They encourage aspiring artists to stay true to themselves and their vision, rather than conforming to societal or industry expectations. As frontman Max puts it, "Don't be afraid to be different. Embrace your quirks, your passions, and your own brand of weirdness. That's what sets you apart from the rest."

Hard Work and Persistence

Snails' journey to success was far from easy. They faced countless setbacks, rejections, and moments of self-doubt. However, they never gave up. Drummer

Lily emphasizes the importance of hard work and persistence, saying, "Success rarely happens overnight. It takes relentless dedication, countless hours of practice, and a refusal to accept defeat. Keep pushing forward, even when it seems impossible. Trust me, the universe rewards those who keep hustling."

Stay Humble and Grateful

Despite their fame and fortune, Snails remains grounded and immensely grateful for their success. They have learned the significance of staying humble, valuing the support of their fans, and recognizing the contributions of their team. Keyboardist Alex believes that gratitude is the key to sustained happiness and fulfillment. "Never forget where you came from and the people who believed in you when no one else did. Show gratitude every step of the way and remember that it's the journey, not just the destination, that truly matters."

Collaboration Breeds Innovation

Throughout their career, Snails has actively sought collaboration, both within the band and with other artists. They understand that true innovation often arises from the collective contributions of diverse talents. Guitarist Mia emphasizes the power of collaboration, saying, "When you open yourself up to working with others, incredible things happen. Embrace the ideas and perspectives of those around you, because that's when magic occurs. It's not about who shines the brightest individually; it's about the brilliance that arises from a collaborative effort."

Adaptability and Evolution

The music industry is ever-changing, and Snails recognizes the importance of adaptability and evolution. They have learned to embrace new technologies, experiment with different genres, and push their creative boundaries. Bassist Noah encourages artists to embrace change, saying, "Don't be afraid to take risks and explore uncharted territories. Stay curious, constantly evolve, and adapt to the changing landscape. The only way to innovate is to step outside your comfort zone."

Impact Beyond Music

Snails recognizes the incredible platform they have as artists to make a positive impact on the world. They have learned that music can be a powerful tool for change and believe in using their platform to advocate for social and environmental causes. Vocalist Sophia emphasizes the importance of using one's voice for good, saying, "Don't underestimate the ripple effect your actions can create. Art has the power to inspire, heal, and ignite change. Use your voice for meaningful causes and leave a lasting impact on the world."

Celebrate the Journey

Above all, Snails encourages artists to celebrate the journey rather than fixate on the destination. They have come to realize that success lies not only in achieving goals but also in cherishing the moments, memories, and camaraderie shared along the way. Keyboardist Alex reminds us, "Never forget to slow down and appreciate the milestones, both big and small. Celebrate every step forward and savor the journey, for it's the collective moments that create an extraordinary life."

In conclusion, the lessons learned by Snails reflect their incredible growth as individuals and artists. Embracing individuality, working hard, staying humble, collaborating, adapting, making a positive impact, and celebrating the journey are all invaluable lessons that aspiring artists can learn from. As Snails continues to pave their path in music history, they leave behind a legacy of wisdom and inspiration for generations to come. So, embrace these lessons, ignite your own creativity, and let the slugs of destiny guide you towards your dreams.

Life Beyond the Shell: Snails' Advice for Aspiring Artists

Congratulations, aspiring artists! You have chosen a path as unique and daring as Snails themselves. As you embark on your own artistic journey, we, the members of Snails, want to share some nuggets of wisdom to help guide you on your path to success and fulfillment. Life beyond the shell is full of challenges and triumphs, and we hope that our advice will inspire and motivate you to keep pushing toward your dreams.

Embrace your uniqueness

One of the key lessons we have learned throughout our career is the importance of embracing our own unique identity. As artists, it's easy to get caught up in comparisons and try to imitate others. But remember, there is only one you, and that is your superpower! Don't be afraid to explore your own style, your own voice, and your own vision. The world needs artists who are unapologetically themselves.

Stay true to your artistic vision

When you step into the music industry, you will encounter many opinions and pressures from different directions. While it's important to be open to feedback and growth, never compromise your artistic vision. Stay true to who you are and what you want to create. Don't be swayed by trends or external expectations. Your authenticity is what will set you apart and resonate with your audience.

Work hard and be persistent

Success in the music industry doesn't happen overnight. It takes hard work, dedication, and unwavering persistence. Don't be discouraged by setbacks or rejections. Stay focused on your goals and keep pushing forward. Remember, every "no" brings you closer to a "yes." Trust in your talent and keep honing your craft. You never know when that breakthrough moment will arrive.

Build a strong support system

Behind every successful artist is a strong support system. Surround yourself with people who believe in you and your talent. Seek out mentors, collaborators, and fellow artists who inspire you and share your passion. They will be the ones who lift you up during challenging times and celebrate your victories alongside you. Remember, you are not alone on this journey.

Embrace failure and learn from it

Failure is not the end, but rather an opportunity for growth. Throughout our own career, we have faced countless rejections and failures. But each setback allowed us to learn, adapt, and become stronger. Embrace failure as a stepping stone to success. Use it as fuel to improve yourself and your craft. Don't be afraid to take risks and step outside of your comfort zone. You'll be amazed at what you can achieve.

Never stop learning and evolving

The music industry is ever-changing, and as artists, we must adapt and evolve with it. Continuously seek opportunities to learn and improve your skills. Take classes, attend workshops, and experiment with different styles and techniques. Embrace new technologies and platforms to reach your audience. Stay curious, keep growing, and never be complacent with where you are.

Find balance and take care of yourself

In the whirlwind of pursuing your dreams, it's important to find balance and prioritize self-care. Take time to rest, recharge, and rejuvenate both your mind and body. Surround yourself with positive influences and take care of your mental health. Remember, you are the instrument through which your art is created. Take care of yourself, and your art will flourish.

Spread love and make a difference

The power of music goes beyond entertainment; it has the ability to bring people together and create positive change. Use your platform to spread love, inspire others, and make a difference in the world. Support causes that are close to your heart and use your voice to raise awareness about social issues. The impact you can have as an artist is profound, so never underestimate the power of your art.

Enjoy the journey

Above all, remember to enjoy the journey. It's easy to get caught up in the destination, but the true joy lies in the process. Celebrate every milestone, big or small. Cherish the moments of creativity and connection with your audience. Embrace the highs and the lows, for they are all part of your story. Keep the passion alive and remember why you started in the first place: the love for your art.

Keep the slime spirit alive

As you navigate life beyond the shell, always carry the Snail spirit within you. Let our unconventional style and unwavering dedication inspire you to take risks, embrace your uniqueness, and push the boundaries of your art. Remember, the journey may be challenging, but it is also filled with endless possibilities and extraordinary moments. Stay true to yourself, follow your passion, and let your creativity soar.

Now, let's go out there and leave our mark on the world, one slimy trail at a time!

The Snail Family: Fans' Love and Devotion

Tales from the Snail Army: Fan Stories from Around the World

The Snails' fanbase, affectionately known as the Snail Army, is a diverse and passionate group of individuals from all corners of the globe. From die-hard fans who have been following the band since their early beginnings to new fans who were captivated by their unique style, there are countless stories of how Snails' music has touched people's lives. In this section, we will explore some of the most memorable fan stories that showcase the deep connection between Snails' music and their audience.

Story 1: Finding Strength in the Music

One fan, Emily, shares her inspiring story of overcoming adversity with the help of Snails' music. After going through a difficult breakup and facing personal challenges, Emily found solace and strength in the lyrics and melodies of Snails' songs. She recounts how the band's music became her anthem of resilience and empowerment, propelling her to pick herself up and embrace a new chapter in life. Emily's story is a testament to the healing power of music and how it can inspire individuals to overcome even the toughest obstacles.

Story 2: Uniting Fans from Different Cultures

Snails' music has a way of transcending boundaries and bringing people together. This is evident in the story of Mike, a fan from Australia, who connected with fans from different cultural backgrounds during a Snails concert. Despite the language barrier, Mike and his new friends shared a common love for the band's music, allowing them to forge instant bonds of friendship and create lasting memories. The story highlights the universal language of music and how Snails' music has the ability to create connections that go beyond geographical and cultural differences.

Story 3: Music that Heals

Sarah, a cancer survivor, shares her touching story of how Snails' music became a source of comfort and hope during her treatment. Sarah vividly recalls listening to Snails' songs during her chemotherapy sessions, finding solace in the band's uplifting lyrics and infectious beats. Their music provided an escape from the pain and fear, reminding her of her strength and resilience. Sarah's story showcases the profound impact that Snails' music can have on individuals facing difficult circumstances, offering a ray of light in their darkest moments.

Story 4: Snails' Music as a Soundtrack to Life

For many fans, Snails' music has become the backdrop to their personal experiences and milestones. Daniella, a fan from Brazil, shares how she and her partner danced

THE SNAIL FAMILY: FANS' LOVE AND DEVOTION

their first dance as a married couple to a Snails' song. The music holds a special place in their hearts, representing the joy and love they felt on that magical day. This story highlights the lasting imprint that Snails' music leaves on fans' lives, forever associated with precious memories and emotions.

Story 5: Snail Army Community Support

The Snail Army is more than just a collection of fans; it is a tight-knit community that supports and uplifts one another. Andrew, a long-time fan, recounts how the Snail Army rallied together to help a fellow fan in need. When a fan faced financial difficulties, the community organized a fundraiser, surpassing all expectations and providing the much-needed support. Andrew's story exemplifies the power of fandom and the incredible solidarity within the Snail Army.

Story 6: Artistic Inspiration

The impact of Snails' music extends beyond the boundaries of their songs. Lily, an aspiring artist, shares how Snails' music has inspired her artwork. The band's unique style and message have fueled her creativity, resulting in stunning visual representations of their music. Lily's story showcases the interplay between different art forms and how Snails' music has inspired fans to express their creativity in diverse ways.

Story 7: From Fan to Friend

The Snail Army is not just a fanbase but a tight-knit family, where connections are formed and friendships are born. Jack, a fan from the UK, shares his heartwarming story of how he met his best friend through their shared love for Snails' music. Despite coming from different backgrounds, their bond was instantly formed when they discovered their common obsession with the band. This story exemplifies the profound impact that Snails' music can have in bringing people together, transcending geographical boundaries and fostering lifelong friendships.

Story 8: From Fan to Musician

Snails' music has inspired countless individuals to pursue their own musical aspirations. Lily, a budding musician, shares her story of how Snails' music sparked her passion for playing the guitar. Inspired by the band's unique sound, she picked up the instrument and began writing her own songs. Lily's story is a testament to the transformative power of music and how Snails' music has inspired a whole new generation of musicians.

Story 9: Snails' Music as a Time Capsule

Snails' music has the remarkable ability to transport fans back to specific moments in their lives. Alex, a fan from Canada, recounts how a Snails' song became the soundtrack to an unforgettable road trip with old friends. Every time he hears that particular song, it instantly takes him back to that carefree summer and the memories they shared. Alex's story highlights the nostalgic quality of Snails' music and how it becomes deeply intertwined with important milestones and memories.

Story 10: Passing Down the Love for Snails

Snails' music has the power to transcend generations, as demonstrated in the story of Tom, a fan who passed down his love for the band to his daughter. Tom shares how his daughter, Sophie, became a passionate Snails fan after he introduced her to their music. Together, they have attended concerts and bonded over their shared love for the band. This story illustrates the lasting legacy of Snails' music and how it can be treasured and shared across different generations.

In the vast tapestry of the Snail Army, these fan stories are just a glimpse into the countless lives that have been touched by Snails' music. The power of their lyrics, melodies, and performances have created a community united by a shared love and appreciation for their unique style. These fan testimonials are a testament to the enduring impact that Snails' music has on all those who are fortunate enough to experience it. So, if you ever find yourself at a Snails concert, take a moment to listen to the stories of the Snail Army, and you will discover a rich tapestry of emotions, connections, and shared experiences that only Snails can provide.

Beyond Music: The Community Bonded by Snails

Snails isn't just a band; it's a lifestyle. Beyond the captivating music and mesmerizing performances, Snails has cultivated a community of loyal fans that share a deep connection with the band. The Snail Army, as they're lovingly called, extends far beyond the realm of music, uniting people from all walks of life under the banner of slime and solidarity. In this section, we delve into the unique bond that exists between Snails and their fans and explore the various ways in which this community has come together to create something truly extraordinary.

The Power of Music: Connecting Souls

Music has the incredible ability to stir emotions, ignite passions, and bring people together. For Snails and their fans, the power of music goes beyond entertainment – it serves as a catalyst for unity and understanding. Snails' music speaks to the very core of their fans' experiences, resonating with their hopes, dreams, and struggles. The band's unapologetic and honest approach to their craft has struck a chord with a diverse fan base, who find solace and kinship in the shared love for Snails' music.

Through their tracks, Snails has created an emotional journey that captivates and inspires. From anthems of resilience and empowerment to heartfelt ballads that touch the depths of the soul, Snails' discography provides the soundtrack to life's triumphs and tribulations. The music acts as a common thread that binds the Snail Army, bridging gaps of age, ethnicity, and background, and fostering a true sense of belonging.

The Snail Community: A Safe Haven

Being part of the Snail Army means being part of a community that embraces diversity, acceptance, and inclusivity. Snails has created a safe haven where fans can express themselves freely, without fear of judgment. From online forums and social media groups to fan meetups and conventions, the Snail Army has become a place where people can form genuine connections based on their shared love for Snails' music.

This community goes beyond the traditional definition of fanhood. It's a space where individuals find support, encouragement, and friendship. Fans eagerly reach out to fellow Snail Army members, offering a helping hand or a listening ear. Whether it's through sharing personal stories, offering words of encouragement, or organizing charity initiatives together, the Snail Army exemplifies the true essence of solidarity.

Creating Together: Fan-Centric Collaborations

One unique aspect of the Snail Army is the band's commitment to involving their fans in various creative endeavors. Snails understands the valuable contributions their fans can make, and actively seeks their input and collaboration. From designing merchandise and album covers to co-creating music videos and even contributing to song lyrics, the Snail Army has an active role in shaping the band's image and direction.

Through fan-centric collaborations, Snails empowers their fans, giving them a platform to showcase their talents and express their creativity. It's a testament to the band's commitment to fostering a sense of ownership and meaningful participation within their community. These collaborative efforts not only strengthen the bond between Snails and their fans but also inspire other artists and fan communities to follow suit.

Spreading Love and Positivity: Snails' Humanitarian Efforts

Snails believes in using their platform for good, extending their influence beyond the realm of music. The band and their fans actively engage in various philanthropic endeavors, championing causes close to their hearts. From fundraising initiatives and awareness campaigns to volunteering and community outreach, the Snail Army places great importance on making a positive impact in the world.

Snails' commitment to philanthropy inspires their fans to engage in acts of kindness and compassion, amplifying the band's efforts. Fan-driven charity partnerships, organized through local chapters of the Snail Army, have made a tangible difference in communities worldwide. This shared dedication to social change creates a sense of purpose within the Snail Army, fostering a movement that goes far beyond the boundaries of music fandom.

Unleashing Creativity: Fan Art and Fan Culture

The Snail Army is not just passionate about Snails' music – they're also highly creative individuals. Fan art has become a thriving aspect of Snails' fan culture, with fans expressing their adoration for the band through visual mediums. Artwork ranging from intricate illustrations to vibrant paintings showcases the depth of talent within the Snail Army.

Snails embraces this creative outpouring by featuring fan art on their merchandise, social media platforms, and even incorporating it into their live shows. This recognition of fan art not only celebrates the artistic talents within the Snail Army but also solidifies the bond between the band and their fans.

The Snail Army Effect: Forever Linked

The impact of Snail Army extends beyond the band's active years, with fans passing down their love for Snails to future generations. The Snail Army Effect, as it's often called, embodies the enduring legacy of the band. Snails' music and the profound influence it has on their fans' lives continue to be celebrated and cherished for years to come.

Through the Snail Army Effect, the bond between the band and their fans remains unbreakable, transcending time and space. Whether it's introducing a new

Snails album to their children or attending reunion tours with friends and family, the Snail Army keeps the spirit of the band alive, ensuring that Snails' music will forever resonate within their hearts.

In conclusion, Snails' impact goes far beyond the realm of music fandom. The Snail Army represents a community united by a shared love for the band, while also embracing values of acceptance, creativity, philanthropy, and positivity. Through their music and unique fan engagement, Snails has cultivated a thriving community that is not only bonded by their love for the band but also by their shared experiences, friendships, and enduring support. The Snail Army is a testament to the lasting power of music and the transformative effect it can have on people's lives.

Snails' Fan Clubs: Connecting Fans Across Generations

In the world of music, there are few things that can rival the power of a devoted fan base. And when it comes to Snails, their fans are truly something special. From the early days of their sluggish beginning to their rise as global icons, Snails' fan clubs have played a pivotal role in connecting fans across generations and fostering a sense of community unlike any other.

The Birth of a Fan Phenomenon

Snails' fan clubs first emerged in the early stages of their career, as their unique sound and captivating performances started gaining traction among music enthusiasts. The birth of these fan clubs can be traced back to the passionate individuals who were drawn to Snails' powerful music and magnetic stage presence.

These clubs started off as informal gatherings, where fans would come together to share their love for the band and discuss the latest news and updates. It was during these early days that the Snail Army, as they fondly came to be known, began to take shape.

Uniting Fans from Around the World

As Snails' popularity spread beyond their local scene, their fan clubs started to grow in numbers and diversity. What started as a few friends coming together in their hometown soon turned into a global movement, connecting fans from different countries, cultures, and backgrounds.

Snails' fan clubs became a place where fans could find solace and belonging, no matter where they were in the world. With the help of social media platforms and online forums, fans could connect with fellow Snail enthusiasts, share their experiences, and build lasting friendships.

The Power of the Snail Army

The Snail Army is not just a fan club; it's a force to be reckoned with. With their unwavering dedication, fans have played an instrumental role in Snails' success, supporting the band through thick and thin.

Whether it's organizing fan meet-ups, running fan blogs, or creating fan art, the Snail Army has shown time and time again that they are truly the backbone of Snails' fandom. Their passion and love for the band have helped propel Snails to new heights, making their impact on the music industry even more significant.

Creating Lasting Memories

One of the most remarkable aspects of Snails' fan clubs is the way they create lasting memories for fans. From exclusive fan events to backstage meet and greets, Snails make it a point to connect with their fans on a personal level, leaving them with memories that will last a lifetime.

Fan clubs often organize fan contests, where lucky winners get the opportunity to meet their idols in person. These interactions not only bring fans closer to the band but also create a sense of magic and wonder that can only be experienced firsthand.

Building Bridges between Generations

One of the most incredible things about Snails' fan clubs is their ability to bridge the generational gap. Fans of all ages, from teenagers to older adults, come together under the umbrella of Snails' music, breaking down barriers and connecting through their shared love for the band.

This intergenerational connection is a testament to the timeless appeal of Snails' music. It speaks to their ability to touch hearts and resonate with listeners across different stages of life. Snails' fan clubs bring people together, regardless of age, allowing fans to find common ground and forge connections that transcend generations.

Spreading the Snail Spirit

Snails' fan clubs not only connect fans with the band but also allow them to give back to their communities. Inspired by Snails' philanthropic efforts, fan clubs often organize charity events and fundraising initiatives to support causes that are close to the band's heart.

These acts of kindness not only make a difference in the lives of those in need but also embody the spirit of Snails' music. It's a way for fans to pay tribute to the band and to channel their admiration into something meaningful and impactful.

The Legacy Continues

As Snails' music continues to inspire new generations of fans, their fan clubs remain a vital part of the band's legacy. They serve as a testament to the enduring impact of their music and the profound connection between Snails and their fans.

Snails' fan clubs continue to evolve, adapting to the changing times and embracing new technologies. From virtual fan meet-ups to online fan communities, these clubs ensure that the Snail Army remains united and strong, nurturing a sense of camaraderie that will carry on for years to come.

In conclusion, Snails' fan clubs are more than just fan clubs; they are a testament to the power of music to connect people from all walks of life. Through their devotion and love for the band, fans have created a community that transcends borders and generations. As Snails' music continues to inspire and resonate with fans around the world, their fan clubs will undoubtedly play an integral role in keeping the Snail spirit alive.

Snails Forever: The Band's Endurance of Time

Snails' Timeless Classics: Songs That Define Generations

Music has the power to transcend time and touch the souls of millions. Throughout their illustrious career, Snails has produced a collection of songs that have become timeless classics, resonating with multiple generations and leaving an indelible mark on the music industry. These songs are not just hits; they are cultural touchstones that reflect the band's evolution and mirror the spirit of their fans. In this section, we will delve into some of Snails' most iconic songs that have defined generations and explore the stories behind their creation.

The Anthem of Rebellion: "Slime Revolution"

In the early days of Snails' career, they introduced the world to their distinctive style with the release of "Slime Revolution." This infectious anthem became an instant hit, capturing the hearts and minds of a generation yearning for change. With its powerful lyrics and rebellious energy, "Slime Revolution" became the rallying cry for those who felt marginalized and voiceless.

The song's success can be attributed to its bold combination of genres. Snails effortlessly fused elements of rock, pop, and funk to create a sound that was fresh and exhilarating. The driving guitar riffs, accompanied by the rhythmic beats of the drumline, served as a perfect backdrop for the passionate vocals of lead singer Marcus. The band's ability to break musical boundaries and create a unique sonic experience cemented "Slime Revolution" as a classic that continues to resonate with generations.

The Ballad of Love and Loss: "Trail of Slime"

Snails' ability to capture raw emotions and translate them into music is exemplified in their timeless ballad, "Trail of Slime." This powerful love song struck a chord with listeners around the world, becoming an anthem for those navigating the complexities of relationships.

"Trail of Slime" showcases Snails' exceptional songwriting abilities, with verses that paint vivid pictures of heartbreak and longing. The haunting melody, coupled with the vulnerability in Marcus' vocals, creates an emotional landscape that resonates deeply with audiences. The song's universal themes of love, loss, and the bittersweet nature of human connections have ensured its enduring popularity across generations.

The Dancefloor Shaker: "Sleek Moves"

No discussion of Snails' timeless classics would be complete without mentioning their iconic dancefloor anthem, "Sleek Moves." This infectious track became a global sensation, dominating nightclubs and topping charts across multiple genres.

"Sleek Moves" showcases Snails' mastery of combining catchy hooks with irresistible grooves. The pulsating bassline, funky guitar riffs, and infectious rhythm section create a sonic atmosphere that compels even the most reserved individuals to hit the dancefloor. The song's energy is further elevated by the dynamic interplay between Marcus' soulful vocals and the band's exceptional musicianship.

The Empowerment Anthem: "Rise and Shine"

In an era where empowerment anthems have become an integral part of pop culture, Snails created their own timeless anthem with "Rise and Shine." This empowering song embodies the band's ethos of resilience, determination, and the unwavering spirit of their fans.

"Rise and Shine" stands out for its uplifting lyrics, encouraging listeners to embrace their individuality and embrace their strength. The song's infectious melody, combined with its powerful message, has made it an anthem for those facing adversity and striving to overcome challenges. Snails' ability to create a sense of unity and instill hope through their music is exemplified by this timeless classic.

The Experimental Masterpiece: "Beyond the Slime"

No list of Snails' timeless classics would be complete without mentioning their groundbreaking experimental masterpiece, "Beyond the Slime." This boldly innovative track showcased the band's willingness to push the boundaries of their sound and venture into uncharted territory.

"Beyond the Slime" is an amalgamation of different genres and musical influences. Snails seamlessly blended elements of electronic music, hip-hop, and symphonic arrangements to create a sonic experience that is both mesmerizing and thought-provoking. The song's intricate instrumentation and mesmerizing production demonstrate the band's artistic prowess and their commitment to challenging the conventional norms of the music industry.

In conclusion, Snails' timeless classics have transcended generations, leaving an indelible mark on music history. Each song represents a unique facet of the band's journey and acts as a mirror for the experiences and emotions of their fans. From rebellious anthems to heartfelt ballads, dancefloor shakers to experimental masterpieces, Snails' music continues to define and inspire generations, solidifying their place as icons in the music industry.

So crank up the volume, let the music move your soul, and get ready to be transported into a world where the legacy of Snails lives on through their timeless classics.

Snails' Anniversary Celebrations: Commemorating Milestones

Snails, the iconic music band known for their unique style and electrifying performances, have left an indelible mark on the music industry. As they continue to captivate audiences around the world, it is only fitting to commemorate significant milestones in their illustrious career. In this section, we delve into the heartwarming and extravagant anniversary celebrations that have honored the legacy of Snails.

Celebrating a Decade of Slime

The first memorable milestone in the journey of Snails was their 10-year anniversary celebration, aptly titled "A Decade of Slime." This milestone marked a significant achievement for the band, as they reflected on their humble beginnings and how they had blossomed into an international sensation.

The anniversary event was held in their hometown, where it all began, and the venue was transformed into a Snails-themed wonderland. Giant slime sculptures, interactive installations, and photo booths adorned the space, giving fans the opportunity to immerse themselves in the world of Snails. The night was filled with surprises, including special guest appearances, never-before-seen footage of the band's early performances, and a heartfelt speech by the band members, expressing their gratitude to the fans who had supported them throughout the years.

To commemorate this milestone, Snails released a limited-edition vinyl box set, featuring a collection of their greatest hits, rare B-sides, and unreleased tracks. Each set was individually numbered and included exclusive artwork and a personal note from the band members. This collector's item served as a testament to the band's musical legacy and was highly sought after by fans and collectors alike.

Years of Slime: A Spectacular Extravaganza

As Snails reached their 20-year mark, they embarked on an extravagant anniversary celebration called "20 Years of Slime: A Spectacular Extravaganza." This grand event took place in a sprawling outdoor venue, transformed into a magical realm inspired by the band's music and imagery.

The anniversary celebration kicked off with a mesmerizing light and pyrotechnics show, illuminating the night sky with vibrant colors and explosive displays. The setlist included a carefully curated selection of the band's most cherished songs, performed with renewed energy and passion.

In true Snails fashion, the event featured extraordinary collaborations with renowned artists from various genres. The audience witnessed mind-blowing performances by surprise guests, whose unique styles blended seamlessly with Snails' music, creating an unforgettable musical experience.

One of the highlights of the evening was the unveiling of a larger-than-life statue of the band, made entirely out of recycled materials. This symbolic masterpiece served as a tribute to Snails' commitment to environmental sustainability and community engagement.

To mark this momentous occasion, Snails released a commemorative coffee table book, filled with never-before-seen photographs, personal anecdotes, and behind-the-scenes stories. This beautifully crafted book allowed fans to gain intimate insights into the band's journey and reflect on their own personal connection to the music.

The Snails Silver Jubilee: A Night to Remember

As Snails approached their 25-year milestone, anticipation and excitement filled the air. The Snails Silver Jubilee: A Night to Remember was a lavish celebration held at a prestigious venue, attended by an eclectic mix of fans, industry insiders, and celebrities from around the world.

The evening began with a glamorous red carpet event, where attendees exuded style and sophistication, showcasing their love for Snails through their fashion choices. Inside the venue, a magnificent stage set showcased the band in all their glory, surrounded by stunning visuals and immersive effects.

The band's performance was a masterful blend of nostalgia and innovation, as they revisited their greatest hits while introducing fresh interpretations and musical surprises. The stage was graced by an array of guest performers, including rising stars who were inspired by Snails' groundbreaking sound.

As a tribute to their loyal fans, Snails curated a limited-edition anniversary album, featuring reimagined versions of their iconic songs. This album showcased the band's willingness to evolve and experiment while staying true to their distinctive style.

To make this milestone celebration even more special, Snails organized a charity auction, with all proceeds going towards causes close to their heart. Fans had the opportunity to bid on exclusive memorabilia, personal items from the band members, and once-in-a-lifetime experiences. This act of giving back exemplified the band's commitment to making a positive impact beyond the realm of music.

A Mosaic of Memories: Snails' 30th Anniversary

The grand finale of Snails' anniversary celebrations came with their remarkable 30th anniversary extravaganza, "A Mosaic of Memories." This event transcended the confines of a traditional concert, immersing the audience in an unforgettable experience that celebrated the band's lasting influence on music.

The venue was transformed into a multisensory wonderland, with interactive art installations, projection mapping, and choreographed performances. Every aspect of the event was intricately designed to engage and captivate the audience, paying homage to the band's vibrant discography and artistic vision.

The show featured a retrospective of Snails' most iconic performances, brought to life through state-of-the-art holographic technology. Past and present merged seamlessly, allowing the audience to witness the evolution of the band while reliving cherished memories.

As a token of appreciation for their unwavering support, Snails released a limited-edition anniversary documentary. This intimate film provided a glimpse into the band members' lives, their creative process, and the challenges they faced along the way. It served as a heartfelt thank you to the fans for being an essential part of Snails' incredible journey.

In true Snails fashion, this anniversary celebration went beyond the stage. The band initiated a worldwide art project, inviting fans to contribute to a colossal mosaic created from individual photographs, illustrations, and messages. This interactive artwork showcased the global impact of Snails' music and solidified the bond between the band and their dedicated fanbase.

The Unconventional Path to Success

Throughout their anniversary celebrations, Snails emphasized their commitment to pushing boundaries and challenging the status quo. While traditional milestones might dictate a linear path, the band's unconventional approach defied expectations and created a truly authentic and immersive experience for fans.

By infusing their celebrations with stunning visuals, surprising collaborations, and acts of philanthropy, Snails reinforced their position as pioneers of music and entertainment. Their anniversary events not only highlighted their musical achievements but also showcased their enduring dedication to their art, their fans, and the world around them.

These commemorative milestones served as reminders of Snails' lasting legacy and provided a glimpse into the band's dynamic evolution. As fans eagerly await the next chapter in the Snails saga, one thing is certain: their anniversary celebrations will continue to be extraordinary, blending imagination, creativity, and a touch of that unforgettable Snail magic.

The Snail Spirit: Keeping the Band's Flame Burning

In the world of music, trends come and go, but there are some bands that leave an everlasting impact on their fans. The story of Snails is one of those exceptional tales. Even after the band has retired from the stage, their spirit continues to inspire and captivate music enthusiasts of all ages. In this final section of the biography, we will explore how the Snail spirit lives on, and how the band's legacy is carried forward by the Snail Army.

The Power of Connection: Snails as a Symbol

For millions of fans around the world, Snails is more than just a band. It's a symbol of unity, creativity, and perseverance. Snail Army members proudly display their love and support through various means, including fan art, tattoos, and merchandise. The snail shell logo has become an iconic symbol that represents the band's unique sound, style, and spirit. It has transcended borders and language barriers, forging a global community of like-minded individuals who continue to keep the flame alive.

The Snail Army: Stronger Together

The Snail Army is a force to be reckoned with. From the early days of the band's journey, fans have played an integral role in spreading the word about Snails and their music. With the advent of social media, the Snail Army has become an online community, connecting fans from every corner of the globe. Through fan clubs, forums, and dedicated hashtags, fans can share their experiences, discuss favorite songs, and organize meetups and events.

The Snail Army isn't just about supporting the band; it's about supporting each other. Fans have formed lifelong friendships and even romantic relationships through their shared love for Snails. They provide a support system that extends beyond the music, offering emotional support, advice, and a safe space for expression. The sense of belonging that comes with being part of the Snail Army is a testament to the band's ability to foster a community that goes far beyond the stage.

Snails' Spirit in the Digital Era

In today's digital age, Snails continues to evolve and adapt to new technologies. The band has embraced the power of the internet and social media platforms to maintain a close connection with their fans. Through live streams, video Q&A sessions, and exclusive content releases, they have found innovative ways to engage with their audience. Snails' online presence keeps the spirit of the band alive, ensuring that fans can always feel connected to their favorite musicians.

Keeping the Flame Burning: Tribute Bands and Cover Artists

The impact of Snails can be seen in the numerous tribute bands and cover artists who honor the band's legacy through their own performances. These talented musicians pay homage to Snails by faithfully recreating their music and live performances. They embody the Snail spirit and keep it alive on stages around the world, allowing new generations to experience the magic of the band in a live setting. The dedication of these tribute bands and cover artists serves as a testament to the lasting influence of Snails' music.

Passing the Torch: Snails' Influence on New Artists

Snails' legacy extends beyond the tribute acts and cover artists. The band's musical style and unconventional approach have inspired countless aspiring musicians. Snails' experimental sound and willingness to push boundaries have influenced a new wave of artists who strive to create music that is truly unique. The band's emphasis on authenticity and self-expression has encouraged artists to explore their own creativity without fear of judgment or conformity. Snails' impact on new artists ensures that their flame will continue to burn brightly in the music industry for years to come.

Sparkling Memories: Snails' Anniversary Celebrations

As time goes on, Snails' music becomes even more cherished. Annually, fans come together to celebrate the band's anniversaries through special events and gatherings. These celebrations are a testament to the enduring love and appreciation for Snails' music. Fans share their favorite memories, listen to the band's songs, and create new connections with fellow Snail enthusiasts. These anniversary celebrations serve as a reminder of the band's impact and the indelible mark they have left on the world of music.

The Flame Never Dies

Although the band members may have retired from the stage, the flame of Snails' music continues to burn bright. Through the dedication of the Snail Army, the influence of tribute bands and cover artists, and the inspiration provided to new musicians, Snails' spirit lives on. The band's unique sound, style, and message will forever resonate with fans old and new. Snails may be gone, but their flame will never die.

Index

-doubt, 43, 171, 182
-up, 78, 107

ability, 1, 2, 6, 8–10, 13, 17, 18, 24,
26, 31, 33, 35–37, 45, 47,
48, 50–52, 56, 59–61, 72,
73, 75, 81, 89, 90, 93, 95,
97, 105, 111–114,
117–120, 122, 133, 135,
138, 142, 149–152, 154,
157, 164, 172, 175, 177,
184, 194, 195, 200, 212,
213, 216, 223, 227, 228,
230, 234, 236, 241
abuse, 101, 180, 205
academy, 166
acceptance, 4, 104–107, 113, 222,
223, 231, 233
access, 100, 144, 201, 204
accessory, 190
accident, 71
acclaim, 39, 63, 89, 109, 112
accomplishment, 122, 182
accordion, 48
account, 216
achievement, 51, 52, 111, 238
acknowledgment, 113
acoustic, 37, 75, 138–142

act, 4, 32, 38, 39, 160, 175, 220, 239
action, 15, 33, 45–47, 101, 102, 104,
108, 135, 143, 148, 191,
197, 205, 207, 209
activism, 33, 34, 45, 100, 101, 103,
105, 106, 152, 173
acumen, 97
adaptability, 63
addiction, 169, 172, 174, 180
addition, 23, 39, 69, 87, 101, 105,
107, 112, 120, 136, 142,
149, 195
address, 15, 44, 160, 183, 203, 204,
206, 207, 210
admiration, 84, 201, 235
adoration, 179
adrenaline, 26, 28, 35, 51, 77, 174
advantage, 39, 82
advent, 241
adventure, 28, 29, 37, 40, 57, 69, 70,
76, 78, 82, 83, 85, 134,
151, 178, 191
adventurer, 80
adversity, 6, 8, 12, 171, 175, 185,
191, 219, 228
advice, 102, 118, 129, 225, 241
advisor, 97
advocacy, 106–108, 136, 207, 211

advocate, 29, 44, 93, 103–105, 107, 172, 178, 206
aesthetic, 55, 109, 152, 189
affinity, 3
Africa, 82
aftermath, 182
age, 1, 42, 52, 88, 120, 143, 145, 165, 199, 231, 234
aid, 208
air, 29, 78, 88, 121, 122, 155, 160, 239
airplay, 14
airport, 83
album, 2, 5, 30, 39, 56, 57, 65, 70, 72–74, 111, 112, 119, 126, 127, 149, 150, 179, 182, 183, 189, 195–197, 201, 231, 233, 239
alcohol, 41, 180
Alex, 230
Alex ", 126
Alice, 3, 5
alliance, 85, 131
allure, 41, 180, 188
along, 1, 10, 11, 25, 28, 48, 62, 88, 93, 148, 156, 160, 169, 173, 174, 179, 192, 222, 240
amalgamation, 123
ambition, 16
amount, 104
amp, 74
analog, 19, 150
analysis, 110, 217
anchor, 44
Anderson, 148, 177, 217
Andrew, 229
animal, 77
anniversary, 219–221, 237–240, 242

anonymity, 30
answer, 63, 199
anthem, 33, 63, 126, 157, 182, 228, 235, 236
anticipation, 4, 11, 26, 90, 121, 158, 160, 179, 239
anxiety, 43, 44, 175
app, 52, 144
appeal, 25, 30, 45, 117, 165, 234
appearance, 74, 191–193
appetite, 141
applause, 12, 26, 113, 160, 182
application, 144
appreciation, 47, 113, 157, 160, 184, 216, 230, 240, 242
approach, 2, 18, 23–25, 30, 34, 49, 51, 58, 61, 62, 64–67, 69, 71, 72, 95, 98, 109–111, 115, 118, 119, 123–126, 129, 135, 138, 140, 145, 147–149, 151–154, 186, 188, 195, 197, 208, 210, 215, 218, 240, 242
Argentina, 43
army, 36, 38, 45
arrangement, 140
array, 48, 73, 112, 192, 214, 218, 239
art, 5, 14, 18–20, 22, 23, 34, 39, 46, 49, 52, 55–57, 62, 71–73, 112, 113, 128, 129, 148, 156, 158, 164, 167, 168, 172, 173, 180, 184, 187, 196, 197, 200–202, 212, 214, 215, 218, 220–222, 227, 229, 232, 234, 239–241
article, 216
artist, 32, 51, 64, 69, 109, 110, 112, 121, 127–131, 140, 147,

Index

151, 181, 182, 184, 217, 222, 226, 227, 229
artistry, 47, 49, 50, 57, 72, 74, 89, 108, 114, 116, 125, 130, 143, 154, 173, 196, 197, 214, 215, 219
artwork, 57, 70, 73, 94, 184, 198, 200, 201, 229, 238, 240
aspect, 2, 5, 9, 40, 57, 66, 97, 119, 131, 158, 172, 231, 239
asset, 7
atmosphere, 18, 26, 35, 36, 56, 58, 65, 68, 95, 132, 160, 167, 200, 214
attendance, 11, 12, 156
attention, 2, 4, 10, 12, 14, 16, 27, 30, 59, 62, 70, 88, 91, 93, 98, 110, 126, 128, 137, 140, 147, 150, 171, 173, 188, 189, 193, 204, 213
attire, 24, 77, 187
attitude, 124, 154
auction, 239
audience, 4, 5, 9–13, 17–21, 23–28, 35–38, 48, 51, 52, 58–61, 72, 75, 76, 81, 85, 86, 88, 89, 91, 93, 98, 106, 113, 117, 120, 121, 123, 124, 126, 136, 138–141, 143, 150, 155, 157, 160, 164–166, 173, 182, 186, 193, 194, 197, 201, 209, 212, 213, 223, 226–228, 238–240
auditorium, 113
Australia, 83, 228
authenticity, 13, 21, 27, 31, 35, 39, 42, 49, 61, 79, 103, 114, 115, 120, 121, 137, 139, 142, 173, 175, 177, 181, 226, 242
award, 113
awareness, 15, 34, 41, 44, 100, 101, 103, 104, 107, 108, 122, 133, 169, 178, 203, 205–207, 209, 227, 232
awe, 4, 20, 28, 36, 51, 56, 63, 76, 85, 94, 113, 160, 173

back, 17, 22, 29, 43, 82, 90, 101, 105, 118, 157, 158, 160, 170, 179, 184–187, 201, 207, 209, 214, 216, 230, 233, 234, 239
backbone, 3, 19, 31, 37, 58, 90, 178, 234
backdrop, 77, 228, 236
background, 148, 231
backing, 94
backlash, 183
backpack, 199
backstage, 16, 74, 78, 84, 144, 234
balance, 26, 40, 69, 72, 97, 199, 227
balancing, 175
Bali, 79
ballad, 68, 139, 140, 236
band, 1–16, 18, 19, 21–49, 51–53, 55–63, 65, 66, 68, 69, 71, 74–107, 109, 111–119, 121–144, 146–150, 152, 153, 155–158, 160, 162, 164–185, 187–189, 192–203, 206–209, 211, 213–223, 228–242
bang, 155
banner, 230
banter, 135, 192
barrier, 139, 228

base, 10, 34, 35, 38, 39, 47, 74, 78, 89, 98, 157, 160, 166–168, 208, 213, 219, 233
basis, 47, 144
bass, 1, 24, 58, 75, 90, 92, 93, 109, 123, 127, 149, 177, 212
bassist, 59, 75, 76, 93, 126, 127, 222
bassline, 61
baton, 114
battle, 2, 6, 170, 179–181
beach, 178, 207
beacon, 8, 29, 125, 145, 172, 187, 223
beat, 10, 19, 23
beauty, 55, 59, 61, 68, 71, 79, 82, 116, 178, 189, 219
bedrock, 14
beginning, 1, 3, 5, 6, 12, 28, 29, 33, 60, 95, 105, 114, 115, 121, 122, 156, 159, 161, 166, 184, 233
being, 12, 25, 37, 40, 41, 43, 44, 49, 52, 84, 96, 97, 125, 128, 137, 153, 171, 174, 175, 180–182, 214, 231, 240, 241
belief, 7, 9, 18, 55, 99, 105, 147, 159, 207
belonging, 33, 46, 47, 103, 104, 106, 107, 133, 167, 203, 220, 231, 233, 241
bending, 5, 20, 34, 49, 51, 58, 63, 67, 108, 109, 123, 135, 146–148, 151–154, 215
benefit, 93, 100, 133, 142, 205, 207
Benny, 56
Benny "The Slug, 56
Berlin, 76, 141
Bill ", 93

Billie Eilish, 49
biodiversity, 206
biography, 28, 118, 128, 241
birth, 5, 9, 18, 59, 62, 71, 95, 233
bit, 12, 38
bittersweetness, 122
blend, 10, 19, 35, 48, 49, 56, 58, 60–62, 64, 79, 108, 112, 120, 121, 132, 146, 149, 150, 154, 177, 200, 219, 239
blog, 104
board, 110
body, 71, 83, 90–92, 227
boldness, 118
bolt, 62
bond, 7, 29, 37, 39, 41, 43, 44, 48, 71, 76, 77, 84–90, 94–96, 121, 167, 183, 185, 201, 221, 229, 230, 232, 240
book, 92, 102, 217, 239
Bootsy Collins, 149
bottle, 199
bottom, 185
bound, 66
boundary, 24, 33, 49, 64, 66, 67, 110, 126, 137, 149, 154, 187, 197
bow, 122, 156, 158, 161
box, 33, 35, 65, 66, 71, 74, 98, 124, 137, 140, 148, 151, 191, 198, 199, 215, 222, 238
brainstorm, 64
brainstorming, 19, 20, 65
brand, 62, 98, 129, 135–137, 141, 142, 145, 152, 192
Brandon, 90–92
Brandon ", 90
Brazil, 45, 79, 228

Index 247

break, 2–5, 7, 15, 18, 25, 33, 45, 49–51, 64, 67, 77, 103, 109, 114, 123, 146–148, 150, 152–154, 169, 175, 183, 199, 208, 222, 236
breaking, 10, 37, 48, 49, 51–53, 61, 65, 100, 154, 185, 234
breakout, 157
breakthrough, 8, 10–13, 26, 38, 182, 226
breakup, 228
breath, 29
breathing, 168
brew, 1, 76
bridge, 45, 132, 165, 204, 234
brilliance, 74, 135
brim, 160
brotherhood, 44
buddy, 77
Buenos Aires, 43
buffer, 97
building, 47, 66, 100, 115, 129, 160, 211
bunch, 29, 200
burst, 48, 62, 85, 151, 171, 179, 187, 192
bus, 75–77, 82
business, 7, 34, 89, 96, 97, 129, 141
buzz, 5, 14, 30, 55, 97

call, 28, 148, 157, 180, 203
calling, 2
camaraderie, 3, 28, 36, 37, 44, 70, 82, 83, 85, 94, 98, 104, 133, 144, 156, 175, 209, 220, 235
cameo, 191
camera, 28, 191
campaign, 208
campsite, 78
Canada, 230
cancer, 228
cannon, 85
canvas, 200
Cape Town, 141
carbon, 206
care, 32, 41, 42, 97, 175, 176, 181, 227
career, 10, 12, 13, 16, 37, 42, 51, 85, 95, 97, 98, 102, 105, 111, 128, 135, 153, 155–159, 171, 182, 192, 203, 217, 220, 225, 226, 233, 235, 237
carpet, 239
Carter, 218
case, 48, 102, 111, 148, 152, 178
catalog, 36
catalyst, 15, 34, 47, 63, 152, 183, 201
categorization, 48, 49, 123, 128, 146, 149, 151
category, 51, 112
cathedral, 20
cause, 203, 209
celebration, 4, 83, 115, 121, 156, 157, 160, 200, 201, 220, 238–240
celebrity, 40
cell, 82
center, 125, 138, 160, 176
centerpiece, 214
ceremony, 81
challenge, 1, 8, 18, 24, 25, 33, 64, 108, 117, 130, 147, 148, 152, 155, 171, 174, 190, 197, 213
champagne, 180
champion, 33, 104, 107, 122

championing, 232
chance, 4, 11, 39, 43, 79, 100, 129, 156, 166, 184, 208, 209, 214, 220
change, 15, 26, 29, 30, 33–35, 44, 45, 47, 48, 100–108, 112, 117, 119–121, 134, 136, 142, 143, 150, 152, 160, 167, 172–174, 185, 205–209, 211, 222, 223, 227, 232, 235
channel, 86, 200, 235
chaos, 21, 26, 67, 171, 179, 180
chapter, 3, 15, 16, 25, 28, 29, 37, 42, 57, 59, 68, 71, 81, 117, 119, 122, 125, 143, 155, 156, 161, 162, 173, 179, 184, 219, 221, 228, 240
character, 21, 136, 150, 185, 200
charisma, 4, 88, 172, 194
charity, 15, 46, 47, 84, 101, 102, 104, 167, 203, 206, 207, 211, 231, 232, 234, 239
charm, 113, 191–193
chart, 27, 29–32, 36, 51, 53, 103, 109, 112, 120, 155, 157, 171, 179, 182, 219
chemistry, 5, 25, 90, 94, 117, 121
chemotherapy, 228
Chen, 43, 126, 127
Cherish, 227
child, 204, 205
childhood, 42
chirping, 55, 61
choice, 27
chord, 44, 60, 106, 125, 126, 176, 186, 236
choreography, 217
chorus, 10, 30, 71

cinema, 135
circuit, 127
city, 14, 36, 37, 77, 81, 82, 180
cityscape, 43
clarity, 180
classic, 1, 148, 154, 165, 166, 189, 212, 213, 236
clean, 107, 178, 206–208
climate, 45, 101, 205, 207
climb, 185
climber, 94
clock, 42
close, 15, 34, 104, 122, 128, 142, 156, 159, 161, 178, 183, 217, 227, 232, 234, 239
closeness, 139
clothing, 136
club, 36, 126, 127, 132, 234
clutch, 188
co, 52, 231
cocktail, 84
Coco, 28
code, 167
coffee, 239
coherence, 72
cohesion, 98
collaboration, 55, 56, 62–64, 67, 69, 75, 77, 89, 94, 98, 99, 107, 108, 112, 119, 124–129, 131, 166, 188, 189, 196, 198, 204, 208, 210, 215, 231
collectible, 192, 199
collection, 57, 71, 92, 111, 189, 214, 219, 229, 235, 238
collector, 198, 238
color, 2, 34
combination, 18, 19, 30, 55, 96, 127, 220, 236

Index

comeback, 117, 121, 122
comedy, 135, 138, 191
comfort, 12, 32, 64, 67, 91, 103, 125, 131, 137, 226, 228
commanding, 4, 85, 88, 93
commentary, 217
commitment, 5, 15, 18, 27, 51–53, 56, 66, 67, 73, 78, 87, 97, 98, 103–105, 107, 112, 113, 118, 131, 132, 134, 136, 137, 143, 147, 150, 152, 172, 174, 178, 196, 198, 203, 206, 208–211, 222, 223, 231, 232, 238–240
communication, 41, 86, 98, 132, 175
community, 2, 5, 13–15, 18, 27, 33, 34, 37, 46, 47, 83, 84, 87, 89, 98, 100, 103–105, 113, 114, 118, 129, 133, 134, 142, 144, 156, 158, 165–167, 175, 200, 201, 203, 213, 220, 229–233, 235, 238, 241
compassion, 209, 222, 232
compendium, 218
competition, 2, 7
compilation, 72
complement, 18, 57, 58, 95, 140, 177, 195
complexity, 9, 149
component, 205
composition, 59, 60, 62, 63, 66, 151
compromise, 41, 175, 181, 226
concept, 20, 59, 72, 110
concert, 11, 12, 17, 35, 36, 52, 75, 77, 84, 85, 89, 93, 104, 136, 138, 157, 167, 180, 196, 214, 228, 230, 239

conclusion, 22, 47, 50, 53, 58, 94, 96, 108, 125, 143, 153, 168, 209, 213, 221, 225, 233, 235, 237
condition, 48, 196, 199
confetti, 85
confidence, 104, 208
confine, 4
conformity, 5, 7, 123, 242
congas, 31
connection, 14, 18, 40, 44, 45, 52, 79, 83–87, 89–91, 94, 137, 139–142, 150, 166–168, 176, 184, 186, 201, 202, 220, 227, 228, 230, 234, 235, 239
conquest, 141
conscience, 108
consciousness, 206
conservation, 33, 101, 133, 178, 205, 206
consideration, 5, 27
construction, 203
contact, 36
contemporary, 43, 112, 120, 154, 165, 216
content, 16, 39, 136, 137, 144, 167
contest, 201
context, 17
continuation, 114, 115, 164
continuity, 102
contract, 2, 97
contribution, 43, 89, 91, 111
control, 21, 34, 52, 90, 145
controversy, 182
convention, 154
conventional, 1, 9, 23, 56, 58, 109, 123, 125, 153
conversation, 78, 107

copyright, 97
core, 55, 85, 95, 120, 137, 183, 212, 222
corner, 3, 6, 41, 152, 180, 241
cosplay, 18
costume, 85
country, 3, 4, 36, 131–133
couple, 229
courage, 104, 105, 128, 133
course, 3, 84, 85, 98, 111, 116, 122
couture, 187
cover, 70, 205, 208, 212, 213, 242
coverage, 97
cowbell, 28
craft, 2, 10, 13, 16, 18, 25, 27, 30, 31, 51, 53, 60, 73, 83, 88, 89, 109–111, 113, 118, 150, 170, 174, 177, 178, 183, 186, 226
craftsmanship, 189
cranny, 73
craze, 188
craziness, 76
creation, 8–10, 63, 65, 74, 110, 209, 235
creativity, 5, 8, 29, 30, 35, 49, 50, 52, 56–60, 62, 66–68, 70, 71, 73, 82, 84–86, 90, 91, 93, 99, 100, 110, 112, 113, 116, 125, 128–131, 137, 143, 148, 150, 152, 154, 155, 162, 166–168, 180, 188, 191, 199, 201, 208, 213, 215, 220, 222, 223, 225, 227, 229, 231, 233, 240–242
credit, 127
crew, 20, 37, 217
crispness, 20
critic, 216
criticism, 7, 60, 122, 171, 182
crooning, 2
cross, 146, 166
crossover, 120
crowd, 2, 4, 7, 11, 12, 14, 17, 18, 26, 28, 35–37, 74, 75, 77, 85, 90, 92, 93, 121, 155, 156, 160, 182, 198
crunching, 65
cry, 235
cuisine, 76
culmination, 156
culture, 34, 41, 46, 47, 49, 66, 76, 79, 82, 118, 128, 132, 134, 150, 172, 173, 193–195, 200, 202, 214, 215, 218, 236
curiosity, 78, 84
curriculum, 129
curtain, 18, 76, 157, 161
curve, 98, 119, 121
custom, 20, 24, 58
cutting, 19, 21, 22, 24, 33, 52, 57
cycle, 25, 100, 179, 180, 201, 208

dance, 5, 23, 26, 27, 36, 60, 77, 90, 91, 93, 126, 127, 132, 173, 193, 229
dancefloor, 236, 237
Daniella, 228
darkness, 186
daughter, 230
Dave Grohl, 149
David ", 127
David Houndstooth, 112
David Thompson, 216
Davis, 62, 75, 90
day, 6, 11, 45, 77, 121, 154, 174, 229

deal, 2, 5, 16, 39, 40
debate, 199
debut, 2, 5, 39, 149
decision, 89, 117, 174, 183, 185
decor, 136
dedication, 2, 12, 16, 18, 27, 30, 31, 47, 51–53, 57, 59, 83, 84, 89, 101, 103, 105, 107, 111–113, 116, 118, 133, 140, 143, 150, 152, 156, 158, 160, 168, 177, 178, 196, 197, 200, 206, 209, 215, 221, 223, 226, 227, 232, 234, 240, 242
defeat, 16
defiance, 124
definition, 231
deforestation, 205
degradation, 205
delight, 81, 85
delivery, 140, 154, 177
demand, 4, 182, 198
demeanor, 177
depression, 103, 175
depth, 9, 18, 20, 59, 61, 73, 79, 90, 93, 94, 118, 138, 140, 149, 177, 196, 200, 201, 216
desert, 77, 82
design, 17, 20–22, 52, 58, 190, 195–197, 215, 217
desire, 3, 5, 44, 62, 64, 88, 100, 104, 123, 126, 138
desk, 42
despair, 186
destination, 79, 227
destiny, 225
detail, 2, 59, 70, 77, 98, 137, 150, 173, 189

determination, 1, 6, 8, 11, 16, 25, 26, 29, 38, 43, 44, 105, 114, 174, 176, 178, 185, 191, 236
development, 136, 143, 222
devotion, 85, 198, 219, 220, 235
dialogue, 165, 204
diary, 81–84
didgeridoo, 9, 56, 147
die, 135, 192, 227, 242
difference, 46, 47, 100–106, 108, 133, 143, 152, 167, 184, 204, 207, 209, 211, 227, 232, 235
dilemma, 199
dimension, 56, 57, 69, 177, 213
direction, 89, 182, 189, 231
disappointment, 4
disaster, 104, 207, 209
disco, 154
discography, 155, 160, 215, 216, 220, 231, 240
discovery, 4, 8, 43, 60, 72, 104, 186, 196
discussion, 23, 107, 236
display, 2, 46, 83, 136, 192, 214, 241
distance, 44
distress, 82
distribution, 145
dive, 8, 13, 16, 32, 35, 59, 68, 71, 76, 79, 84, 99, 144, 169, 191, 193, 198, 210, 219, 221
diversity, 30, 45, 82, 147, 167, 231, 233
DJ Shelltop, 56
DJ Sluggo's, 127
DJ X, 109, 110
DJ X credits Snails, 109
DJ X's, 109

djembe, 31
documentary, 136, 192, 240
documentation, 83
domination, 113, 118
door, 63, 155
doubt, 43, 171, 182
down, 5, 7, 19, 33, 37, 45, 75, 82, 85, 114, 138, 140, 142, 157, 160, 165, 168, 171, 177, 180, 222, 230, 232, 234
drama, 16, 135, 136, 138, 191
dream, 12, 29, 32, 39, 42, 52, 53, 114
drive, 90, 148, 150
drone, 147
dropping, 20, 23, 37, 158
drum, 23, 28, 36, 58, 91, 146
drumbeat, 61
drumline, 236
drummer, 4, 42, 58, 59, 71, 74, 75, 93, 126, 177, 221
Drummer Lily ", 127
Drummer Max ", 149
drumming, 3, 5, 90, 92, 93, 126, 149, 177
Dublin, 42
dubstep, 123
duo, 177
dynamic, 10, 17, 20, 43, 65, 72, 93, 109, 141, 149, 177, 200, 240

ear, 68, 96, 231
earning, 112, 177, 192
earth, 177
ease, 117, 177
eco, 205, 206
ecstasy, 182
Eddie "Speedy" Ramirez, 94

edge, 16, 19, 21, 22, 24, 33, 52, 57, 109, 148, 154, 198
edition, 142, 167, 197–199, 208, 238–240
education, 100, 129, 133, 204–206, 208
effect, 49, 73, 101, 154, 233
effort, 87, 181
elaborate, 5, 23, 34, 138, 140, 142, 155, 173, 213
electronica, 8, 151
elegance, 189
element, 2, 20, 31, 61, 95, 212
Ella Fitzgerald, 146
embodiment, 44, 168
embrace, 2, 4, 8, 12, 16, 18, 22, 25, 28, 29, 32, 43, 47, 49, 59, 61, 63, 66–68, 71, 74, 75, 78, 91, 92, 103–105, 109, 120, 121, 125, 127, 128, 130, 145, 147, 148, 150, 152–154, 183, 184, 188–190, 195, 201, 213–215, 221–223, 225, 227, 228
embracing, 7–9, 21, 31, 33, 35, 43, 46, 49, 50, 60, 62–67, 82, 104, 110, 120, 125, 128, 132, 143, 147, 154, 155, 165–168, 172, 181, 185, 191, 206, 222, 223, 225, 233, 235
emergency, 203
Emily, 84, 103, 177, 178, 228
Emily ", 177
Emily Lewis, 217
Emily, 84
Emma, 44, 105, 126
Emma ", 126

Index

Emma "Slow Tempo" Thompson, 1
Emma Johnson, 19
emotion, 9, 31, 155, 157, 160, 196
emphasis, 18, 242
empire, 135–138, 141, 143, 192, 193
empowerment, 10, 103, 104, 106, 220, 223, 228, 231, 236
emptiness, 180
encore, 51, 83, 160, 192
encounter, 15, 28, 43, 74, 82, 222, 226
encouragement, 83, 96, 103, 231
end, 4, 73, 76, 90, 101, 121, 122, 129, 148, 155–158, 160, 161, 184, 186, 187, 226
endeavor, 126, 164
ending, 25, 84, 159
endurance, 51
energy, 2–5, 8, 11, 13, 16–19, 21, 26, 28, 29, 32, 33, 35, 36, 38, 43, 48, 51, 62, 63, 68, 72, 75, 86, 88, 90–94, 108–111, 113, 117, 121, 126, 127, 138, 139, 146, 148–151, 155, 157, 160, 165, 166, 177, 180, 182, 191–195, 200, 206, 212, 235, 238
engagement, 34, 37, 87, 107, 108, 138, 201, 233, 238
engineering, 19, 22
ensemble, 188
entertainment, 33, 135, 137, 171, 172, 192–195, 227, 240
enthusiasm, 34, 38, 89
enthusiast, 217
entrance, 74
envelope, 18, 145

environment, 45, 61, 66, 86, 89, 97, 98, 129, 130, 143, 203, 205–207
environmentalist, 178
episode, 138, 192
equipment, 6, 11, 19, 58, 65, 97, 150, 214
era, 33, 98, 114, 117–122, 143, 144, 146, 148, 151, 153, 155–157, 160, 161, 236
Eric, 58
escapade, 77
escape, 12, 180, 228
essay, 64, 110, 128
essence, 5, 21, 29, 36, 56, 57, 59, 60, 68, 70, 73, 82, 109, 112, 115, 120, 138, 140, 149, 165, 179, 188, 189, 199, 200, 212, 214, 216, 218, 221, 231
establishment, 211, 214
esteem, 104
eternity, 159
ethnicity, 231
ethos, 21, 109, 153, 236
euphoria, 86, 182
evaluation, 72
evening, 78, 238, 239
event, 11, 84, 104, 121, 238–240
evolution, 8, 10, 26, 47, 79, 111, 115, 117, 118, 123, 125, 127, 133, 148, 150–152, 164, 182, 185, 198, 215, 217, 235, 240
examination, 216
example, 10, 34, 68, 98, 113, 125, 133, 147, 154, 182, 183, 186, 197, 211, 213
excellence, 52, 53

exception, 6, 55, 61, 92, 93, 119, 140, 169, 184, 208, 216
exchange, 81
excitement, 2, 11, 13, 35, 36, 74–77, 81, 85, 160, 195, 239
exercise, 140
exhibit, 214, 215
exhibition, 112
exhilaration, 137
expansion, 45, 141
expense, 23, 36, 42
experience, 2, 5, 10, 13, 17, 18, 20, 22–24, 35, 36, 38, 48, 49, 52, 56, 57, 59, 61–63, 65, 67, 68, 70–73, 75, 77, 78, 82, 89, 90, 93, 94, 113, 116, 119, 125, 126, 128, 129, 132, 135, 137–140, 142–144, 146, 147, 150, 151, 158, 173, 178, 184, 193, 195–197, 199, 205, 214–220, 230, 236, 238–240, 242
experiment, 7, 10, 19, 23, 32, 55, 56, 60, 61, 63, 66, 69, 71, 91, 95, 117, 123, 126, 130, 137, 138, 140, 147, 150, 197, 213, 216, 226, 239
experimentation, 8–10, 48–50, 58, 65, 66, 69, 71, 86, 109–111, 119, 124, 125, 147, 149–155, 179, 201
expertise, 97, 99, 132, 210
exploitation, 205
exploration, 9, 10, 33, 49, 55, 56, 64, 65, 67, 71, 82, 84, 86, 110, 118, 124, 125, 127, 128, 146, 151, 153, 154, 216, 218

explosion, 35
exposure, 11, 38, 41, 129, 166
expression, 33, 53, 63, 100, 103, 118, 124, 128, 132, 147, 154, 162–164, 167, 189, 193, 197, 200, 217, 222, 241, 242
extent, 133
extravaganza, 36, 77, 239
eye, 24, 32, 36, 77

fabric, 85
facade, 174
face, 6, 8, 12, 41, 44, 50, 88, 95, 128, 133, 170, 171, 174–176, 219
facet, 237
fact, 87
factor, 119
fade, 156, 218, 219
failure, 6, 7, 124, 226
faith, 164
fame, 3, 6, 16, 25, 28, 29, 32, 38, 40–42, 44, 88, 89, 97, 100, 114, 142, 170, 171, 174, 175, 179–181, 183, 192, 198, 206, 216, 217
family, 1, 15, 41, 44, 94, 181, 217, 229, 233
fan, 10, 14, 18, 23, 34–39, 46, 47, 74, 75, 78, 84, 85, 87, 89, 98, 102, 103, 107, 127, 133, 138–140, 143, 144, 157, 158, 160, 166–168, 182, 192, 200–202, 208, 209, 212, 213, 219, 220, 228–235, 241
fanbase, 1, 5, 7, 11, 13–15, 18, 27, 40, 41, 84, 87, 101, 104,

106, 107, 117, 120, 129, 132, 133, 138, 150, 153, 166, 175, 200, 201, 211, 227, 229, 240
fandom, 220, 229, 232–234
fanfiction, 200, 220
fantasy, 17, 173
farewell, 155–161, 168
farmer, 74
fascination, 42
fashion, 6, 24, 27, 49, 104, 136, 142, 152, 168, 172, 173, 187–189, 191, 197, 198, 214, 238–240
fashionista, 190
father, 43, 44, 178
favorite, 13, 23, 47, 75, 128, 140, 193, 199, 201, 212, 219, 241, 242
fear, 7, 95, 104, 124, 179, 228, 231, 242
fearlessness, 65, 66, 104, 127, 150, 153, 155
feast, 20, 23, 58, 213
feat, 28, 51, 55, 212
feature, 25
feedback, 140, 226
feeling, 75, 180, 182
fellow, 52, 55, 79, 89, 128, 130, 140, 200, 206, 213, 214, 226, 229, 231, 233, 242
fervor, 11, 160
festival, 11, 26, 196
fever, 5, 13, 158
fi, 20
fiction, 167, 218
field, 206
fight, 43, 45, 76, 173
figure, 74

figurine, 199
fill, 74
film, 94, 142, 240
filmmaking, 135
finale, 35, 239
finesse, 90
fingerwork, 5
finish, 70
fire, 16, 35, 42, 78
Fitzgerald, 146
flair, 92, 168
flame, 29, 86, 158, 221, 241, 242
flash, 51
flavor, 1, 5, 65, 91
flight, 184
floor, 77
fluidity, 3, 72
focus, 92, 96, 97, 178, 179, 211
folk, 79
following, 2, 4, 9, 12, 84, 109, 131, 144, 228
food, 76, 208
foot, 26
footage, 144, 238
footprint, 206
footwork, 23
foray, 135
force, 2, 16, 25, 33, 36, 43–47, 59, 72, 85, 88, 93, 95, 97, 107, 110, 111, 142, 143, 158, 167, 178, 189, 207, 234, 241
forefront, 93, 128, 137, 208
forest, 37
form, 63, 70, 71, 77, 98, 110, 124, 134, 148, 172, 176, 177, 200, 217, 231
format, 139
formula, 96

fortune, 40, 174
foundation, 7, 9, 59, 61, 86–88, 90, 93, 95, 98, 99, 115, 149, 177, 200, 209–211
fragrance, 199
framework, 217
freedom, 29, 95, 99, 128, 130
frenzy, 187
frequency, 24
friend, 97, 229
friendship, 7, 43–45, 47, 82, 87, 94–96, 228, 231
front, 36, 85, 137, 179
frontman, 1, 13, 42, 59, 61, 88, 89, 93, 94, 113, 126
frustration, 78
fuel, 4, 8, 16, 38, 59, 79, 82, 83, 92, 150, 167, 175, 226
fulfillment, 225
fun, 23, 75, 188, 190
fund, 6
funding, 100, 204, 206
fundraiser, 229
fundraising, 107, 167, 203, 211, 232, 234
funk, 1, 4, 8, 26, 28, 38, 48, 62, 79, 88, 111, 148, 149, 151, 152, 212, 236
fury, 90
fusion, 4, 9, 26, 29, 33, 38, 39, 48, 56, 62, 63, 69, 79, 109, 117, 127, 146–148, 154, 215
future, 3, 12, 35, 37, 46, 49, 50, 65, 91, 105, 115, 118, 122, 125, 131, 148, 150, 151, 153–156, 159, 166, 168, 201, 204–206, 208, 211, 215, 232

game, 40, 86, 172, 193–195
gap, 115, 132, 165, 204, 234
garage, 6, 25, 26
garde, 9, 67, 126, 152, 187, 189, 197
Gary ", 68
gas, 206
gateway, 73, 144
gathering, 139, 141, 160
gem, 69
generation, 34, 49, 52, 64, 67, 91, 100, 109, 114–119, 121, 125–131, 134, 137, 145, 147, 150, 152, 154, 158, 164, 166, 172, 208, 213, 215, 230, 235
generosity, 84, 209, 211
genesis, 16, 17, 183
genius, 59, 74, 164, 170
genre, 9, 18, 34, 35, 48–51, 56, 63, 64, 66, 89, 109–112, 114, 119, 123, 128, 140, 146–149, 151–154, 177, 201, 213, 215, 217
Georgia, 94
Germany, 81
gesture, 21
ghost, 78
gift, 88
gig, 2, 182
glam, 28, 29, 81, 140, 173–175
glamor, 44
glamour, 43, 181
glass, 61, 65
glimmer, 103, 184, 219
glimpse, 39, 81, 135, 144, 192, 214, 218, 230, 240
glitter, 5
glitz, 28, 29, 43, 44, 81, 140, 173–175, 181

globe, 6, 45, 62, 76, 79, 81, 83, 132, 137, 141, 167, 199, 214, 227, 241
glory, 42, 122, 239
glue, 44
goal, 85, 95, 98, 141
good, 34, 81, 107, 142, 206, 211, 232
goodbye, 156, 159–161
goodness, 103
grace, 14, 158, 186
grandeur, 79
grandfather, 44, 88
gratitude, 83, 121, 122, 132, 133, 156, 157, 159–161, 201, 238
greatness, 7, 8, 10, 26, 95, 98, 123, 125, 176
Greece, 82
greenhouse, 206
greet, 87
greeting, 132
grit, 16
groove, 1, 60, 71, 91, 92, 154
ground, 95, 183, 209, 234
groundbreaking, 10, 29–31, 52, 53, 62, 63, 66, 95, 108, 111–113, 123, 124, 126–128, 146, 152, 154, 157, 158, 179, 189, 214, 216, 237, 239
group, 1, 3, 10, 25, 27, 45–47, 78, 81, 83, 84, 92, 111, 152, 160, 168, 170, 179, 192, 227
growth, 8, 63, 65, 96, 97, 117, 118, 121, 125, 150, 171, 172, 175, 181, 183–186, 201, 222, 223, 225, 226

Gucci, 189
guerrilla, 14
guest, 37, 74, 130, 140, 192, 213, 220, 238, 239
guidance, 7, 98, 128–130
guide, 13, 41, 55, 91, 92, 102, 131, 191, 225
guitar, 1, 3, 5, 9, 10, 26, 36, 43, 56, 58, 67, 74, 75, 85, 88, 90, 94, 125, 139, 148, 153, 177, 198, 212, 219, 229, 236
guitarist, 43, 58, 74, 75, 94, 125, 222

hair, 188
hall, 77, 214
halt, 77
hammer, 61
hand, 5, 74, 84, 98, 113, 130, 177–179, 199, 207, 208, 215, 231
handful, 5, 38
happiness, 42, 174
hardship, 103
harmony, 60, 91, 94, 146
haven, 86, 231
Hawaii, 82
head, 5, 8, 25, 48, 83, 103, 171, 173, 174, 184, 185
headline, 39, 182
headlining, 39
headpiece, 191
healing, 172, 207, 228
health, 33, 41, 44, 48, 103, 169, 171, 172, 175, 176, 178, 181, 203, 217, 227
healthcare, 100, 133, 204
heart, 3, 26, 35, 43, 72, 80, 92, 97, 99, 118, 135, 155, 156,

166, 171, 176, 183, 207, 227, 234, 239
heartbeat, 59, 93, 177
heartbreak, 61, 175
heartwarming, 74, 84, 191, 229, 237
heist, 191
help, 11, 28, 41, 44, 47, 71, 80, 82, 92, 93, 96, 103, 104, 110, 121, 130, 140, 156, 165, 171, 174–176, 181, 225, 228, 229, 233
Herbie Hancock, 149
heritage, 44, 132
hero, 31, 32
hiatus, 121, 183
hideout, 68
high, 4, 18, 26, 29, 32, 36, 38, 51, 63, 72, 90, 127, 138, 182, 188
highlight, 85, 140
hip, 23, 30, 49, 63, 119, 123, 126, 146, 147, 152, 153
historian, 216
history, 3, 35, 37, 59, 62, 78, 111, 114, 116, 157, 166, 173, 195, 198, 218, 225, 237
hit, 7, 10, 14, 28, 30, 31, 39, 51, 65, 68, 71, 84, 85, 112, 119–121, 126, 135, 136, 157, 179, 182, 192, 195, 235
hole, 77
Hollywood, 28, 29
homage, 44, 82, 109, 115, 132, 154, 189, 200, 202, 215, 220, 240, 242
home, 14, 71, 111, 136, 203
homeless, 203
homelessness, 203, 204, 206
hometown, 4, 121, 155, 233, 238

homogeneity, 34
honesty, 84, 103
honor, 112, 115, 155, 158, 242
hop, 23, 30, 49, 63, 119, 123, 126, 146, 147, 152, 153
hope, 8, 29, 68, 103, 105, 106, 160, 172, 176, 181, 184, 186, 187, 207–209, 211, 219, 223, 225, 228
host, 192
hotel, 37, 78, 81, 180
house, 81
household, 42, 115, 195
housing, 203
hub, 58, 144, 200
humility, 113
humor, 77, 192, 193, 195
hunger, 21
hurdle, 8
husband, 44
hush, 160
hybrid, 123

Iceland, 149
icon, 88, 93, 126
idea, 4, 5, 59, 62, 68, 81, 208
identity, 1, 9, 17, 23, 24, 43, 46, 66, 88, 104, 117, 120, 131, 148, 196, 215, 217, 225
illustration, 200
image, 4, 24, 25, 97, 117, 176, 180, 231
imagery, 9, 60, 112, 238
imagination, 72, 191, 199, 240
imagine, 19
imitation, 110
impact, 3, 5–7, 12, 13, 15, 18, 23, 29, 32–35, 37, 39, 40, 42, 44, 47–49, 52, 64, 66, 67,

79, 83, 84, 87–89, 93, 98, 100–105, 107–112, 114–118, 121, 128, 131–138, 142, 143, 146–148, 151–157, 159–161, 164, 167, 172, 173, 181, 184, 187–189, 193–195, 197, 200–203, 206, 207, 209–211, 214–220, 222, 223, 225, 227–230, 232–235, 239, 240, 242
importance, 8, 12, 23, 41, 42, 44, 79, 85, 96, 98, 100, 114–118, 120, 128, 129, 131, 141, 147, 165–167, 171, 174–176, 178, 180, 181, 185, 203, 205, 207, 209, 225, 232
impression, 17, 24, 37, 61, 83, 84, 88, 111, 114, 116, 152, 221
imprint, 229
improvement, 185
improvisation, 66, 67, 140
incident, 81
inclination, 42
inclusivity, 34, 107, 167, 195, 231
income, 203, 204
incorporation, 61, 154
independence, 125
individual, 7, 41, 60, 63, 66, 71, 85, 88, 92, 94–96, 117, 118, 125, 127, 130, 156, 162, 164, 176, 178–180, 183, 184, 240
individuality, 4, 7, 18, 21, 27, 32, 49, 91, 93, 94, 104, 105, 125, 126, 131, 152, 154, 167, 168, 177, 189, 191, 195, 200, 216, 221, 223, 225
induction, 111, 113
indulgence, 180
industry, 1–10, 12, 15–17, 23–35, 39, 42, 43, 45, 48, 49, 51–53, 56, 62, 64, 66, 72, 89, 93–98, 100, 107, 108, 111–121, 124–126, 128, 129, 131, 133, 135, 138, 143, 145–148, 150–158, 162, 164, 166, 171, 172, 174, 175, 178–180, 182, 186, 187, 189, 192, 193, 195, 197, 206, 212–217, 226, 234, 235, 237, 239, 242
inequality, 203
influence, 6, 14, 46–50, 79, 89, 91, 100, 102, 107, 109–111, 133, 134, 137, 142, 147, 149, 151–154, 158, 168, 172, 173, 187, 189, 195, 200–202, 204, 206, 207, 214–217, 219, 232, 239, 242
infrastructure, 97, 208
ingredient, 18, 94, 96
initiative, 100, 129, 166, 178, 204–206, 208
injustice, 173
innovation, 21, 26, 33, 35, 50, 53, 57, 58, 61, 63, 64, 67, 109, 110, 114, 115, 118, 123–125, 128, 131, 137, 143, 147, 150–155, 166, 204, 206, 208, 239
innovativeness, 110
input, 165, 231
inspiration, 1, 7, 9, 12, 20, 40, 43,

44, 46–48, 53, 55, 56, 59, 61, 62, 68, 71, 79, 88, 94, 103, 105, 109, 110, 114, 115, 118, 125, 145, 147–151, 154, 155, 160, 172, 174, 176, 178, 186, 187, 201, 206, 209, 216, 220, 223, 225, 242
installation, 196
instance, 9, 42, 65, 68, 74
instant, 126, 127, 135, 136, 228, 235
institution, 111
instrument, 6, 57, 73, 147, 177, 227, 229
instrumental, 9, 10, 13, 34, 59, 97, 107, 140, 183, 234
instrumentation, 48, 65, 67, 126, 128, 151
integration, 21, 49, 62, 146, 151
integrity, 16, 32, 89, 145, 147, 181, 183
intensity, 3, 36, 51, 61, 151, 155, 178
interaction, 17, 102, 142
internet, 136
interplay, 138, 139, 229
interpretation, 141
interview, 109
intimacy, 36, 144
intrigue, 59, 61, 140, 151
intro, 61
introduction, 77
introspection, 79, 172, 175, 179, 183
invasion, 13–16, 40, 171, 218
invincibility, 175
invitation, 4, 28, 81, 158
involvement, 102, 106, 209
Ireland, 42
Isabella, 43–45
Isabella ", 93

Isabella "The Serpent", 43
issue, 101, 203, 204
item, 199, 238

Jack, 229
Jack ", 148
Jaco Pastorius, 149
Jake, 180
Jake "Groovy Beats" Martinez, 1
jam, 36, 37, 44, 55, 60, 66, 74, 75, 81, 86, 138, 180
James Anderson, 217
James Brown, 48
Japan, 43, 81
Jason Gianni - A, 92
Jason Jay, 126
jaw, 23, 37, 158
Jay, 126
Jay-Z, 63
jazz, 1, 8, 56, 62, 63, 69, 91, 146, 148, 149, 152, 182
jealousy, 41
Jenkins, 216, 217
Jim, 76, 77
Jimi Hendrix, 88, 148
Jimmy Fallon, 28
job, 143, 203
Joe, 58
Joe "Sluggo" Carter, 160
John Bonham, 149
John Lennon, 212, 213
Johnson, 56, 68, 74, 90, 93, 97, 148, 178, 216
journalist, 216, 217
journey, 1, 3–10, 12–14, 16, 22, 25–32, 35, 38, 39, 42, 43, 47, 52, 55, 56, 59, 60, 67, 68, 71, 72, 79–81, 83, 84, 86, 88, 89, 92, 94–96, 99,

Index   261

100, 102–105, 114, 115, 117, 118, 121–123, 126, 128, 130, 131, 133–136, 140, 143, 144, 150, 155–157, 160, 164, 166, 169, 171–176, 179, 181–187, 192, 195–198, 213, 215–218, 220, 222, 223, 225–227, 231, 237–241

joy, 75, 81, 83, 160, 199, 209, 227, 229
judgment, 95, 104, 231, 242
jungle, 77
justice, 33, 101, 108, 136

karaoke, 81
kazoo, 69
key, 17, 31, 38, 60, 62, 65, 66, 87, 90, 95, 96, 99, 115, 119, 129, 138, 151, 185, 188, 205, 206, 210, 225
keyboard, 43, 63, 149
keyboardist, 93, 222
Kid Beats, 147
kind, 8, 52, 61, 69, 75, 82, 126, 196, 198
kindness, 83, 84, 101, 106, 167, 222, 232, 235
kingdom, 69
kit, 58
kitchen, 61
knack, 36, 56, 212
knowledge, 80, 89, 93, 97, 118, 129, 144, 166, 182
koto, 81
Kraftwerk, 49

label, 2, 5, 16, 27, 34

labor, 205
labyrinth, 77
lack, 82, 203, 204, 208
landscape, 3, 24, 33, 35, 48, 49, 52, 61, 64, 67, 69, 74, 98, 108–110, 117, 119, 123, 124, 128, 143, 145, 148, 149, 151, 153–155, 185, 195, 214, 216
lane, 25, 27, 157
language, 34, 81, 90, 132, 134, 141, 150, 228, 241
Larry, 75
Larry "The Smooth Operator", 75
last, 12, 46, 155, 156, 160, 234
laughter, 74–76, 78, 113, 177, 194
layer, 2, 9, 36, 57, 69, 75, 178
lead, 1, 3, 12, 31, 43, 66, 74, 75, 94, 125, 179, 181, 191, 221, 236
leader, 88, 89, 93
leadership, 89, 207
leap, 27, 126, 164
leave, 11, 16, 17, 24, 28, 29, 37, 51, 71, 83, 88, 95, 102, 115, 131, 148, 150, 155, 160, 197, 211, 212, 221, 222, 225, 227, 240
Led Zeppelin, 48, 154
legacy, 24, 29, 32, 34, 35, 44, 47, 49, 50, 53, 64, 85, 87, 91, 102, 103, 105, 109, 111, 114–118, 122, 125, 131, 134, 138, 143, 147, 148, 152–156, 158, 160, 161, 164–166, 168, 173, 186, 193, 195, 202, 209, 211, 214, 215, 217, 219–221, 225, 230, 232, 235, 237,

238, 240–242
legion, 109
length, 39
lesson, 120
letter, 184
level, 10, 13, 17, 20, 26, 31, 39, 48,
    60, 74, 89, 91, 93, 95, 102,
    111, 114, 124, 128, 132,
    135, 138, 140–143, 150,
    157, 165, 172, 177, 181,
    183, 188, 195, 220, 222,
    234
Lewis, 217
lexicon, 46
Liam, 42–45
licensing, 97
life, 2, 8, 10, 11, 17, 19, 20, 25–28,
    31–33, 35–37, 41–46, 51,
    56, 58, 60–62, 68, 71, 76,
    78, 81–83, 86, 88, 103,
    106, 110, 119, 139, 160,
    167, 170, 172, 177, 178,
    182–184, 187, 191, 193,
    195, 196, 200, 212–215,
    221, 222, 227, 228, 230,
    231, 234, 235, 238, 240
lifeline, 103
lifestyle, 25, 41, 174, 180, 230
lifetime, 46, 84, 140, 234, 239
light, 5, 20, 23, 33, 35, 52, 82, 92,
    110, 134, 136, 138, 142,
    171, 172, 184–187, 217,
    228, 238
lighting, 20, 52
lightning, 1, 5, 51, 62, 90, 93, 94
Lily, 229
Lily ", 148
limelight, 3, 28, 40, 171
limit, 136, 163

line, 41, 66, 67, 142, 212
lineup, 4, 43
lining, 82
Lisa, 3, 5, 93
Lisa "Slime Queen" Martinez, 93
Lisa Martinez, 93
Lisa Roberts, 217
list, 237
listener, 10, 67, 139
listening, 70, 72, 81, 96, 126, 147,
    196, 228, 231
literature, 9, 216–218
live, 2, 5, 7, 10, 21, 23, 24, 33,
    35–39, 49, 51, 89, 97, 98,
    129, 134, 136, 141, 142,
    153, 156, 158, 161, 173,
    179, 182, 193, 195, 196,
    198, 209, 214, 217, 218,
    220, 232, 242
living, 25, 27, 168, 171, 182, 205,
    206
local, 2, 3, 10–16, 25–27, 74, 76, 79,
    81, 82, 84, 105, 107,
    131–134, 141, 203, 207,
    208, 232, 233
lodge, 77
logo, 46, 188, 241
London, 78
longevity, 94, 96, 119, 120, 166
longtime, 140
look, 10, 31, 61, 69, 72, 77, 79, 90,
    119, 136, 142, 152, 156,
    186–188, 192
loss, 43, 44, 60, 180, 205
lot, 41, 55, 57, 68, 77
Louis Carter, 217
love, 3, 5, 7, 11, 13, 15, 16, 27, 34,
    39, 41–47, 60, 68, 69, 71,
    75, 82–85, 87, 89, 104,

105, 107, 136, 142, 156, 158, 160, 165, 167, 168, 178, 188, 192, 198–200, 208, 213, 220, 222, 223, 227–236, 239, 241, 242
low, 24, 90, 204
loyalty, 45, 158, 221
luck, 12, 38, 75
luxury, 81
lyric, 156, 160, 186

madness, 85, 198
maestro, 43
magazine, 216, 218
magic, 2, 19–22, 55, 68, 69, 71, 75, 86, 90, 96, 116, 121, 140, 156, 188, 212, 214, 215, 220, 234, 240, 242
magnetism, 88
mainstream, 7, 25, 151, 152
makeover, 213
makeshift, 6
makeup, 168, 188
male, 43
management, 97, 198, 206
manager, 96–99, 178
manifest, 89
manner, 47, 196, 218
mantra, 103, 123, 221, 222
mapping, 20, 23, 239
Marcus, 3
Marcus "Squish" Simmons, 177
Marcus "The Magician, 43
Marcus Johnson, 97
Marcus Turner, 93
mark, 7, 11, 12, 15, 28, 29, 33, 35, 48, 51, 72, 89, 95, 107, 108, 111, 113–115, 122, 125, 128, 131, 134, 135,

148, 150, 151, 153, 155, 156, 158, 163, 166, 172, 180, 187, 191, 193, 195, 202, 212, 213, 221, 227, 235, 237–239, 242
marketing, 14, 15, 97, 99, 129
marvel, 21
mask, 170, 180
master, 3, 23, 177
mastermind, 68
masterpiece, 2, 30, 56, 57, 63, 71, 72, 112, 127, 135, 179, 237, 238
mastery, 43, 90
match, 57, 188
matcha, 81
material, 121
matter, 5, 15, 74, 186, 187, 233
Max, 90–92, 177, 178
Max "Slimestick" Martinez, 177
Max "Slimy" Thompson, 126
Max "The Beat Machine", 90
maze, 68
mean, 6, 120
meaning, 68
means, 51, 53, 113, 141, 143, 146, 168, 185, 205, 208, 231, 241
measure, 42
media, 13, 23, 28, 39, 40, 46, 47, 87, 97, 98, 102, 107, 108, 135, 138, 144, 165, 166, 168, 171–173, 191, 192, 200, 201, 213, 221, 231–233, 241
mediocrity, 72
medium, 110, 135, 216
medley, 160

meet, 14, 47, 78, 82, 87, 133, 167, 179, 201, 220, 234, 235
meeting, 7, 29, 37, 81, 168
Melissa Foster, 19
melodica, 140
melody, 19, 59–61, 71, 180
melting, 23
member, 1, 5, 6, 10, 18, 25, 36, 41, 42, 44, 56, 58, 59, 64, 65, 76, 77, 85, 86, 88, 92–96, 118, 125, 129, 138, 144, 148, 155, 156, 160, 162, 164, 169–171, 177, 180, 181, 183, 184, 199, 213, 216
memorabilia, 239
memory, 3, 76, 78, 157
mentor, 44, 97, 114, 129
mentorship, 45, 118, 129, 131, 166, 207
merch, 198
merchandise, 27, 40, 46, 84, 135, 136, 142, 167, 172, 192, 197–199, 201, 211, 231, 232, 241
merchandising, 197, 201
message, 4, 10, 14, 34, 46, 59, 72, 103–107, 122, 126, 160, 167, 168, 176, 187, 213, 219, 223, 229, 242
metal, 56, 146, 149
method, 198
mettle, 25
Mexico, 42
Mia Gonzalez, 196
mic, 4, 141
Michael Jenkins, 216
Mick Berry, 92
Mick Jagger, 148

microphone, 58, 71, 150, 160
middle, 75, 77, 82
midst, 140, 180
Mike, 228
Mike ", 149
Miles Davis, 62
milestone, 2, 39, 171, 220, 227, 238, 239
million, 52
mind, 5, 20, 35, 51, 57, 58, 67, 81, 108, 109, 135, 143, 227, 238
mindfulness, 41
mindset, 143
minibar, 180
minute, 51
mirror, 171, 235, 237
misfortune, 78
mission, 44, 207, 209, 210
mix, 1, 11, 23, 88, 135, 160, 188, 239
mixture, 161
model, 206
mold, 25, 50, 67, 88, 146–148, 152
moment, 4, 12, 13, 18, 26, 27, 36, 39, 43, 44, 68, 71, 74–76, 81, 83, 84, 88, 111, 121, 155, 160, 161, 180, 182, 187, 198, 209, 226, 230
momentum, 7, 14, 15, 131
money, 100, 104, 107, 198
monotony, 3
mood, 57, 68, 110, 140
moonlit, 139
morning, 77, 78
mosaic, 240
mosh, 36
motif, 189
motion, 21

Index

motivation, 223
mouth, 13, 76
move, 11, 13, 23, 56, 74, 75, 90–92, 118, 177, 179, 237
movement, 4, 9, 14, 15, 23, 27, 232, 233
movie, 86, 135, 191
multimedia, 112, 135, 137, 138, 141, 143
multitude, 110, 144, 151
museum, 214, 215
mushroom, 196
music, 1–18, 20–37, 39–53, 55–75, 79–129, 131–135, 137, 138, 140–168, 171–187, 189, 191, 193–203, 205–209, 211–221, 223, 225–242
musicality, 126, 140
musician, 6, 32, 62, 80, 88, 89, 105, 125, 126, 128, 130, 184, 229
musicianship, 13, 138
myriad, 6, 154
mystery, 78, 170, 216
mystique, 176, 218

name, 4, 23, 27, 30, 46, 115, 117, 191, 195
namesake, 24
narrative, 17, 57, 68, 72, 197, 198, 217
Nathan "Slick" Johnson, 1
nation, 28
nature, 2, 7, 9, 20, 24, 61, 65, 67, 69, 85, 110, 138, 142, 174, 177, 178
necklace, 188, 190

need, 41, 93, 100, 104, 105, 119, 129, 167, 175, 180, 204–211, 229, 235
negotiation, 97
neon, 196
nest, 55, 58, 118
network, 47, 129, 167, 181, 204
networking, 204
neutrality, 206
New York, 141
newfound, 25, 29, 78, 118, 185
news, 121, 233
niche, 26, 64
night, 4, 6, 12, 26, 28, 29, 37, 44, 51, 76–78, 81, 82, 86, 141, 156, 160, 161, 180, 192, 193, 195, 238
Nirvana, 212
none, 178
nonprofit, 209, 210
nook, 73
norm, 7, 18, 123
nostalgia, 121, 156, 164–166, 220, 239
note, 4, 11, 14, 16, 19, 35, 44, 111, 156, 160, 238
notice, 2, 5, 16, 39
notion, 103, 189
novelty, 4
number, 42

obscurity, 6, 30
observation, 59
obsession, 229
obstacle, 25, 85, 117
occasion, 75, 84, 121, 239
octane, 18
octopus, 76
odd, 6

odyssey, 164
off, 9, 11, 12, 14, 49, 76, 82, 86, 90, 94, 121, 141, 142, 155, 156, 160, 172, 185, 233, 238
offer, 129, 192, 216, 218, 220
offering, 1, 22, 72, 81, 98, 103, 104, 129, 135–137, 142, 183, 203, 217, 228, 231, 241
offstage, 39, 178
Oliver, 58
on, 1–8, 10–21, 23, 25–29, 31–45, 47–50, 52, 53, 56, 58–62, 64, 66–72, 74–99, 102, 103, 105–119, 121–148, 150–158, 160–167, 171–185, 187–189, 191–198, 200–203, 206, 207, 209, 211–222, 225–235, 237–242
one, 3, 8, 18, 21, 33, 36–38, 43, 44, 47, 50, 52, 60, 61, 63, 69, 71, 74, 75, 81, 83, 84, 88, 95, 96, 104, 111, 113, 114, 120–122, 126, 129, 140, 150, 154, 155, 160, 168, 170, 172, 175–177, 179–183, 185, 196, 198, 199, 213, 225, 227, 229, 240
opening, 4, 12, 32, 38
operation, 178
opportunity, 5, 8, 11, 12, 28, 36, 38, 39, 62, 64, 78, 82, 129, 132, 133, 136, 140–142, 156–158, 161, 171, 175, 201, 207, 208, 211, 213, 220, 226, 234, 238, 239
orchestra, 63

orchestration, 119, 126, 127
order, 119
organization, 102, 143, 207, 209
origin, 147
original, 11, 122, 136, 140, 153, 199, 201, 212, 213
originality, 66, 114
other, 7, 9, 18, 24, 25, 30, 32, 33, 36, 38, 41, 44, 46, 47, 51, 60, 63, 66, 69–71, 74, 75, 77, 82, 83, 86–91, 94, 95, 98, 104, 108, 110, 118, 124, 131, 132, 136–138, 144, 146, 147, 151, 153–155, 163, 164, 167, 171, 177–179, 185, 186, 195, 198–200, 202, 208, 210, 212, 220, 232, 233, 241
outfit, 188
outlet, 171
outlook, 8
outpouring, 232
output, 34
outreach, 232
outside, 32–35, 64–67, 71, 86, 91, 98, 124, 125, 131, 137, 140, 151, 169, 191, 198, 215, 222, 226
ownership, 172, 232

pace, 51, 93
package, 199
packaging, 199
pain, 43, 61, 185, 186, 228
paint, 83
painter, 94, 196
painting, 200
pair, 188, 190
palette, 73, 109

pan, 51
panel, 220
panic, 76
paparazzi, 41, 179
paradise, 155
paragraph, 64
park, 193
part, 5, 7, 14, 17, 24, 36, 40, 46, 48, 52, 60, 61, 70, 85, 97, 105, 128, 156, 161, 182, 200, 201, 203, 206, 207, 211, 215, 227, 231, 235, 236, 240, 241
participation, 232
partner, 228
partnering, 64, 93, 133, 136, 205
partnership, 16, 27, 98, 119, 146, 189, 207
party, 41, 77, 180
passage, 77, 219
passersby, 14
passion, 5, 8, 10, 11, 13, 15, 16, 18, 26, 27, 43–47, 51, 53, 59, 62, 69, 73, 79, 87–89, 102, 105, 114, 116, 117, 121, 122, 126, 131, 132, 142, 143, 150, 158, 161, 175, 177, 183, 185, 207, 220, 221, 223, 226, 227, 229, 234, 238
past, 48, 165, 172, 192
Patagonia, 79
path, 6, 8, 12, 15, 16, 28, 42–44, 124, 131, 145, 152, 155, 157, 172–174, 179, 185, 199, 221, 225, 240
pattern, 71
peace, 213
pearl, 188, 189

peek, 55, 81, 198
pencil, 42
penthouse, 180
people, 12, 33, 38, 45, 47, 52, 74, 79, 81–83, 86, 101, 112, 134, 159, 175, 177–179, 182, 189, 200, 201, 210, 216, 220, 221, 226–231, 233–235
pep, 96
perception, 25, 67, 147
percussion, 31, 43, 127
percussionist, 94, 127
perfection, 18, 21
performance, 2, 4, 5, 8, 10–13, 17–19, 26, 28, 36–38, 51, 52, 66, 74, 75, 77, 81, 83, 84, 90, 92, 93, 129, 137, 139, 155, 157, 160, 173, 182, 186, 191, 196, 239
period, 9, 25, 73, 117, 130, 165
perseverance, 8, 10, 12, 31, 39, 89, 105, 106, 114, 116, 126, 174, 176, 186, 219, 223, 241
persistence, 2, 9, 221, 226
person, 19, 201, 234
persona, 36, 88, 93, 176, 180
personality, 18, 25, 89, 93, 170, 178, 199
perspective, 45, 56, 59, 60, 65, 115, 131, 165, 213
Peter Smith, 19
phase, 9, 10, 60, 122–124, 182
phenomenon, 13, 39, 121, 140, 141, 154, 187, 216
philanthropic, 15, 89, 100, 102, 106, 112, 133, 207, 208, 211, 232, 234

philanthropy, 101, 102, 105, 134, 143, 152, 208, 209, 232, 233, 240
philosophy, 21, 58, 67, 164, 221
phone, 28
photo, 238
physicality, 18
pianist, 3, 44, 146
piano, 5, 43, 61, 139, 180
picture, 139
piece, 43, 110, 128, 136, 172, 184, 187, 191, 198, 223
pilgrimage, 43
pillar, 95, 183
pinnacle, 182
pioneer, 111
pitch, 5, 158
place, 15, 30, 32, 35, 37, 43, 47, 57, 58, 62, 82, 105, 111, 112, 116, 120, 121, 124, 150, 156, 160, 164–166, 173, 180, 186, 187, 192, 203, 204, 227, 229, 231, 233, 237, 238
plan, 131
planet, 45, 79, 101, 178, 205
planning, 97, 134
planting, 101, 206, 207
platform, 15, 29, 33, 34, 41, 44, 48, 93, 100–105, 107, 108, 112, 115, 122, 129, 133, 136, 142, 152, 166, 169, 171, 172, 175, 178, 201, 203, 208, 209, 211, 227, 231, 232
play, 60, 146, 160, 165, 213, 235
playing, 2, 4, 5, 25, 28, 38, 74, 90–92, 149, 165, 180, 215, 229

pleasure, 199
pocket, 90
point, 4, 19, 27, 46, 82, 123, 180, 185, 234
policy, 203
pollination, 146, 166
pool, 193
pop, 33, 109, 110, 118–120, 134, 152, 153, 172, 173, 185, 215, 218, 236
popularity, 2, 3, 5, 9, 27, 37–40, 100, 136, 164, 179, 233
population, 203
portal, 214
portion, 142, 208
portrayal, 217
position, 96, 111, 118, 120, 125, 141, 240
positivity, 46, 102, 106, 167, 193, 222, 223, 233
poster, 198
pot, 23
potential, 2, 16, 26, 32, 55, 64, 97, 99, 100, 128, 137, 138, 143, 164, 208
poverty, 100, 208
power, 1, 8, 9, 12, 15, 16, 31, 32, 35, 39, 41–43, 45–48, 50, 52, 64, 67, 72, 74, 75, 80, 81, 83, 86, 87, 89, 100–103, 105–107, 114, 115, 121, 125, 127–129, 133–136, 141–143, 147, 156, 158–161, 165–168, 174, 176, 178, 180, 181, 185, 186, 191, 205, 207, 209, 213, 217, 219, 221, 222, 227–230, 233, 235
powerhouse, 4, 93, 94, 177

Index

practice, 3, 110, 200
praise, 147
prank, 74
pre, 76, 167
precision, 3, 57, 59, 93
presence, 2, 4, 5, 10, 13, 14, 16–19, 24–26, 28, 35, 41, 43, 47, 49, 57, 78, 85, 88, 89, 91, 93, 94, 98, 108, 111, 113, 121, 131, 141, 144, 148, 153, 155, 165, 168, 170, 172, 177, 178, 191, 192, 195, 200, 212, 214–216, 233
preservation, 111
press, 97
pressure, 7, 29, 43, 171, 175, 179, 180, 182
prevention, 204
price, 40, 41, 174, 217
pride, 44, 203
Prince, 8, 88
principle, 152
print, 77
priority, 14, 79
privacy, 40, 171, 179
probability, 122
problem, 204, 206
process, 19, 20, 32, 35, 55–57, 59, 60, 62, 65, 66, 68, 69, 71, 72, 86, 89, 95, 99, 110, 128, 134, 136, 165, 179, 183, 213–215, 227, 240
prodigy, 3
producer, 2, 109
product, 148
production, 5, 19, 24, 49, 69, 71, 99, 124, 129, 131, 138–140, 142, 154

profession, 87
professional, 40, 41, 83, 94, 97, 171, 174, 175, 181
proficiency, 90
profit, 207
program, 100, 129–131, 204, 206
progress, 6
project, 72, 126, 183, 203, 207, 240
projection, 20, 23, 239
promotion, 14
proof, 105
property, 97
protection, 97
prowess, 9, 10, 39, 63, 91, 94, 135, 143, 212
pub, 81
public, 14, 30, 32, 97, 101, 107, 108, 180, 205
punk, 26, 111, 151
purpose, 73, 88, 183, 185, 232
pursuit, 7, 15, 18, 28, 38, 53, 124, 125, 133, 171, 174, 192
puzzle, 59

quality, 9, 86, 204, 220, 230
Queen, 154, 212
quest, 119, 130
question, 25, 158
quirkiness, 4, 5, 124
quo, 33, 109, 213, 240

race, 92
radio, 14
Radiohead, 154
rally, 11, 101, 204
rallying, 46, 235
Ramirez, 126, 127
range, 1, 8, 24, 48, 49, 72, 100, 112, 119, 123, 126, 147, 148,

152, 154, 163, 177, 191, 193, 195
rap, 63, 126
rapper, 63
rapture, 160
rawness, 151
ray, 228
reach, 8, 16, 27, 45, 51, 60, 98, 120, 121, 135, 141, 143, 187, 189, 209, 210, 221, 226, 231
reality, 17, 68, 136–138, 145, 173, 180, 214, 221
realization, 143, 160
realm, 3, 33, 47, 109, 110, 112, 135, 141, 143, 145, 154, 163, 173, 177, 198, 214, 218, 230, 232, 233, 238, 239
rebellion, 4, 123, 217
rebuilding, 208
recognition, 10, 13–16, 27, 39, 46, 47, 111–113, 129, 153, 179, 200, 201, 232
record, 2, 5, 7, 12, 16, 27, 37–39, 51–53, 97, 103, 112, 119, 145
recording, 2, 10, 25, 40, 49, 57, 68–71, 130, 150
recovery, 174
redemption, 172, 173, 181, 184–187
reflection, 2, 4, 83, 118, 128, 151, 156, 157, 172, 175, 219
reforestation, 206
refusal, 31, 147, 154
reggae, 91, 147, 152
region, 131, 141
rehabilitation, 208
reign, 58, 111
reinterpretation, 213

reinvention, 50, 123, 125, 183
rejection, 4, 7, 16
relatability, 195
relationship, 18, 41, 97–99, 183, 221
release, 39, 51, 150, 179, 182, 186, 198, 235
relevance, 119
relief, 174, 203, 207, 209
remain, 21, 41, 53, 89, 119, 120, 134, 156, 181, 235
reminder, 5, 8, 12, 31, 42, 47, 50, 53, 61, 63, 75, 77, 79, 81, 82, 115, 122, 125, 148, 157, 161, 180, 181, 186, 219–222, 242
reminiscence, 156
rendition, 139, 212, 213
repertoire, 212, 219
replica, 214
replication, 214
representation, 5, 34, 58, 60, 201
reputation, 7, 13, 25, 41, 65, 127, 177
research, 100, 217
residency, 130, 131
resident, 93
resilience, 6, 7, 25, 28, 41, 43, 45, 61, 72, 77, 83, 105, 106, 160, 161, 172, 174–176, 181, 183, 187, 217, 228, 231, 236
resistance, 147
resolve, 83
resourcefulness, 82
respect, 85, 89, 94, 95, 98, 99, 132, 134, 156, 167, 168
responsibility, 7, 42, 133, 207, 222
rest, 32, 46, 55, 59, 227
restaurant, 76

Index 271

result, 62, 63, 67, 69, 138, 140, 146, 183, 213
retrospective, 240
return, 121, 122
reunion, 117, 118, 122, 233
revelry, 180
revenue, 98, 145
reverberation, 20
revolution, 33, 35
reward, 73
rhythm, 4, 28, 59, 61, 90–93, 177
richness, 20, 93, 132, 149, 177
ride, 35, 62, 71, 82, 89, 171, 181, 184, 192, 193, 222
riff, 10, 67, 212
right, 88, 90, 110, 125, 168, 199, 204
rise, 3, 6, 10, 15, 16, 25, 27–29, 32, 34, 38, 49, 89, 97, 105, 114, 134, 172, 176, 185, 187, 188, 192, 198, 216, 233
rivalry, 76
road, 6, 32, 36, 59, 62, 71, 75–78, 80–83, 185, 186, 230
roadside, 75
roar, 160
Roberts, 217
rock, 1, 3, 4, 8–10, 23, 26, 28, 30, 33, 38, 42, 44, 48, 49, 59, 62, 67, 79, 81, 88, 94, 109, 111, 112, 123, 124, 126, 127, 139, 140, 146, 148, 149, 151, 153, 154, 177, 180, 185, 191, 212, 213, 219, 236
rocket, 16
rockstar, 41, 174
role, 6, 10, 14, 34, 59, 88, 89, 96–98, 102, 112, 128, 134, 149, 165, 168, 189, 191, 206, 231, 233–235, 241
roll, 48, 59, 111, 191
rollercoaster, 36, 171, 172, 181, 183, 184, 192, 222
roof, 61
room, 30, 75, 179, 180, 214
root, 203, 211
Rossi, 43
row, 36, 85, 137
runway, 189
rustling, 61

s, 1–6, 10, 12–21, 24, 25, 27, 28, 30, 32, 34–37, 40–47, 49, 51, 52, 55–63, 67–69, 71–79, 81–102, 104–107, 109–115, 117–122, 125–127, 129, 131, 132, 134–142, 144, 146, 148, 149, 152–158, 160, 164, 166–168, 170–173, 177–183, 187–196, 198–202, 206–211, 213–223, 225–242
sadness, 160, 161
safari, 77
saga, 15, 240
sale, 167
Sally ", 69
salsa, 28
salvage, 6
Sam, 3–5
sampling, 49, 69
sanctuary, 44, 57
Sarah, 104, 228
Sarah "Keys" Thompson, 149
Sarah Johnson, 216
saving, 186

saw, 2, 26, 69, 123, 141, 143, 149
saxophone, 56, 69, 75, 153
saying, 156, 207
scale, 15, 83, 113
scene, 1, 11, 13, 14, 16, 23, 25–27, 48, 62, 64, 76, 82, 132, 134, 151, 171, 179, 187, 197, 233
scent, 180
schedule, 25, 77, 82, 175
scholarship, 208
school, 42, 90
scrapbook, 84
screen, 29, 135, 191, 193–195
script, 138
scrutiny, 32, 40
sculptor, 196
sculpture, 110
sea, 2, 156, 160, 180, 188
seal, 199
seashell, 20
seat, 16
secrecy, 176
secret, 8, 18, 68, 94, 96, 98, 198
secretion, 5
section, 6, 8, 10, 12, 16, 19, 23, 25, 29, 32, 33, 35, 40, 48, 51, 55, 59, 61, 62, 64, 72, 76, 85, 88, 90–93, 96, 99, 103, 105, 108, 110, 111, 123, 125, 128, 138, 141, 145, 148, 151, 153, 164, 166, 169–172, 174, 177, 179, 181, 191, 195, 197, 200, 203, 216, 221, 223, 228, 230, 235, 237, 241
seed, 68, 88
selection, 72, 238

self, 4, 8, 32, 41–43, 60, 72, 103, 104, 106, 118, 162, 167, 168, 171, 172, 175, 176, 180–182, 185, 186, 189, 196, 222, 227, 242
sensation, 56, 135, 236, 238
sense, 4, 11, 13, 24, 33, 36, 44, 47, 61, 72, 78, 79, 85, 98, 103, 104, 106, 107, 122, 129, 133, 134, 139, 142, 144, 151, 156, 165, 167, 172, 175, 177, 180, 182, 187, 195, 201, 203, 209, 220, 231–235, 241
Serena, 58
serenade, 139
series, 127, 131, 135, 136, 142, 146, 157, 191, 192
serve, 12, 37, 46, 47, 58, 63, 73, 113, 115, 129, 164, 167, 176, 178, 179, 220, 235, 242
service, 82, 101, 205
session, 36, 68, 74, 75, 138, 180
set, 3–5, 11, 20, 25, 26, 28, 33–37, 46, 49, 51, 52, 59, 63, 66, 68, 75, 78, 81, 89, 112, 132, 133, 140, 143, 146, 151–155, 160, 170, 171, 198, 203, 213, 226, 238, 239
setback, 6, 16, 78, 171, 175, 183, 226
setlist, 11, 52, 139, 238
setting, 1, 9, 12, 38, 42, 72, 97, 113, 142, 171, 175, 242
setup, 20, 158
shape, 1, 12, 50, 67, 77, 79, 86, 94, 110, 131, 143, 154, 155, 176, 184, 233
share, 1, 4, 5, 11, 15, 23, 25, 28, 38,

Index 273

    41, 43, 44, 47, 69, 76, 77, 79, 82–84, 86, 94, 104, 107, 128, 129, 139, 165, 167, 168, 170, 186, 210, 213, 220, 223, 225, 226, 230, 233, 241, 242
shell, 12, 56, 58, 162, 164, 177, 188, 189, 191, 209, 225, 227, 241
Shelly, 28
shelter, 84, 203, 208
Shimmer, 94
shimmer, 188
shine, 11, 32, 85, 141, 187, 188, 191, 209
shortage, 198
shoulder, 96, 98, 183
show, 24, 28, 75, 76, 78, 84, 136, 138, 140, 156–158, 160, 191, 192, 194, 195, 238, 240
showcase, 5, 11, 12, 28, 38, 39, 85, 98, 138, 140, 142, 149, 166, 188, 200, 201, 212, 215, 216, 220, 228, 231
showmanship, 121
shrine, 199
side, 15, 40, 75, 99, 129, 138, 140, 160, 170, 171, 179–181, 199, 217
sight, 5, 7, 14, 27, 83, 85, 87, 120, 176
signature, 1, 2, 5, 8, 19, 23–25, 28, 31, 36, 38, 58, 63, 89, 93, 109, 113, 115, 117, 120, 121, 126, 177, 185, 187, 194, 212, 213, 219
significance, 107, 176, 216
silence, 73

silver, 29, 82, 135, 191
sing, 36
singer, 191, 221, 236
single, 30, 51, 112, 119, 157, 182, 195
sitcom, 192
situation, 75, 208
skepticism, 9, 122, 147
sketch, 20
skill, 90
skin, 182
sky, 29, 77, 139, 238
Slammer, 58, 74
sleep, 82
sleeve, 198
Slick, 1
slime, 2, 5, 13, 25, 29, 35, 55, 58, 61, 83, 85, 103, 128, 155, 156, 170, 173, 176, 179, 187–189, 191, 193, 211, 219, 221–223, 230, 238
Slimy, 127
Slimy Sirens, 154
slot, 4
sluggishness, 13
Sluggo, 28
sluggy, 192
Slumbersville, 155
smash, 28
Snail, 37
snail, 2, 13–16, 23, 24, 27, 55, 57, 58, 68–71, 77, 85, 92, 93, 155, 160, 177, 188, 189, 191, 192, 197–199, 209, 212, 218, 241
Snailmania, 187–189, 191
Snailverse, 144
snare, 58
sneak, 198

society, 44, 89, 105, 112, 133, 136, 142, 206, 207, 209, 211, 222
software, 20
solace, 1, 43, 47, 82, 103–105, 167, 174, 175, 180, 183, 185, 186, 228, 233
solidarity, 229–231
solo, 74, 118, 125–128, 140, 162, 164
song, 10–12, 30, 52, 56, 57, 59–61, 65, 67, 68, 70, 71, 73, 79, 84, 91, 92, 118, 121, 126, 130, 139, 140, 154–156, 160, 171, 182, 212, 213, 219, 223, 229–231, 236, 237
songwriting, 39, 43, 55, 56, 58–62, 68, 69, 86, 99, 129, 138, 149, 215
Sophia "Slick Keys" Lee's, 126
sophistication, 239
sorrow, 160
soul, 38, 43, 73, 90–92, 99, 118, 139, 155, 166, 176, 178, 183, 185, 231, 237
soulmate, 44
sound, 1–4, 6–10, 14, 16, 19–21, 23, 25, 26, 28, 30–33, 35, 38, 39, 43, 48–51, 55, 57, 58, 60–62, 64, 65, 69, 73, 79, 80, 86, 88–91, 93–95, 99, 108–112, 115–120, 123–126, 128, 130, 132, 138, 140, 141, 146–155, 165, 177, 179, 182, 185, 195, 197, 212–216, 219, 221, 229, 233, 236, 237, 239, 241, 242

soundcheck, 74
soundtrack, 104, 230, 231
source, 7, 46, 47, 53, 109, 150, 174, 178, 181, 201, 220, 223, 228
South Africa, 77
South America, 82
southwest, 77
space, 68, 86, 103, 104, 109, 171, 231, 232, 238, 241
spark, 59
sparkle, 58
speak, 177, 179
spectacle, 2, 13, 17, 20, 35, 36, 76, 155, 179
speech, 113, 238
speed, 51, 53
Speedy, 94
spellbinding, 37
spin, 212
spine, 78, 177
spiral, 185
spirit, 6, 10, 16, 18, 29, 34, 47, 48, 53, 57, 60, 61, 66, 67, 71, 77, 81, 83, 87, 89, 92, 93, 109, 110, 113, 138, 141, 143, 145, 150, 155–158, 164–166, 168, 176, 186, 187, 191, 194, 213, 218, 220, 227, 233, 235, 236, 240–242
splash, 7, 194
spontaneity, 21, 66, 75
spot, 72
spotlight, 2, 6, 27, 39, 125, 171, 175, 180, 209
spread, 2, 4, 14, 25, 38, 41, 45, 102, 107, 131, 187, 222, 227, 233

Index

Squish, 177, 178
stability, 98, 208
stack, 71
stadium, 36, 156, 171
stage, 2–5, 10, 11, 13, 14, 16–26,
    28, 33, 35–38, 42–44, 49,
    52, 57–59, 74, 75, 77,
    82–86, 88, 89, 91–94, 98,
    102, 111, 113, 117, 121,
    122, 125, 129, 131, 138,
    140–143, 148, 152, 153,
    155, 156, 158, 160, 168,
    170, 173–178, 181, 185,
    187, 189, 192, 195–197,
    199, 200, 212, 214–217,
    233, 239–242
stagnation, 183
stamina, 51
stamp, 109
stand, 7, 23, 85, 101, 120, 173, 198
standard, 37, 49, 152, 154
standout, 139, 192, 216
Stanton Moore - A, 92
staple, 188
star, 24, 27, 81, 119, 147, 180
stardom, 16, 28–30, 32, 34, 38, 39,
    134, 135, 171, 174
start, 11, 16, 68, 70, 114, 204
starting, 19, 36
state, 20, 52, 57, 129, 240
statement, 188, 190, 199
station, 14
statistic, 51
statue, 238
status, 10, 24, 26, 33, 39, 40, 109,
    111, 114, 115, 127, 158,
    182, 187, 194, 213, 240
steel, 23, 48
Stella Jones, 119
stench, 55, 59, 61, 62, 71
step, 18, 32, 36, 56, 62, 64, 67–69,
    71, 91, 92, 111, 124, 125,
    129, 148, 158, 181, 185,
    226
stereotype, 43
Stevie Ray Vaughan, 148
stigma, 169, 171, 175
sting, 182
stone, 2, 158, 226
stop, 3, 20, 26, 36, 48, 56, 63, 74, 75,
    78, 84, 85, 142, 199, 212
storm, 36, 117, 126, 188, 193
story, 1, 3, 8, 12, 17, 25, 28, 30, 31,
    42, 44, 50, 57, 72, 79, 85,
    103, 105, 136, 169, 184,
    186, 187, 199, 219, 223,
    227–230, 240
storyline, 138
storytelling, 5, 9, 10, 19, 52, 56, 73,
    135, 137, 142, 145, 197,
    198, 218
stranger, 147
strategy, 14, 165
streaming, 98, 136, 160
street, 55, 76, 82, 188
streetwear, 188
strength, 43, 44, 83, 103, 106, 167,
    171, 172, 175, 178, 181,
    185, 217, 228
string, 30
structure, 67
struggle, 16
studio, 10, 57, 59, 68–71, 89, 130,
    144, 150
study, 43, 217
style, 1, 3, 5, 7–11, 14, 18, 23–27,
    29, 30, 33, 38, 39, 48, 51,
    56, 58, 61–63, 66, 69, 86,

88, 92, 100, 104, 110–112,
    114, 115, 117, 130, 133,
    136, 140, 142, 148, 149,
    151–153, 155, 156, 158,
    164, 168, 172, 177,
    187–189, 193, 194, 199,
    201, 203, 212, 214, 216,
    217, 225, 227–230, 235,
    237, 239, 241, 242
substance, 180
success, 1, 4, 6–8, 12, 14, 15, 25, 27,
    30–32, 34, 39, 42, 43, 45,
    51, 59, 60, 85, 87–90,
    93–100, 103, 105,
    112–114, 119, 120, 128,
    131, 135, 137, 138,
    141–143, 153, 169, 171,
    174, 175, 177–182, 209,
    216, 217, 221–223, 225,
    226, 234, 236
successor, 115
suit, 110, 232
suite, 180
sum, 60, 95
summary, 16, 218
summer, 26, 230
sun, 78
sunshine, 4, 40
superpower, 225
superstardom, 28, 29
support, 2, 6, 7, 13, 14, 27, 32, 34,
    41, 43–45, 47, 78, 83–89,
    96–99, 101–104, 107,
    121, 122, 128–133, 136,
    156–158, 160, 167, 168,
    171, 172, 174, 178, 181,
    183, 203, 204, 206–208,
    210, 211, 213, 220, 221,
    226, 229, 231, 233, 234,
    240, 241
supporter, 103
supreme, 24, 58, 111
surprise, 61, 73–75, 77, 78, 102,
    133, 198, 213, 238
surrounding, 46, 78, 175, 181, 182,
    202, 216
survivor, 228
sushi, 76
sustainability, 205, 206, 238
swagger, 168
swap, 56
sweaty, 26
swing, 81, 146
sword, 179, 181
symbol, 5, 14, 23, 29, 40, 45, 46,
    198, 241
symbolism, 112, 217
symphony, 56, 57, 63, 127
sync, 93
synchronicity, 3, 59
synergy, 21, 65, 86, 91, 121
synth, 73, 93
system, 32, 34, 41, 77, 86, 96–99,
    104, 171, 178, 181, 220,
    226, 241

t, 4, 5, 7, 8, 10, 11, 20, 25–29, 32,
    36, 39, 48, 56, 58, 62, 63,
    72, 74, 75, 81, 82, 84, 85,
    91, 93, 121, 136, 140–142,
    145, 156, 167, 169, 180,
    182, 188, 191, 192,
    197–199, 207, 212, 213,
    225, 226, 230, 241
table, 32, 59, 65, 76, 93, 95, 115,
    148, 198, 239
tactic, 14
tale, 3, 16, 77, 191

Index 277

talent, 2–4, 16, 25, 26, 28, 38, 39, 43, 53, 62, 71, 85, 88, 89, 99, 111, 113–115, 121, 128, 129, 134, 136, 138, 140, 141, 143, 157, 164, 166, 171, 179, 191, 193, 195, 201, 203, 213, 220, 221, 226
talk, 26, 28, 172, 191–195, 199
tape, 69
tapestry, 18, 43, 79, 148, 154, 230
task, 10
taste, 29, 192
tea, 81
team, 2, 20, 21, 27, 32, 60, 96, 97, 130, 138, 178, 198
teamwork, 8, 62
tear, 83, 179
technique, 24, 56, 68, 177
technology, 17, 19–22, 33–35, 52, 53, 57, 65, 112, 119–121, 137, 143, 145, 240
teenager, 104
television, 136, 142, 191, 193–195
tempo, 51, 90
temptation, 85
tenacity, 27
tension, 175
term, 120, 203, 208
territory, 127, 148, 155, 237
test, 41, 71, 94, 144
testament, 3, 8, 10, 11, 21, 31, 35, 37, 43, 45–48, 50, 52, 53, 57, 67, 73, 74, 77, 80, 81, 83, 86, 89, 111–114, 116, 117, 120, 125, 134, 147, 150, 156, 158, 160, 164, 167, 168, 171, 176, 177, 186, 195, 200–202, 212, 213, 215, 219, 222, 223, 228, 230, 231, 233–235, 238, 241, 242
texture, 61, 73
thank, 156, 158, 240
the City of Angels, 29
theater, 173
theatricality, 2
theme, 72, 74, 192, 193
themed, 77, 84, 85, 191, 238
therapy, 172, 174, 181
theremin, 9, 23, 48, 69, 151
thing, 150, 156, 199, 240
thinking, 35, 48, 98, 194, 222
thirst, 123
thought, 9, 14, 48, 51, 59–63, 73, 111–113, 118, 127, 197, 213, 218
thread, 231
threat, 205
thrilling, 3, 13, 25, 75, 76, 81, 193, 194
throne, 121
ticket, 28, 122
Tim ", 74
Tim "Sticky" Johnson, 125
time, 3, 5, 9, 15, 17, 20, 21, 32, 44, 49, 52, 68, 71, 74, 75, 77, 81–83, 85–87, 90, 94, 107, 111, 114, 115, 117, 121, 130, 143, 151, 154, 155, 157, 159, 160, 162, 164, 165, 175, 178, 181, 183, 184, 203, 213, 214, 219–221, 227, 229, 230, 232, 234, 235, 242
timing, 90, 177
tin, 61
title, 72, 216

today, 3, 42, 49, 55, 110, 125, 154, 158, 195
toe, 5, 83
token, 240
Tokyo, 43, 45, 76, 79, 141, 149
toll, 25, 40, 43, 83, 174, 175, 180, 217
Tom, 230
tomorrow, 110
tone, 60, 68, 72, 92, 167
Tony, 178
Tony ", 178
tool, 33, 98, 102, 104, 144, 208
toolbox, 58
top, 1, 27, 30, 121, 184, 185, 187, 188
topping, 27, 29–32, 36, 51, 53, 109, 112, 126, 155, 157, 171, 179, 182, 219, 236
torch, 91, 105, 116, 118, 131, 158
torrent, 160
touch, 21, 56, 59, 79, 92, 102, 106, 109, 124, 145, 166, 176, 185, 188, 209, 212, 216, 221, 231, 234, 235, 240
tour, 3, 36–39, 45, 62, 74–79, 81–84, 86, 97, 117, 121, 122, 129, 131, 150, 155–159, 196, 198
touring, 25, 34, 40, 76–79, 82, 132, 141, 174, 175, 206
town, 1, 3, 5, 6, 25, 42, 74, 81, 82, 84, 88, 104
toy, 136
track, 2, 10, 20, 27, 62, 63, 67, 72, 73, 112, 119, 126, 147, 153, 154, 219, 236, 237
tracking, 21
traction, 9, 62, 233

trademark, 2, 9, 31, 75, 124, 191, 193
tradition, 212
tragedy, 44
trail, 13, 25, 70, 71, 103, 211, 222, 223, 227
trailblazer, 197
training, 203
trajectory, 26
transformation, 26, 72, 88, 117, 172
transition, 72, 117, 119–121
transparency, 39, 41, 171
trap, 123
travel, 79–84, 98
traveling, 82
treasure, 137
treat, 173, 180
treatment, 34, 228
tree, 101, 206, 207
trend, 23, 144
tribute, 44, 115, 212, 213, 235, 238, 239, 242
trick, 198
trip, 75, 157, 230
triumph, 6, 60, 122, 176, 186
trophy, 111, 112
trumpet, 62
trust, 16, 85, 86, 95, 96, 98, 99, 175
truth, 219
tug, 139
tuition, 205, 208
tune, 30, 140
tunnel, 184, 186, 187
turn, 8, 44, 48, 55, 75, 76, 78, 88, 201
turning, 4, 25, 27, 38, 43, 56, 82, 123, 180
twist, 9, 56, 154, 217

UK, 229
umbrella, 234
unconventionality, 27, 66
underbelly, 171
underdogs, 1
understanding, 7, 19, 45–47, 90, 91, 95, 117, 138, 166, 175, 215–218
unfamiliar, 127
uniqueness, 31, 32, 43, 49, 69, 104, 127, 130, 223, 227
unit, 3
unity, 7, 10, 37, 40, 45, 46, 72, 79, 84, 85, 87, 106, 107, 126, 132, 161, 167, 168, 171, 185, 201, 209, 241
universe, 20, 22, 57, 197, 214
unpredictability, 2, 21, 123
unveiling, 238
up, 7, 11, 27, 29, 38, 39, 42, 43, 46, 47, 50, 53, 60, 62, 63, 65, 66, 71, 74, 75, 78, 81, 90, 92, 94, 96, 97, 105, 107, 109, 119, 127, 129, 146, 147, 150, 151, 158, 160, 171, 173, 176, 179, 180, 182, 186, 198, 203, 207, 213, 222, 225–229, 237
upheaval, 175
uplift, 34, 87, 103–105, 167, 172, 213
urge, 90
usage, 69, 124, 147
use, 9, 17, 19, 23, 24, 31, 33, 34, 48, 49, 53, 60, 65, 66, 68, 101, 107–109, 131, 146, 147, 150, 152, 172, 197, 200, 209, 211, 215, 227

value, 8, 114, 115, 142, 172
variety, 1, 88, 191, 210
vehicle, 33, 35
veil, 176
venture, 67, 125, 138, 237
venue, 11, 12, 36, 77, 121, 156, 160, 238, 239
versatility, 10, 11, 56, 63, 75, 91, 98, 118, 123, 126, 138, 140, 142, 191, 194, 212
version, 71, 140, 141, 212
vibe, 93
victory, 112
video, 19, 112, 173, 195, 213
view, 180
vintage, 19, 150
vinyl, 198, 208, 238
vinyls, 197
violence, 101
violin, 56, 63, 140, 151
virtuosity, 126
virtuoso, 177
vision, 1, 2, 5, 9, 16, 19, 20, 24, 27, 31, 32, 34, 60, 70, 72, 78, 83, 85, 89, 94–97, 109, 112, 113, 115, 120, 123, 135, 138, 143, 147, 154, 179, 201, 210, 225, 226, 240
visionary, 49, 89, 135, 142
visit, 82, 102
visual, 2, 5, 17, 18, 20, 21, 23, 24, 36, 49, 56–58, 70, 73, 109, 110, 112, 135, 152, 173, 189, 195–197, 201, 213–215, 217, 229
vocal, 13, 34, 101, 104, 111, 126, 128, 148, 154, 177
vocalist, 4, 58, 94, 126, 127, 177

voice, 2, 4, 43, 58–61, 93, 94, 98, 101, 124, 128, 130, 131, 148, 160, 172, 173, 177, 225, 227
volume, 237
volunteer, 106, 107, 167, 208
volunteering, 15, 232
vomitstep, 123
vortex, 67
vulnerability, 7, 84, 103, 141, 172, 175, 181, 184, 186

wake, 13, 25, 154, 223
wardrobe, 188
warmth, 177
waste, 206
water, 65, 208
watering, 76, 77
waterphone, 56
wave, 13, 29, 39, 66, 67, 106, 108, 147, 151, 154, 157, 242
way, 1, 3, 5, 10, 12, 13, 16, 17, 25, 28–30, 33, 34, 40, 46, 49, 51, 57, 62, 64, 66, 68, 69, 75, 79, 82, 84, 85, 88, 91, 95, 119, 124, 125, 127, 129, 136, 137, 141, 148, 151, 153, 154, 156, 169, 173, 174, 181, 183–188, 192, 214, 222, 223, 228, 234, 235, 240
weakness, 175
weapon, 8, 177
weight, 7, 16, 160, 182
well, 4, 25, 38, 40, 41, 43, 56, 97, 98, 121, 135, 171, 174, 180, 181, 200, 213
whimsy, 188

whirlwind, 5, 27, 28, 34, 37, 44, 76, 81, 171, 180, 227
whiskey, 180
whole, 7, 20, 26, 28, 49, 55, 57, 64, 66, 68, 74, 75, 77, 81, 91, 120, 125, 136, 142, 207, 230
wilderness, 77
wildfire, 2, 4, 25
wildlife, 77
willingness, 5, 8, 10, 58, 61, 63–65, 79, 91, 114, 124, 127, 137, 147, 149, 150, 152, 170, 173, 237, 239, 242
win, 208
wind, 147
window, 83
wisdom, 44, 131, 223, 225
wit, 192, 193
wizard, 93
wizardry, 57
woman, 43
wonder, 151, 156, 198, 234
wonderland, 193, 238, 239
word, 11, 13, 14, 16, 25, 28, 50, 84, 241
work, 2, 12, 19, 38, 39, 52, 57, 60, 71, 95, 97, 98, 101, 102, 105, 110, 119, 129, 130, 143, 151, 152, 154, 158, 160, 167, 171, 173, 177, 179, 184, 186, 197, 198, 209, 211, 215, 217, 221, 226
working, 85, 119, 165, 178, 204, 206, 208, 225
world, 1–7, 12, 13, 15–17, 19, 21, 22, 24, 26, 28–30, 32, 35, 38, 39, 41–47, 49, 51, 52,

Index

55, 56, 58, 59, 62–65, 68, 70, 71, 73, 79–84, 88, 89, 92–94, 96, 100, 102–109, 112, 114, 115, 118, 119, 121, 125, 126, 129, 131, 134–137, 141–143, 146, 148, 149, 151–153, 155–158, 160, 161, 168, 172, 173, 179–181, 187–189, 191, 192, 194–197, 200–203, 205, 207, 209, 211, 212, 214, 216, 218, 221–223, 225, 227, 232, 233, 235–242

worth, 4, 120

woven, 43, 85, 154
writing, 68, 71, 78, 229

x, 189

y, 68, 71
year, 238, 239
your, 13, 16, 19, 32, 50, 53, 64, 67, 69, 71, 80, 81, 90–92, 110, 128, 130, 131, 140, 141, 181, 184, 186–188, 190, 191, 199, 225–227, 237
youth, 100, 165, 205

zone, 12, 32, 64, 131, 226